# Economic Development in the Middle East

By examining economic development in the aftermath of the Arab Spring, this textbook introduces undergraduate and postgraduate students to the most pressing and topical economic issues in the contemporary Middle East. Although development failures contributed to the popular discontent in much of the Arab World, this comparative study also highlights development success, especially in Turkey and the Gulf.

Organised thematically, a full range of topics are discussed, including:

- the impact of demographic changes, not least the dramatic decline in birth rates and the implications for future employment
- the role of banks and capital markets in the region's development
- the advances in oil and gas production and attempts to diversify
- the effects of the region's economic development on international and intra-regional trade.

Through discussing the region's problems of the past as well as the present and future challenges, this book provides students with a compact and manageable review of the state of economic development in the Middle East.

**Rodney Wilson** is Emeritus Professor at Durham University, UK, and Visiting Professor at the Qatar Faculty of Islamic Studies. His research interests include Islamic finance and the political economy of development in the Middle East.

# Economic Development in the Middle East

## Second edition

**Rodney Wilson**

Routledge
Taylor & Francis Group

LONDON AND NEW YORK

First published 1995
by Routledge

This second edition published 2013
by Routledge
2 Park Square, Milton Park, Abingdon, Oxon OX14 4RN

Simultaneously published in the USA and Canada
by Routledge
711 Third Avenue, New York, NY 10017

*Routledge is an imprint of the Taylor & Francis Group, an informa business*

*British Library Cataloguing in Publication Data*
A catalogue record for this book is available from the British Library

*Library of Congress Cataloging in Publication Data*
Wilson, Rodney.
  Economic development in the Middle East / Rodney Wilson – 2nd ed.
    p. cm.
  Includes bibliographical references and index.
  1. Middle East–Economic conditions–1979- I. Title.
  HC415.15.W545 2012
  330.956–dc23
               2012010660

ISBN: 978-0-415-49126-6 (hbk)
ISBN: 978-0-415-49127-3 (pbk)
ISBN: 978-0-203-09578-2 (ebk)

Typeset in Times New Roman
by Taylor & Francis Books

Printed and bound in Great Britain by the MPG Books Group

# Contents

# Tables and figures

## Tables

# Figure

# 1  Introduction

## Aim

This book was first published by Routledge in 1995 and received encouraging reviews. The aim is to provide a long-overdue second edition which has been substantially revised and expanded from the first edition. The basic structure in terms of chapter headings and subheadings still seems appropriate and has stood the test of time. However, all the data presented have been updated and much of the text rewritten to take account of recent events, not least the Arab Spring. This new edition should be suitable for use by final year under-graduates and MA students in and from the Middle East, as well as outsiders interested in this rapidly changing region.

The objective of this present study is to provide an account of the recent experience of development in the Middle East that will enhance the readers' understanding of how the development process works or fails in an important region of the world with several unique characteristics. This should encourage the reader to question the universality of the neo-classical approach to devel-opment. Are western economic concepts and values applicable in societies whose priorities may be very different, reflecting not only their stage of development, but differences in religion and culture? All too often economists neglect such issues.

In most courses on economic development the standard classical and neo-classical approaches are employed, so that students become acquainted with the conventional models, concepts and issues which are central to the subject. The meaning and measurement of development is the starting point, with the historical context emphasised. Growth and structural change are discussed in terms of one sector and two sector models. Concepts of dual economies are introduced as well as unbalanced growth and the notion of leading sectors.

One aim of this book is to reinforce the students' understanding of these basic concepts, by drawing on the experience of one specific geographical region. The Middle East economies are taken as case studies to illustrate and explore further the usefulness of the material the students have learnt. Through this exposure to a region with a distinctive culture, religion and value system, readers are challenged to rethink their assumptions about development, and indeed the premises of much of modern economic history.

## The context

The economies of the Middle East have developed remarkably since the first edition was written, partly due to the second oil-price boom and the much better management of surplus revenue. The role of the state has changed with improvements in institutional capability, although the economic competency of governments and ministries varies more than ever as the gap between best practice and poor administration widens. The private sector plays a much greater role in the economies of the region, and home-grown multinational companies have now emerged, but it is often difficult to delineate the boundaries between the state and the private sector.

Economic power has shifted from the northern Arab countries to the Gulf, with Saudi Arabia by far the largest economy in the region, and the economy of the United Arab Emirates (UAE) now larger than that of Egypt on some measures. Capital flows from the economies of the Gulf Co-operation Council (GCC) to the northern Arab states have taken off and are having a profound economic impact on the region as a whole. Labour flows remain limited however, and the policy of prioritising employment for local citizens in countries such as Saudi Arabia and Kuwait has resulted in less mobility of Arab labour, apart from that of the more educated professionals. Regional integration therefore remains limited, and most trade is externally focused.

Iran is included in the study as an integral part of the region, with most of its trade flowing through the UAE. Although Iran's economy has suffered because of continuing sanctions by the United States and the European Union, the Islamic Republic's economic problems are mainly due to internal mismanagement. Nevertheless, high oil and gas prices have helped the economy, and commercial relations with Asia are flourishing, and far from the economy collapsing, there is some reason for optimism. In neighbouring Iraq it is much harder to be optimistic, and although there have been significant economic changes since the United States invasion, sustainable economic development will not be possible until the security situation improves and politics becomes more stable, although since 2009 there has been some encouraging progress, with interest by foreign investors in Iraq increasing.

The Middle East receives more media coverage than any other area of the developing world. As a result of its deep-seated conflicts the region is a major focus of attention for specialists in international relations and political scientists. Academics involved in development studies, and consequently their students, have much less knowledge of the Middle East. Indeed western economists and sociologists have been much more active in African and Latin American studies and most case study material used in development courses relates to these areas.

In recent years development specialists have been pre-occupied with the economies of East and South East Asia, and to a lesser extent South Asia as, despite the Asia crisis of 1997, these are seen as much more promising cases of economic growth, especially given the Chinese and Indian experiences. In contrast the Middle East has been overlooked, with the growth in the GCC states simply attributed to oil and gas exports, rather than being viewed in the context of successful economic diversification strategies.

This relative neglect of the Middle East from the perspective of development studies is partly a result of the limited range of books and articles on the region written by British or American economists and sociologists. There are a number of books in English by Arab writers, but most adopt a country or sub-regional perspective, and do not treat the Middle East as an entity. Furthermore, most of these authors are little-known in development studies circles apart from notable exceptions such as Samir Amin.[1] Even he, however, has comparatively little to say on the Middle East, being regarded as more of an African specialist.

**Approach**

The intention has been to write a subject-oriented book rather than a country-by-country study. The approach is analytical rather than descriptive, with the analytical tools drawn from the theories of economic development. The objective is to complement established texts in development economics such as that by Michael Todaro and Stephen Smith, now in its tenth edition,[2] Frederick Nixson, now in its second edition,[3] or Peter Cramp, now in its fourth edition.[4] The first is the leading US text, while the latter two are aimed at the UK market. These mainstream texts use the tools of conventional economic theory, and demonstrate how economists such as W. Arthur Lewis have constructed models from these premises which can be applied specifically to developing countries.[5] Such approaches are categorised by economists as neo-classical, and are often described as technocratic by political scientists and international relations specialists.

There are of course many alternative approaches to development, and this book is also designed to appeal to those who have followed these traditions. The text by Michael Todaro and Stephen Smith draws on a wide range of economic concepts and theories at an introductory and intermediate level. It is specifically targeted at economics students in developing countries, and draws on economic theories and concepts which are felt to be useful to explaining development problems. Todaro places more stress on comparative economic systems, and there is a fuller discussion of the merits of the command versus the market economy, issues which are pursued here.

A fundamentally different approach is that of Wilber and Jameson whose readings are designed for students of development studies generally and not only economists.[6] The readings are written from a political economy perspective, and the contributors include committed Marxists such as Paul

Baran. Overall the text is well-balanced, however, and it has been a popular recommendation for courses in development offered by sociology departments. The chapter by Howard Wiarda on non-ethnocentric theories of development is especially relevant for this study, as it considers views from those in emerging economies on development objectives. There is a highly critical contribution on privatisation by John Waterbury who has considerable Middle Eastern experience. The lack of further editions illustrates that radical approaches to development became less fashionable in recent years, undoubtedly reflecting the demise of socialism. Whether there is a revival of such approaches in the post-2008 financial crisis era remains to be seen, although so far this does not appear to be the case.

Amartya Sen's book on development as freedom is also worth consideration in a Middle Eastern context.[7] He sees the free and sustainable agency of people as a major engine of development, and the violation of freedoms resulting from a denial of civil and political liberties as an impediment to development. The debate concerning whether there is a link between development and democracy has received much attention in the Middle East, not least in the context of the invasion of Iraq being justified in terms of its liberation from a tyrannical regime in the interests of economic development. Sen, however, also stresses the importance of the maintenance of local peace and order for economic development, conditions clearly not present in post-Saddam Iraq.

The overthrow in 2011 of President Ben Ali of Tunisia, President Mubarak of Egypt and the Gaddafi regime highlighted the failure of autocratic governments, despite the international view that they were stable states. Youth unemployment and rising prices were the underlying causes of the revolutions, demonstrating the significance of economic factors. These, together with the popular perceptions that the regimes were corrupt, and that the ruling families were siphoning off the wealth of the country, resulted in a climate of resentment that many outside observers failed to spot. Interestingly it was the self-immolation of a young market trader who had not got the necessary permits to sell his fruit and vegetables that triggered the initial protests in Tunisia. The demand was simply for the government to allow free markets to operate and not interfere with those who tried to be enterprising. Whether the new governments create a better climate for honest business remains to be seen.

## Perspectives on development

Attitudes towards development may be different in the Middle East to those prevailing in Europe or North America. Is development merely the improvement of personal or family material well-being? Can economic history be viewed as the story of continuous long-term progress, with minor setbacks at times of recession, and temporary downturns during economic slumps?

This, perhaps naïvely optimistic, view has prevailed in the Christian and lapsed Christian West for most of the twentieth century. The Islamic Middle East has more recently entered its fourteenth century, but a common perception is that the last hundred years compares unfavourably with the early centuries of Islamic civilisation. Yet not many envy the West. In the opinion of at least some in the Middle East any economic gains the West has achieved have been outweighed by the social costs. One perception is that material advance has undermined human values, and even religion itself has been under threat in the West, leaving the populations in a state of spiritual confusion. If this view is taken, the western path of development, far from being a role model, is to be avoided if at all possible.

More fundamentally the question must be asked whether the traditional economists' tools for measuring and evaluating development are relevant for a region where many do not share western aspirations. If judged by yardsticks such as per capita gross domestic product rises or the development of modern manufacturing, many of the economies of the Middle East may be seen as failures. But are they? Is it the methods and measures of evaluation which have failed rather than the economies themselves? Is neo-classical economics only applicable to North American or European area studies programmes because of its western ethnocentricity? Are development economists, western governments and international agencies trying to promote a style of living that many in the region simply do not want?

The early twenty-first century has seen rapid economic growth in so-called emerging economies when measured by conventional criteria such as per capita GDP or structural change indicators such as the share of manufacturing in GDP. Economic growth has been particularly impressive in India, with which the states of the Gulf have had close relations historically, and in China, with which historical relations have been more limited. In contrast economic growth in the so-called developed economies seems to have lagged, especially since the financial crisis of 2008 which had such a negative effect on the economy of the United States and encouraged yet more introspection in the European Union, cumulating in the Eurozone crisis.

The economies of the Middle East can also be seen as emerging economies but for the most part with much less impressive growth rates than those of India or China.[8] Nevertheless it is unlikely that these economies will be seen as role models in the Middle East as there are deep cultural differences. Indeed it is arguably less plausible that the Middle East will become "east-ernised" in the twenty-first century any more than it became "westernised" during the twentieth century. Even though the Middle East is sometimes referred to as Western Asia, the designation Middle East remains meaningful not merely because it is between East and West in a geographic sense, but also due to the fact that it is influenced by its regional neighbours. It nevertheless maintains its own distinctive identity in terms of both economics and political economy, and it is not simply absorbing the ideas and concepts of others. The Middle East has, however, yet to become a knowledge-based economy in the modern sense and it remains more a recipient of technology transfers rather than a provider. The long-term challenge is for the Middle East to become an economic core rather than a periphery in the way it was during the early centuries of Islam when it was a centre of civilisation, indeed perhaps the centre.

## Geographical coverage

Geographically the Middle East will be defined to include all the Arab states including those of the Maghreb. The core area is taken as Egypt, the countries of the fertile crescent and the Gulf states. Reference will also be made to the experiences of Sudan and Libya where appropriate. From the point of view of geography Tunisia, Algeria and Morocco may not be part of the Middle East, but they are part of the Arab World. In terms of culture and religion they have much in common with the core states of the Middle East, and arguably this is also the case in the economic sphere. The non-Arab states covered include Iran and Turkey, as there are many parallels between the development of these countries and those of the Arab region. There are, for example, important lessons for Egypt from the Turkish experience of economic liberalisation and structural adjustment in the 1980s.[9]

Israel has economic and political structures that are different in many ways from the other states of the region. Nevertheless, despite its unique beginnings as an outcome of basically European wars, it should not be considered a nation apart from the region in which it is located. Israel is in essence a theocratic state with religion enshrined in the constitution and it is contrary to Zionist ideology to describe it as secular. In legal terms it already is what many of its faith-inspired neighbours would wish their nations to be. Those Israelis who live in hostile surroundings in West Bank settlements are not materially motivated. Their aspirations are spiritual, like those of their Muslim neighbours whom they rarely meet. In any study of Middle Eastern economies the Israeli experience is of positive interest in the specific context of water resource management and in the more general context of how a knowledge economy can be created. Perhaps of more negative interest are developments affecting the Palestinian Arabs, which have on-going adverse effects on the economies of the West Bank and Gaza, and in the longer term will inevitably affect the sustainability of Israel's economy, if not the state itself.

In a global economy which is increasingly made up of economic blocks, a regional perspective seems both relevant and appropriate. The Middle East does not constitute an economic entity, however, as there are no pan-regional structures similar to the European Union, the Association of South East Asian Nations (ASEAN) or the North America Free Trade Area (NAFTA). The Arab League has an economic directorate, but it has no clear mission, and members of the League are not subject to any binding commitments that are economically significant. Any there have been in the past have been of a negative nature rather than trade-promoting, the Damascus boycott of trade with Israel being the most notable.

At the sub-regional level there have been several attempts at economic groupings, the most notable of which, the Arab Common Market, was created out of the ruins of the United Arab Republic when Egypt and Syria split in 1961. Like the earlier union, Nasser's common market venture never became an economic force, though both Jordan and Iraq did reap some benefits. The Gulf Co-operation Council has arguably been more successful as an economic if not as a military alliance, and it is interesting to ask why. Is it because the states have common economic interests, is structural similarity the key factor, or is it simply the openness of these oil economies?

In a region such as the Middle East there are enormous economic differences and disparities between the states. On one shore of the Red Sea lies Sudan, one of the poorest countries in the world, while on the other side is Saudi Arabia, the world's largest oil exporting nation, rivalled only by Russia. Clearly any regional study of economic development must recognise these differences. At the same time, one of the merits of treating the Middle East as an entity is the richness of the development experience that results from the diversity. Common cultural, linguistic and ethnic roots do not breed economic similarity, as the enormous contrasts in the English-speaking world demonstrate.

A sub-regional classification of the Middle Eastern economies gives some indication of their diversification. A three-way split can be made, based on development characteristics. The oil-rich states with limited populations represent one obvious category; this group includes the Arabian Peninsula states plus Libya. All these states remain dependent on primary extractive activity as the main pillar of economic support, despite the tremendous efforts made to diversify. Another group might be the larger and more populous states of the region where significant market size has offered some scope for nationally centred development and import substitution. Egypt, Iran and Turkey clearly fall into this category. The factor endowments of these states are not dissimilar to those of newly industrialising countries in East Asia and Latin America which have successfully established modern manufacturing activity.

A third, and perhaps more controversial, grouping might include those states whose economies have been severely distorted by conflict and wars. Obvious candidates include Israel, Lebanon, Iraq and perhaps Jordan and Syria. In the case of the latter two economies it has been more the risk and anticipation of conflict, together with spill-over effects from neighbouring states, which has caused much of the damage rather than actual hostilities, although in Syria the end game of the Assad dynasty brought severe economic disruption that was internally generated. The economic literature on expectations and concepts such as external diseconomies may have particular relevance to these states, together with other analytical tools used by economists when examining countries involved in conflict.

## The period under review

Historically the period examined starts from the 1950s, the time of the young officers' coup in Egypt and the revolutions in Syria and Iraq.[10] These resulted in major changes in economic policy, and a reorientation in development for these states. For the Gulf the 1950s marked the beginning of the rapid rise in oil revenues, with dramatic consequences for development and an ultimate transformation of economic activity.

The study is not an economic history any more than it is an economic geography. Development theories and approaches are best tested by considering the historical experience. This may involve the evaluation of qualitative infor- mation as well as computation using hard data. Statistics for Middle Eastern economies must be treated with caution. This applies especially for the period prior to 1970 when data collection techniques were much less reliable than they have since become. Nevertheless, there are advantages in taking the 1950s as a starting point and a sixty-year time span. By evaluating a relatively long period the increased number of observations improves the statistical significance of any econometric analysis. Such analysis is not attempted in this study, but for the more technically minded reader some of the articles referred to in the bibliography contain this type of work. The evaluation of qualitative information also becomes more reliable, as, for example, it is easier to assess the impact of Turkey's more market-oriented policies in the 1980s if the outcomes of the more interventionist approaches of the three previous decades are understood.

There are a number of excellent texts on the economic history of the Middle East, the books by Roger Owen[11] and Charles Issawi[12] deserving particular mention. The former covers the 1800 to 1914 period on a chronological basis, and is essentially concerned with the impact of the European powers. Issawi's work covers the period up to 1980, but the latter period is inevitably dealt with rather thinly given the scope of the book. Like the present volume, Issawi adopts a subject-oriented approach, the major theme being the impact of the West through trade and finance and the Middle Eastern response through agricultural expansion, de-industrialisation and re-industrialisation.

Books in economic history do not date of course, but since the early 1980s there have been no new substantive volumes on the Middle East. The book edited by George Sabagh is worth noting, however, especially the chapters on labour mobility by Roger Owen, oil and economic development by Homa Katouzian and educational change by Carter Findley.[13] An earlier edited volume that contains some interesting contributions on Egypt, Iran and Turkey is the work by Elie Kedourie.[14] Labour issues figure prominently, and the chapter by Marius Deeb on "Bank Misr and the Emergence of the Local Bourgeoisie in Egypt" is undoubtedly a classic in its field.

## Issues and themes

It is of course an ambitious task to write a book examining the development experience of an entire region such as the Middle East. There is nevertheless much merit in treating the region as a single entity, despite its diversity of experience. Islam is the dominant religion throughout the region, and Muslim beliefs have important implications for the economic value systems that can win popular acceptance. Oil is another matter of regional significance, not only for the oil-exporting states, but also for those dependent on Gulf aid and remittances.

Although the coverage is wide-ranging, there is selectivity in the topics chosen, with the concentration being on those development issues which are especially relevant for the Middle East. Area studies specialists are clearly most interested in development concepts that are applicable in their region of interest. Looked at from the point of view of development studies, the focus is on those topics where the Middle Eastern experience is deemed to be particularly illuminating in highlighting both constraints and possibilities.

Apart from the issues of Islamic economic values and oil resources, there are other development subjects where the Middle Eastern experience is important. Conflict and war is clearly one such topic, even though this is neglected in traditional development texts. There is conflict weariness in the Middle East, not least because issues such as the aspirations of many Palestinians for their own independent state seem further away from resolution than ever. The nuclear ambitions of Iran are also of great concern to its Arab neighbours, especially in the Gulf, and there is dismay at the changed power structure in Iraq which seems to have played into the hands of Tehran, even if that was never the intention of the United States. Elsewhere, the situation in Lebanon remains volatile, and the leadership succession creates uncertainty in some states otherwise deemed to be stable, notably Saudi Arabia.

Many outside analysts depict the Middle East as an unstable and conflict-prone region and present a rather depressing picture especially as the regional conflicts appear impossible to resolve. In reality, however, prior to the Arab Spring there had been few changes of regime; and the revolutionary fervour of the 1950s and 1960s disappeared in the subsequent four decades. Possibly because of disenfranchisement many people in the region, perhaps the majority, have become politically apathetic. The expectation that government can solve problems, whether political or economic, has diminished. Arguably there is an increasing realism that people have to solve their own problems, and not rely on the state. Government failure is viewed as the norm by sceptical populations, but in contrast business is seen as business, and there is less concern with market failure. Nevertheless, the Arab Spring showed that autocratic rulers cannot ignore popular discontent resulting from economic deprivation. A re-politicisation occurs if economic conditions become unbearable, with no obvious way forward for the youthful poor.

Corrupt government is seen as a fact of life, which is difficult to change given the societal culture.[15] Businesses react in two ways – either by seeking government favours, including by illicit payments, so that they can enjoy the greater benefits and privileges of a rentier economy, or alternatively by adopting a low profile, and avoiding "bully praetorian states".[16]

Emphasis in this study is placed on the role of markets in the development process. Efficiency may be hindered by poor information flows and high transactions costs. In the Peter Bauer tradition there is a focus on traders and their role as development agents.[17] Popular development texts such as that by

Michael Todaro and Stephen Smith cited earlier stress the importance of market signals. The role of development planning is downgraded, as the evidence suggests it has never worked adequately in the Middle East. Do markets best determine resource allocation rather than the state? Should the role of governments in the Middle East be to facilitate instead of direct? The rich and diverse experience of the countries under review should shed some light on these matters.

Even less attention is paid by development economists to the workings of *bazaar* or *souk* economies, but this is obviously a topic of importance in the Middle East context. How efficient are such markets, and how do they evolve with change and development? This area of investigation has often been left to social anthropologists, but the operation of such markets must be of interest to anyone trained in economics. Interesting questions include whether bargaining constitutes competition, the transactions costs with heterogeneous products and the economics of search in an informal sector context.

The economies of the Middle East always have been and remain trading based.[18] Nationalistic and socialist government policies may have inhibited trade, but the economy of the *bazaar* and *souk* has survived, and indeed has enjoyed a revival in the last decade. In some economies such as Lebanon and Syria the informal sector has taken over from the formal as the most vibrant. State economic enterprises stagnate or decline while the black market flourishes.

Islamic economists view trading as a desirable and productive activity, and in the *Qur'an* the virtues of trade are stressed:

> Rejoice in the bargain which you have concluded: that is the achievement supreme.[19]

Trade must be conducted honestly, and in the *Qur'an* there are several passages warning those who would try to take advantage of others through sharp practices, one of the most quoted being:

> Woe to those that deal in fraud. Those who, when they have to receive by measure from men, exact full measure, but when they have to give by measure or weight to men, give less than due. Do they not think that they will be called to account?[20]

The influence of Quranic economic strictures has been considerable on all Muslim societies, and in recent years there has been a revival of interest in Islamic economics. For many the challenge is to apply the teachings and concepts to modern economies, and it is evident that considerable progress has been made in developing the ideas. Islamic ideology may be as incompatible with capitalism[21] as it was with communism, but it does provide an economic system of its own. This recognises private property, but redistribution can occur, at least within families, through the *shari'ah* religious laws on inheritance. It recognises the value of markets and exchange, but avoids being capitalistic through the prohibition of *riba* or interest. There is even a well thought-out critique of the Western literature on economic development, which may interest readers of this volume.[22]

As elsewhere in the developing world, privatisation has become a major issue in the Middle East.[23] The policies of the state financing and managing import substitution industries are now rather discredited and the emphasis switched to economic liberalisation from the 1980s.[24] Nationalised industries have been sold and controls over economic activity reduced. Prices play a larger role in resource allocation, with private business activity not only permitted, but even actively encouraged. The implications of these developments may, however, be different in the Middle East than in other parts of the Third World. An attempt is made to show how business attitudes have been shaped by the social and cultural environment.[25] Labour conditions are quite different to those in the western world, and entrepreneurs survive and react within a business climate which in many respects is unique.

One major theme of this work is that the economic progress of the Middle East has been unsatisfactory. It is not only outside observers who have this perception, but more importantly the majority of economists in the region itself. There has admittedly been enormous economic change, amounting in many cases to a structural transformation. Rapid urbanisation has been accompanied by relative agricultural decline. The share of services in gross national product has grown. Primary extractive industry, namely oil, has dominated economic activity, but its peak of the early 1980s is already long gone despite the buoyancy of oil prices in recent years. The benefits and costs of oil have been much debated.[26] During the early oil boom years economic growth rates were, of course, impressive, but how productive an inheritance has it left? Much less was achieved than the crude figures suggested, but the legacy has been uneven. Much of the oil revenue in Libya was wasted on projects lacking viability, and this was also the case in Algeria and Iran, which also benefited from gas as well as oil revenue. Natural resources contributed more to current consumption spending, especially in expanding the state bureaucracy, rather than to investment. In the monarchies of the Gulf the results were more impressive, however, as oil revenue transformed the infrastructure and opened up the economies. There has also been massive expenditure on education in the Gulf, although there are issues about the quality of what is provided, and frustration in Saudi Arabia in particular that it does not always increase employability.[27]

The evidence on trends in international trade and capital flows points to a growing global interdependence, which has affected the Middle East as much as other areas. Many countries in South East Asia and even Latin America have, however, achieved international competitiveness with their exports of manufactured goods. Unfortunately this is not the case for most Middle Eastern countries despite the efforts to industrialise. Only petrochemical exports have proved successful, but there are issues of feedstock pricing, and such exports by definition still depend on oil and gas production. The region remains very dependent on primary products, and for the non-oil producers, and even some of the OPEC states, balance of payments deficits are increasing. Many developing countries argue for trade, not aid, but from some states in the Middle East such as Yemen, the call for aid gets ever louder, as the countries have so little to offer in trade. This external trading weakness may seem paradoxical in a region where cities and towns have historically thrived and developed through their trade.

What has gone wrong with the region's development? Why has so little been achieved despite the enormous efforts and sacrifices? Is the outside world to blame, or are the causes of failure internal? Clearly there are no simple answers, but it can be argued that there are several factors distorting the development pattern, and inhibiting healthy growth.

First, oil revenue may have provided development finance, but it has also encouraged consumption rather than non-oil production. Rentier economies have been created, whose growth is entirely dependent on oil and overseas financial assets.[28] Oil wealth has been translated into current income, but there has been little alternative domestic wealth creation.

Second, regional conflicts have also severely distorted the pattern of development, and been much more than distractions. More is spent on armaments by Middle Eastern nations than in most other developing economies. Yet the countries import most of their weapons, and with the exception of Israel, local manufacture of military equipment has failed to develop. Iraq's much-discussed armaments facilities were usually so-called turn-key plants, with foreign technology and even foreign personnel. Since the invasion and the overthrow of Saddam Hussein the dependence on external weapons has increased. Iraq's armed forces are almost exclusively trained by the Americans and have all their equipment sourced in the United States. Technologically the gap is widening between the Middle East and the West, and indeed the industrial East. This is perhaps surprising given the huge numbers going through the region's school systems, and the enormous enthusiasm for education.

Overall the aim has been to write a book with themes which will be familiar to all those involved in contemporary development studies. This should be instructive for Middle Eastern specialists, who may not perceive their region to be of interest in such terms. At the same time the uniqueness of the Middle East is emphasised. Often development theorists believe their theories have universal applicability, but the Middle Eastern experience shows this is not necessarily the case. Selectivity and adaptation are certainly required, and this is undoubtedly the central theme of the study.

## Regional versus country perspectives

In any single volume covering a whole region it is impossible to go into depth and detail on the economies of particular countries. This is not the objective of the present work. The aim is not to describe particular economies or even to analyse their peculiarities. Rather, the intent has been to identify regional themes and issues, and to draw on the Middle Eastern experience for illustrative purposes.

There are a number of useful country studies to which the interested reader should refer. The study by Amuzegar was the first in English to examine in detail developments in Iran since the Islamic revolution.[29] The study by Massoud Karshenas on Iran covers a longer period, with a particular focus on oil and industrialisation.[30] A more recent study by Kazem Alamdari attempts to explain the reasons for Iran's development failures.[31] Iran has nevertheless strived to reform its economy in recent years, but as the study by Abdelali Jbili, Vitali Kramarenko and José Bailén shows, the results have been mixed.[32]

For the Turkish economy Z.Y. Hershlag's book provides a useful introduction, with an interesting contrast between the state interventionist policies of the 1970s and the more liberal market-orientated approach of the 1980s.[33] The volume edited by Tevfik Nas and Mehmet Odekon provides some important insights into the background surrounding Turkish economic liberalisation.[34] A more recent study by Ziya Öniş and Fikret Şenses is also worthwhile reading,[35] as is the more radical work of Zülküf Aydın.[36]

Not surprisingly given its population size and economic significance, Egypt has been much-researched in recent years by economists and economic historians. Interested readers can refer to the volume edited by Roberto Aliboni on its economic potential,[37] although it is now rather dated. Reform issues were addressed by Gouda Abdel-Khalek who provides an excellent review of developments in the 1990s.[38] A longer-term economic history is provided by Khalid Ikram who puts reform issues into a broader perspective.[39] The study by Robert Bowker is also informative as he gives a view of Egypt in the context of the wider Arab World.[40] Another recent book which provides insights into the workings of Egypt's economy is the study by Frederic P. Miller, Agnes F. Vandome and John McBrewster.[41]

There are several excellent books on the economy of Israel and the Palestinian Territories, a good starting point being the study by Assaf Razin and Efraim Sadka, despite it being somewhat dated.[42] A more recent edited volume by Avi Ben-Bassat examines in detail economic reform in Israel involving the financial, goods, services and the labour market.[43] A more critical political economy approach is taken in the book by Jonathan Nitzan and Shimshon Bichler which is worth reading.[44] For over a century, even before the state of Israel was declared, Palestine has been divided into separate Jewish and Arab economies. The economic history by Jacob Metzer highlights these divisions, and helps explain how the modern disparities arose.[45] Some Arabs of course ended up living in Israel, and became Israeli citizens, but they faced much economic discrimination as Raja Khalidi shows.[46] More ended up in the limbo of what became the Occupied Territories, subject to exploitation and even repression, according to Shir Hever's controversial book.[47]

In recent years increasing attention has been paid to the economy of Saudi Arabia and its smaller Gulf neighbours. The early work by Ali Johany and associates on the economy of Saudi Arabia is worth citing,[48] as is the work by

Khouja and Sadler on Kuwait.[49] Other notable studies on oil economies include the volume edited by Khader and El-Wifati on Libya.[50] Of greater contemporary interest is the work by Paul Aarts and Gerd Nonneman on Saudi Arabia[51] as are the books by Tim Niblock[52] and Steffen Hertog.[53] The studies by Christopher Davidson on Dubai[54] and Abu Dhabi[55] represent essential reading for those concerned with the political economy of the UAE.

Volumes dealing with the region as a whole are much rarer, my own earlier book on the economies of the Middle East being a good example.[56] This study adopted a country-by-country approach, rather than each chapter being subject based, as is the case with this book. The main competing volume is the text by Alan Richards and John Waterbury, *A Political Economy of the Middle East: State, Class and Economic Development.*[57] The work is a good study, but in many ways better suited for political science students than economists. The coverage of the Gulf is perhaps the weakest part of the book, and has been to some extent already been overtaken by events. One disadvantage of the Richards and Waterbury volume is its length. It is almost five hundred pages long, which is rather off-putting for the undergraduate reader or for those interested in comparative development experiences rather than the Middle East alone. This study is only half that length, and therefore represents a more compact and manageable review of the state of economic development in the Middle East, and the problems of the past, as well as present and future challenges.

# 2   Modelling Middle East economic development

## Three theoretical explanations of underdevelopment

Which development theories are applicable to the Middle East? In this chapter three main types of theories are considered: those that assume an historical progression; those that attribute underdevelopment to non-economic behaviour; and political economy theories that concentrate on the role of the state as a facilitator or impediment to development. Arguably all these approaches have at least some relevance to the Middle East, which is why they are considered here. Ultimately the question of what theories are most relevant can only be settled empirically. This can involve qualitative evaluation, taking the experiences of particular countries as examples. This is the approach taken in this chapter. Quantitative measures of development are considered in the next chapter, where the actual measures of gross national product growth and changes in economic structures in the Middle East are cited.

Before examining the three approaches to Middle East development in detail, it is useful to provide a brief overview of some of the issues raised with each of them. This gives a perspective on the extent to which the approaches are complementary, or whether they are best regarded as non-reconcilable substitutes.

Some economists claim their theories are universal, in that they are relevant for all countries for all time. Such theories can be historically based, identifying a series of stages of development through which countries pass. Marxist theories and Rostow's stages of economic growth theories were of this type, classifying economies as subsistence-based, feudal, and capitalist.[1] Human behaviour changes at each stage according to Rostow, with enterprising entrepreneurs emerging to facilitate the take-off into self-sustained growth, ideas that draw on those of Schumpeter.[2] For Marxists human behaviour differs according to social class, capitalists attempting to maximise their own gains through the exploitation of their employees if necessary, while workers have more altruistic attitudes that shape the relations in a socialist society.

Are the economies of the Middle East at different stages of development, and are the more backward following a path already taken by the more developed? How can the differences in economic performance be explained both within the region and when comparing the region to other parts of the developing world? Is human behaviour the key, with those in the less advanced countries simply not being materialistic enough in their motivation? If development is seen in purely material terms, however, this becomes tautological, in the sense that people get what they aspire to. Neo-classical economists have a particular concept of economic man looking after his self-interest in market dealings. Indeed this type of maximising behaviour may well be necessary if markets are to function efficiently, which neo-classical economists see as a pre-condition of development. Do markets in the Middle East function efficiently, and if not, can this be explained by individual non-maximising behaviour and cultural conditioning?

Political economists are especially concerned with the role of the state, a subject with a huge development literature. How is the state to be viewed in the Middle East where politics and economics are especially entwined? Is the state protective, productive, dirigiste, predatory, rent seeking, authoritarian or totalitarian, or some combination of some or all of these attributes? Whether economic development is possible without some measure of citizen empowerment is an especially relevant question for the Middle East, where there has been less democracy than anywhere else in the Third World.[3] The Arab Spring has raised hope that this may finally be starting to change, but the consequences for development will take many years to emerge.

## The stages of economic growth in the Middle East

The economies of the Middle East are perhaps the most difficult to categorise in terms of the stage of development they have reached. Most have progressed beyond the subsistence stage and have economic relations characterised by the exchange of goods and services based on monetary transactions. In economies such as Yemen, the Sudan and Upper Egypt barter is still prevalent, but it is only in very remote rural areas where farmers largely grow crops and keep animals for their own subsistence needs. Many of the cities and towns of the ancient Middle East were important trading centres long before commerce developed in Europe, so it would be misleading to regard such developments as a relatively recent phenomenon.

Marxists would with certainty classify the economic relations in much of the region as feudalistic, or at least pre-capitalist in many respects. The means of production in agriculture are often still controlled by large landowners who provide a type of paternalistic protection for their tenants, many of whom remain sharecroppers. The land reforms of the 1950s and 1960s in Egypt, Syria, Iraq and Iran reduced the traditional feudalistic land tenure arrangement in agriculture, but apart from in Egypt where over 15 per cent of agricultural land was redistributed, their scope was limited.[4] Under the Shah's so-called "White Revolution" in Iran, for example, landlords were restricted to owning one village, but this still meant they controlled thousands of acres. In Egypt the ceilings on land ownership were progressively reduced, but many landlords got round this by nominating other members of their family as owners. In Syria and Iraq, where much of the land expropriated remained under nominal state control, the government officials controlling the land started to act in a similar way to the former landlords, with no real checks on their activities, as long as they maintained their allegiance to the state.[5]

The failure of indigenous capitalism to develop in most Middle Eastern states can be attributed to the strength of the traditional feudal structures. A strong attachment to the land prevails in much of the Middle East, and even where there has been considerable migration into towns and cities, traditional loyalties to rural kinship and tribal groupings remain. Investment in land and property is valued more than putting funds into productive enterprises, as there is a physical acquisition that can be used for the benefit of the immediate family and more distant relations. More uncertain investment in industry not only means personal risk, but also is potentially irresponsible, as it is regarded as gambling with the assets of the wider family and kinship group. There is also a reluctance to go outside the family group for business finance, as the external providers of capital, whether a bank or equity investors, could potentially wrest control from the owner. For this reason, most businesses in the Middle East are family-owned and -run, and rely on internal sources of finance. Large-scale private enterprises have failed to develop in most of the economies of the region, and there are few indigenous multinational companies.

## The theory of dependency and the "flying geese" metaphor

Dependency theory may have particular relevance in the Middle East as a consequence of the failure of local capitalism to develop. From the nineteenth century European capitalism became dominant in the Middle East as British and French companies increasingly penetrated the region. Trade became directed to Europe, with the Middle East serving as a supplier of raw materials in exchange for British and, to a lesser extent, French manufactured goods. Economic historians such as Alexander Gerschenkron have pointed out the disadvantage that countries face which are late developers, largely with reference to the Eastern European experience.[6] His theories may also be applicable in the Middle East where capital markets were slow to develop, giving established markets such as London a marked advantage. By the time capital became available in the Middle East with the oil revenue boom, it was too late for the financial infrastructure to catch up, and as a result the dependency on western markets continued.

Gerschenkron stressed that as modern industrialisation needed a huge amount of investment, companies based in developed capital markets were in a privileged position. It could be argued that it was this that placed Middle East companies in a disadvantaged position, and it is the supply of capital rather than the demand for capital that matters. Modern capital markets have to some extent been globalised, but this does not imply that economic geography is irrelevant. Middle Eastern companies and even governments have to pay a country risk premium for funds raised in international markets, which western multinationals can avoid.

The theories of the dependency school have become less fashionable in recent years, partly because of the collapse of communism, but also due to the lack of evidence to support the notion of capitalist exploitation through imperialism. It is over five decades since the final withdrawal of the European colonial powers from the region, Aden and Algeria being the last to be freed. Although some assert that British and French colonialism has been replaced by American neo-colonialism, the facts seem to contradict this. The United States may be strong militarily, with considerable political influence in the region, but in economic terms the European Union and Japan are of more significance for the Middle East.

To explain the development rankings of East and South East Asia there was a so-called "flying geese" metaphor, with Japan in the lead, Singapore and Honk Kong just behind, then Taiwan and Korea, followed by Malaysia and Thailand, with the Philippines, Indonesia and China, bringing up the rear.[7] The use of such a metaphor was based on growing regional interdependence in ASEAN and beyond to Japan and China, and the notion that development of the economies is linked, so that it is not a matter of one country moving forward at the expense of the others. Could such a metaphor be applied to the economies of the Middle East? What is the development ranking within the region, and are the economies moving forward together? It is not even so straightforward to identify a lead country in the position of Japan from the 1960s to the 1980s and China subsequently. Which country could be considered the lead economy in the Middle East?

Israel could potentially be seen in this role, but although it is the most developed country within the region on most criteria, its economy is small. Its supply capacity is very limited in relation to China or Japan, and it lacks the purchasing power to transmit substantial multiplier effects to other Middle Eastern countries that would help their exports.[8] Such effects could possibly occur with respect to the Palestinian territories, and perhaps Jordan, but it is hard to see how it could have much impact on the larger regional economies such as Egypt, Syria, Turkey or even Iran. All this assumes, of course, a normalisation of trading relations between Israel and its neighbours. The Damascus boycott of trade with Israel as a result of conflict with the Arabs prevented this in the past. Peace could change the situation, but there is still a tendency in many Arab countries to view development as a zero-sum game, with one country developing at the expense of its neighbours, rather than complementing their economic progress.

Turkey, because of its size and the extent of its industrialisation, could also be seen as a leader of any "flying geese" in the Middle East, but in its case the metaphor may also be unrealistic.[9] Its main regional trading partner in the 1970s and 1980s was Iraq, from whom it imported oil in exchange for manufactured goods and construction supplies. The Gulf War brought an abrupt end to this trade, and although economic links between Saudi Arabia and

Turkey have subsequently increased, they have no common frontier. Since the collapse of the former Soviet Union, Turkey has concentrated on developing its economic relations with the Muslim Turkish speaking countries of central Asia, and there has also been an increase in trans-Black Sea trade. This new northern orientation for Turkey and the continuing strong economic links with the European Union to some extent marginalised its economic position in the Middle East, although the government of Recep Tayyip Erdoğan, which has been in power since 2003, has sought to revive relations with the Arab World, with Saudi Arabia becoming Turkey's major regional trading partner.

## Pre-conditions for self-sustaining development

To advance from feudalism to a modern capitalist economy, it may be necessary for a type of "take-off" to occur, an idea put forward by the economic historian W.W. Rostow.[10] This concept will be discussed in the next chapter in the section on industrialisation, but it is also relevant here as it is take-off that enables countries to break out of external dependency into self-sustaining growth. Such internal generation is achieved only when several pre-conditions are met, although economists, as always, disagree about what these are.

One pre-condition on which there is agreement is that the workforce should have a reasonable level of education, at least up to secondary level. This is the case in most Middle Eastern states, with the exception of Yemen and the Sudan, although it could be argued that this only applies to the younger generation. Just what qualities the education imparts to assist development is more controversial. Critical thinking is especially valued in western education, but arguably less so in the Far East, where there is more emphasis on the absorption of knowledge. Yet most countries in the Far East have taken off, and out-performed the West for the last two decades. In some respects the education systems in the Middle East are more like those of the Far East, yet economic performance is notably weaker, and take-off seems far away. Education encourages team effort in the Far East; perhaps this is the missing ingredient in the Middle East.

What determines the timing of any take-off into self-sustained growth? Is it influenced by external or internal shocks or do countries simply evolve into take-off position? In the Middle East, development has been far from a smooth continuous process as there have been the politically determined shocks associated with war and revolution that have had far-reaching economic implications, not only for the region, but also for the rest of the world. The 1973 oil price shock was an example of this, a direct outcome of the October war between Israel and its Arab neighbours. The subsequent embargo on oil supplies to the United States caused the oil price to rise from under $3 per barrel to over $11 per barrel, bringing a substantial increase in revenue to the oil-exporting states of the Middle East, which could be used to finance development. Similarly in 1979, the Iranian revolution not only had profound implications for the development of that country, but also resulted in a further doubling of oil prices, which brought windfall gains for the other oil-exporting states.

The oil price rises propelled the oil-exporting states forward in terms of the growth of their gross domestic product, and enabled them to build very modern infrastructures to facilitate industrialisation and commercial development. In some respects the Gulf states attained the development preconditions that they had hitherto lacked, at least in physical if not in human terms, given the long lead times necessary for investment in education and training to have much effect. The economic balance between the Gulf states and their northern Arab neighbours was transformed overnight, with the latter becoming more dependent on the former for finance, although the dependence was not entirely one way, as the Gulf states needed labour from Egypt, Jordan, Syria and Lebanon.[11] Nevertheless, the ranking of states in the development hierarchy changed abruptly. Some of the "flying geese" surged ahead, while others fell back. Take-off into self-sustaining development has, however, remained elusive. Arguably, all the physical and human pre-conditions were fulfilled in none of the states of the region. The "geese" relied even less on each other, and more on the outside world.

To see why this was the case, it is perhaps pertinent to examine the structures of how markets operate in the Middle East, and the behaviour of economic agents in a market context. This is considered in the next section. The role of government may also be crucial. Theories on this, and their relevance to the Middle East, will be considered in the final part of this chapter.

## Middle East markets as *bazaar* economies

Markets are crucial for economic activity as within them the forces of demand and supply interact and prices are determined. The literature on economic development has increasingly focused on the role of market efficiency in facilitating development, and competition as a force encouraging that efficiency in transactions.[12] How efficient are markets in the Middle East, and how does the nature of transactions correspond with that depicted in the standard economic models? The traditional markets of the Middle East, the *souks* of the Arab world and the *bazaars* of Turkey and Iran, are renowned for their bargaining, but bargaining is not the same as competition. Clifford Geertz considered how far a *bazaar* economy is efficient in a study of Morocco, and concluded that in its own terms that it was,[13] but other more aggregate studies of distribution and pricing in the Middle East lead to rather different conclusions.[14] Mark-ups on imported goods are often high, the system of exclusive agents reduces competition and choice, bribery is prevalent to circumvent import controls, all of which means countries get relatively poor value from their development budgets.[15]

If Middle Eastern markets function differently to those of the West, as Geertz suggests, it is worth examining some of their characteristics, and the behaviour of those involved in transactions, to ascertain the implications for development. Does the *bazaar* mentality have to be replaced before development can occur? The economics of information and search clearly have relevance for *bazaar* economies, with prices seldom marked, and normally if a seller is asked to quote a price, the quotation will depend on his view of the buyer's cash position, his perceived interest in actually purchasing the good, and if he is expected to wish to bargain or not. The parties are in asymmetrical positions. The seller for his part will have an advantage in terms of both knowledge and skills over the buyer. When bargaining commences he will have been in the situation hundreds, perhaps thousands, of times before, with an experience of buyer psychology acquired over many years in what is perhaps one of the best "schools of commerce", the *bazaar*.

In these circumstances search can be a daunting and potentially unproductive task. It may be advisable to concentrate on dealing with a particular seller, and try to obtain the best deal through bargaining rather than seeking alternative quotes. Sellers are of course aware of this and may aim to ensure enduring customer relations are established. Geertz described the process of building up goodwill with regular customers as "clientelization". Loyalty to particular suppliers reduces the time buyers spend shopping around for their purchasers, or in other words the search time. This can be considerable in *bazaar* economies where the products on offer are heterogeneous rather than homogenous and where the buyer has therefore to take quality into account as well as price. Decision making with two variables, one of which is non-quantitative and judgemental, becomes a much more complex affair than merely deciding on the basis of the lowest price.

In the *bazaar* the goods on offer tend to be imperfect substitutes, and it is this that makes search important. Particular foodstuffs are differentiated with regard to characteristics such as place of origin, size, taste and maturity. Infinite variety is possible, with no two items on offer exactly the same. Textiles and clothing sold in the *bazaar* are often the product of cottage industries or even manufactured in small workshops within the *bazaar* itself. Each garment is unique, indeed it is often tailored to the requirements of particular customers. Clients are prepared to spend time selecting particular cloths, being measured for fittings and then return to the tailor several times while adjustments are made to a particular garment. It could be said that they are actually involved in the manufacturing process directly, rather than being mere final consumers.

In some *bazaars* there may be a clustering of establishments according to religious affiliation, as with the Jewish merchants in Isfahan in Iran and Fez and Rabat in Morocco. This, however, is the exception rather than the usual situation in the Middle East. Normally establishments are grouped according to the kind of trade that they are involved in or the type of activity performed. Establishments selling herbs and spices, for example, may be all located in one area of the *bazaar*, while those selling gold and jewellery will be found in a different location. In the case of the latter the location may be adjacent to the establishments offering money-changing and money-lending facilities, which will also be clustered together.[16]

The bazaars of the Middle East seem much more enduring than the traditional retailers in the western world. Street markets in the West exhibit some of the characteristics of the oriental *bazaar* but they account for only a small share of retail transactions. Will economic development result in the *bazaar* becoming less important in the Middle East? This is of course the reverse of the question already posed, whether the *bazaar* mentality and methods of transacting are conducive to economic development. Are *bazaars* efficient or would their replacement result in lower prices and better service? In neoclassical economics competition is usually seen as a prerequisite for market efficiency, the notion being that monopolies create distortions and result in overpricing. *Bazaar* activity is better analysed formally with the tools of modern game theory, however, as the simple assumptions of perfect competition have little relevance in a market with complex interactions.

Social preferences are shaped by value systems and cultures. Although governments are concerned to promote development in the Middle East as elsewhere, and ordinary people have material aspirations, there is little support for the "westernisation" of commerce and business methods. The family business, rather than large publicly quoted corporations, remains the backbone of the private sector and the emphasis is on personal dealing. The *bazaar* mentality permeates business culture, with trading regarded as a productive and honourable activity. Competition implies bankruptcy for the unsuccessful, and monopolistic competition a significant amount of take-over and merger activity. Such practices would be out of keeping with the ethos of *bazaar* society, as it involves the positions of entire families being threatened.

## Theories of the role of the state

If markets do not function efficiently in the Middle East because of the transactions costs associated with *bazaar* economies, this could be one justification for direct government intervention in resource allocation. The literature on economic development in the 1950s and 1960s was largely biased towards state intervention, but disillusionment with how the governments of many developing countries actually managed their economies resulted in a swing of the pendulum towards less state interference since the 1980s and 1990s.[17] How effective are Middle Eastern governments in economic management? Can state action overcome market failure or does it merely result in a different type of failure? To answer these questions it is important to identify what government economic objectives actually are. The new theories of political economy can help in this, and it is certainly worth considering their relevance to the Middle East.

The role of the state in developing economies can be classified as protective, productive, dirigiste, authoritarian or totalitarian.[18] There is obviously diversity in forms of government in the Middle East, and most do not fit neatly into one particular category. Despite the Arab Spring, governments in the region are mostly authoritarian, in the sense that power is vested in a dynasty, the military or other ruling elite. The development objectives of the state then tend to be identified with those of the ruling group. This is not simply a matter of the material enrichment of the elite, although this may be important, but it is also a question of the self-aggrandisement of the ruling group by increasing the country's economic power. Hence more general societal objectives may be involved, going well beyond the material satisfaction of the ruling group.

Few, indeed perhaps none, of the governments of the Middle East could be described as totalitarian. This applies where a single party dominates all political institutions and controls absolutely all the instruments of economic power for its own ends. Syria and Iraq under the Baathists came closest to this model, as opposition parties and groups were ruthlessly suppressed, but the control of governments in both states was far from being absolute. Black economies flourished in these two countries beyond state control,[19] opposition groups continued their activities underground, and disputes within the ruling groups themselves seemed never ending. The apparatus of government was arguably not effective enough for totalitarianism to prevail. Saddam Hussein and Hafez Assad, despite their criminal acts, never operated on the scale of Stalin or Hitler or in such a comprehensive manner, as although dissents were ruthlessly dealt with, for most of their populations it was life as usual.

The state has become more significant as nationalism has grown, but there are many other loyalties to family, kinship group, tribe, religious sect and even the wider Arab nation or Muslim community. It could also be argued that external interests prevented the emergence of powerful totalitarian regimes in the Middle East in any case, especially given the West's interest in the region's resources.

A protective state exists where there is minimal government intervention but the state is concerned with national security, internal law and order and the protection of property rights. The Ottoman Empire could be characterised in this way despite the authoritarian nature of its governments. The state only interfered in economic transactions by imposing taxes to keep itself functioning, but the citizens were largely free to pursue their business activities, the major limitations being the need to adhere to social norms rather than any constraints imposed by government.[20]

It would be possible to classify the Ottoman state as a rentier rather than a productive state, and regard the so-called oil rentier economies of the last four decades as inheriting this outlook, but the term rentier is used in a different sense in the new theories of political economy to its use by some economists from the 1970s onwards with respect to the Gulf states. It is seen not as "unproductive" but rather as an interest group approach to politics, seeking to redistribute excessive returns over opportunity costs.[21] This new definition is perhaps more applicable to the Middle East than the rather simplistic "unproductive" notion. To elaborate on this it is necessary first to consider the characteristics of productive states to see if these are present in any of the economies in the Middle East. The question of rent-seeking is a separate issue, not the opposite extreme.

Modern political economy draws on neo-classical welfare analysis to define the productive state. The aim of government is to maximise social welfare, as the state represents the whole citizenry. Governments may intervene, both to increase efficiency where market failure occurs, and to redistribute income, not simply to promote equity, but because welfare is increased when money is redistributed from the richer members of society who get less utility or satisfaction from their marginal income than their poorer neighbours. The government recognises diminishing marginal utility, and acts as a beneficial agent for the good of society as a whole. Given this definition of the productive state, it is hard to see its relevance to the Middle East, where governments usually represent interest groups rather than the whole citizenry. Redistribution can occur, as with the land reforms in Egypt, Syria and Iraq, but this was motivated by a political objective, the desire to break the economic power base of the landed class, not to increase the income of the powerless peasants.

Governments in the Middle East may not be productive but they have assumed some of the role of the dirigiste state. This is sometimes regarded as one step beyond the productive state, but the categories are not a progression so much as alternatives that can exist simultaneously. The dirigiste state draws on structuralist theory, and assumes there is a group of agents committed to maximising the national interest. This is not necessarily the same as the interests of all the citizens, but can be defined in terms of national power, military might, regional and even international prestige and other nationalistic objectives. In order to play this dirigiste role, the state has often to assume the levers of economic power, so that there are not internal challenges to weaken its position. This may involve nationalisation of the commanding heights of the economy, allocating resources through the public sector and regulating private economic activity. Middle Eastern governments have taken all these actions in pursuit of the national and their own interests.

Supporters of the dirigiste state point to the stability it brings in conditions where a more laissez-faire approach would only result in uncertainty in economic decision making, and hazardous outcomes.[22] The governments in the Middle East often last for three decades or longer, in contrast to the situations in western democracies where governments seldom hold power for more than two electoral terms (with some notable exceptions). Changes in government do not bring economic disruption where there is a considerable amount of policy consensus among the different political parties or groupings, but this is rarely the case in the Middle East. There, a change of government often brings revolutionary economic as well as political change, as with the young officers' coup in Egypt in 1952, the Iraqi revolution of 1958, the return of Khomeni to Iran in 1979, the Turkish military coup of 1980 and the aftermath of the Arab Spring of 2011. Even the death of a leader and the accession of a colleague can bring major economic change, as when Sadat succeeded Nasser and launched his "open door" policy to the West.[23] In these circumstances it can be argued that the less frequent are changes in government the better. On the other hand it can be asserted that under strong dirigiste leadership pressures for change build up, and it is this that brings revolutionary discontinuities. If more responsive democratic institutions were in place, then the adjustment could be more evolutionary. This has been the experience in Jordan for example, where a degree of parliamentary democracy has provided an outlet for economic frustrations, and helped ensure a continuous and healthy review of development policy.[24]

Dirigiste governments in the Middle East have often been predatory in the sense of maximising their own self-interest at the expense of the public interest, resulting in an erosion of constitutional constraints on state action. Power in the region has often corrupted the rulers, and been corrosive for both economic and political institutions. Checks and balances have seldom been maintained, and it is far from clear that the highly centralised and concentrated decision making has been for the public good. Arguably it would have been better to have business decisions taken by those actually involved in production and trade rather than the political and military elites. In an unregulated market there are many economic agents taking decisions, so the consequences of bad decision taking are less far reaching, and the law of large numbers usually ensures the overall outcomes are satisfactory. When power is concentrated and bad economic decisions are made, the results can be wasteful and potentially disastrous. The Algerian experience illustrates this, with most of the country's substantial oil and gas revenue spent on ill-conceived industrial projects.[25]

As already mentioned, the economies of the Middle East have often been described as rentier states, and there is a considerable amount of literature referring to the oil-exporting states in this way from the 1970s onward. Definitions of what exactly was meant by the term rentier seemed to vary, one theme being that it implied living off the income of a non-renewable resource, from which a rent could be earned because of its scarcity value. After the oil price rises of 1973 and 1979, the price of Middle Eastern oil seemed to bear little relation to its cost of production. The issue was then to whom the rent should accrue – the oil company, the government of the producing country or the government of the consuming country. These issues will be explored further in the chapter on oil revenue and development, but here it is worth noting its relation to the theory of the dirigiste state, and even the notion of predatory behaviour by government.

It could be argued that oil revenue increased the power of the dirigiste state, and gave it the resources to reinforce its role. Accountability became less important, as there was less reliance on the citizens of the state for tax income. There is of course the slogan "no taxation without representation". Jordan, where the government has to impose high levels of personal taxes to cover its expenditures, enjoys a considerable measure of parliamentary democracy. In contrast, in the Gulf states where revenue largely accrues from oil there are some consultative processes but no real popular accountability for expenditure by government. The link between democratic institutions and development is, of course, both complex and a source of considerable controversy. Whether democracy is a pre-condition for development or an outcome of it has been much debated by political economists. If development implied empowering the individual, democracy may be even regarded as an integral part of the process. The Middle East is possibly the least democratic region of the developing world, but the extent to which this can be explained by the nature of the region's income and wealth must remain a debatable point.

## Theorising on Middle Eastern development

All three approaches discussed in this chapter yield some interesting insights into the development failures in the Middle East. Examination of the historical stages of economic growth approach might lead to the conclusion that despite the many economic changes in the region, none of the economies had reached the take-off stage for self-sustaining growth to occur. External dependency continues, and the "flying geese" metaphor that has been applied to the successful economies of South East Asia would not appear especially relevant to the Middle East given the absence of a lead economy and weak regional linkages, especially in relation to trade. The deficiencies in the internal generation of development could be attributed to market failures. There is certainly evidence that markets function inefficiently in the Middle East, with high transactions costs. Government failure may be as serious a problem as market failure, however, with autocratic governments making poor decisions, and an emphasis on short-term rent seeking and the politics of patronage. There is almost a reluctance to permit the emergence of new sources of economic power in case it threatens the state monopoly. These issues will arise again in later chapters of this book, but first we turn to quantifying the exact state of Middle East development, to ascertain the extent of any shortcomings and the scale of the task ahead. This is the subject for Chapter 3.

# 3 Growth and structural change

## The economic inheritance

The Middle East has a rich economic inheritance and was one of the first regions of the world to have a developed civilisation. Both the physical and human achievements were considerable and mankind as a whole owes a great debt to the pioneering efforts of the Egyptians in agriculture and irrigation, the Persians in crafts and the Phoneticians in trading. The spread of Islam was to result in a resurgence of scientific discovery in the region that was only later followed by Europe at the time of the Renaissance. In the sixteenth century the city of Isfahan had more artisans than Paris, Europe's leading metropolis, while Shiraz was a major centre for scholarship and learning.[1] By the late nineteenth century Cairo had a sophisticated financial infrastructure, including a stock exchange, while Alexandria was one of the leading ports of the Mediterranean, its prosperity based on cotton exports, with Egypt being the leading world supplier.[2]

It is against this background that the economic performance of the region during the second half of the twentieth and early twenty-first century must be judged. Much has been achieved, and the last seventy years have witnessed greater changes than the last five centuries. The population of the Middle East has increased to over 300 million, and continues to grow by 8 million each year. Turkey and Iran each have populations exceeding 70 million and Egypt has a population exceeding 80 million.[3] The urban rural balance has changed drastically, and most Middle Eastern societies now have over half of their populations concentrated in cities and large towns. The population of Cairo exceeds 15 million, while Tehran has over 6 million inhabitants.

In the Malthusian view, such a rapid increase in population can only bring misery and hardship. The additional population is regarded as a liability rather than an asset. It adds to consumption pressures without contributing to production. Yet social indicators for Middle Eastern states do not support such a gloomy view. Life expectancy rose from around 55 years on average in 1970 to over 70 years by 2010, reflecting better diets and improved health care. This compares very favourably with sub-Saharan Africa and south Asia, although life expectancy is higher in China and most Latin American countries. Daily calorie intakes are more than adequate throughout the region, apart from Sudan. School enrolments have increased from only half of the population aged from 7 to 17 to over 90 per cent. Two-thirds of the region's population can now read and write, with illiteracy largely confined to the older generation. Literacy levels are much higher than those in South Asia, although below those of China and most of Latin America. There has been a particularly dramatic increase in the numbers of girls in schooling, indicating that Islam has not been detrimental to female educational advancement.

The substantial investment in human capital has not been matched by a corresponding investment in physical capital in the poorer countries of the region, and this mismatch may be one factor accounting for their relatively poor development performance. In countries such as Egypt, Sudan and Iran there has been major economic change, but these changes have often not been for the better, and material living standards for the majority of people remain low, and in many cases are actually deteriorating. The measurement of development is a huge and controversial subject in itself. A useful first step is to review the major conventional indicators.

## Gross domestic and gross national product (GDP and GNP)

Figures for GDP and GNP can give a very misleading impression in the Middle East, especially for the major oil exporting states, but it would be incorrect to dismiss them as useless indicators. They represent real purchasing power internationally, and for small open economies this is highly significant. Alternative measures of development cannot be ignored, including structural indicators, but GDP and GNP are good starting points. They highlight the huge differences within the Middle East in terms of economic muscle and also demonstrate just how weak the position of the region is in relation to other parts of the world.

It is important to distinguish between GDP and GNP when making comparisons over time and between countries. Both measures are available for Middle Eastern economies. GNP includes net property income from abroad, which has been and remains highly significant for the OPEC states of the region with substantial overseas asset holdings. These movements tend to be erratic, reflecting changes in conditions in international financial markets rather than economic developments within the region. Inflows can also result from changes in fiscal policy, but these may be distorting. Government spending in excess of tax revenues can be financed by the sale of overseas assets, which adds to GNP. This, however, is a sign of economic weakness rather than strength.

Remittances also account for GDP and GNP differences. An Egyptian or Syrian working in Saudi Arabia contributes to the GDP of the Kingdom rather than the GDP figures for Egypt or Syria. However, the remittance inflows contribute to Egyptian and Syrian GNP even though no domestic production is directly involved. There will be spin-off effects for the domestic economies as the families receiving the remittances spend locally, resulting in increased retail business and perhaps even a stimulus to Egyptian and Syrian manufacturing activity and construction.

The economic weakness of the region can be illustrated by international gross national product comparisons. Egypt's GDP was around $500 billion in 2010, well below the GDP of $623 billion for Saudi Arabia, a much smaller country in terms of population. The disparity between the Middle East and the more dynamic areas of the developing world is becoming more marked, even taking comparisons with other Muslim countries. Egypt's GDP was almost 50 per cent higher than that of Thailand in 1970, a country with a similar population size, but by 2010 the latter was well ahead with a GDP of $589 billion. Iran's GDP was much higher than that of Turkey in 1970s, but by 2010 the latter's GDP was $969 billion, the highest in the Middle East, compared to $888 billion for Iran, yet Turkey has no indigenous oil or gas. The relative change in the global position of the Middle East is more encouraging, however, as growth in the advanced industrialised countries slows. As a region the Middle East accounted for 1.8 per cent of world GDP in 1970, but by 2010 this proportion had risen to 3.5 per cent.

Per capita GNP is the most widely used indicator for measuring changes in living standards both within countries over time and for international comparisons.[4] For the Middle Eastern economies it illustrates just how poor living standards are for over 90 per cent of the region's inhabitants, and how standards in recent years have been falling rather than rising. In Iran for example, GNP per capita contracted at an annual rate of 1.2 per cent over the 1985 to 2010 period. In Jordan the annual rate of decrease was 4.0 per cent over the same period and in Syria GNP per capita was stagnant. Saudi Arabia fared better, however, with a 1.5 per cent annual increase in per capita GNP, partly a consequence of the oil production and oil price rises.

Oil production distorts GNP figures, and for the Arabian Peninsula states in particular, much of the change reflects oil price decreases and production swings. It is often asserted that for OPEC countries per capita income is a totally misleading indicator of the level of economic development as the high figures merely reflect oil production, not successful advance through economic diversification. What constitutes successful development is a matter for value judgement, and there are no objective criteria. The very high levels of per capita income for the less populous countries do give an indication of the ability to consume imported goods and services, which has implications for individual and social welfare. It is not the measure that is wrong, but the interpretation.

There is also the question of whether to calculate the GNP per capita figure by dividing GNP by the number of local citizens or the total population including expatriates. In the cases of Qatar and the UAE the expatriate population greatly exceeds the local population. In practice the total population headcount is used, which results in the per capita GNP of local citizens being seriously underestimated.

Another criticism of gross national product per capita comparisons is that a common unit of measure has to be used, most frequently the United States dollar. A dollar standard was appropriate when the United States currency underpinned the international monetary system but the dollar's role has diminished considerably in recent years and its exchange rate has been volatile in relation to the yen and euro. As a consequence the dollar is no longer a very attractive store of value or medium of exchange, but in a multicurrency trading system there is no single satisfactory alternative, especially as the Eurozone crisis has damaged confidence in using euros rather than United States dollars.

In any case for the countries of the Middle East the United States dollar arguably remains a better yardstick than other currencies, not least because the price of oil is denominated in dollars. External aid inflows and soft loans to the poorer states are also dollar denominated, which means that the dollar is certainly an appropriate standard for balance of payments receipts. It is on the import side, however, where the dollar is less relevant as, apart from in the field of defence equipment, the United States is an insignificant supplier. Most civilian imports come from China, Japan and Korea or from the countries of the European Union. This applies as much in the case of capital equipment as consumer goods, with Far Eastern and Turkish contractors winning most infrastructure tenders.

The problem for the Middle Eastern states is that with balance of payments receipts largely dollar denominated but expenditure obligations euro and yen denominated, exchange rate fluctuations between the United States, European and Japanese currencies affect the Middle Eastern countries as third parties. An appreciation of the dollar helps the states of the region; depreciation results in economic damage. For most of the thirty-year period since 1980 the fluctuations and deprecations in the dollar harmed the Middle Eastern economies, undermining the region's international purchasing power.

Table 3.1 shows purchasing power parity (PPP) per capita GNP comparisons for nine leading Middle Eastern economies. The PPP figures reflect the real value of per capita income, taking account of variations in the cost of living, which are not reflected in the exchange rates. For all the countries of the region the PPP per capita GNP figures are much higher than the actual figures, indicating that the countries may not be as poor as crude comparisons

*Table 3.1* GDP rankings for highest-income countries in the Middle East

| Country | GDP per capita $ | World rank | GDP $ billion |
|---|---|---|---|
| Qatar | 88,222 | 1 | 150 |
| UAE | 47,439 | 6 | 248 |
| Kuwait | 38,775 | 14 | 139 |
| Israel | 29,602 | 28 | 219 |
| Bahrain | 26,932 | 34 | 30 |
| Oman | 25,492 | 35 | 76 |
| Saudi Arabia | 22,607 | 41 | 623 |
| Libya | 13,846 | 64 | 91 |
| Turkey | 13,577 | 65 | 969 |

Source: International Monetary Fund, Washington, 2011

*[handwritten margin note: ME uses US Dollar as the rate of fluctuation between Euro & Dollar hurts M.E]*

*Table 3.2* GDP rankings for lowest-income countries in the Middle East

| Country | GDP per capita $ | World rank | GDP $ billion |
|---|---|---|---|
| Sudan | 2,380 | 142 | 95 |
| Yemen | 2,606 | 138 | 64 |
| Iraq | 3,548 | 127 | 114 |
| Syria | 5,126 | 113 | 108 |
| Jordan | 5,767 | 107 | 35 |
| Egypt | 6,417 | 104 | 499 |
| Algeria | 6,966 | 99 | 252 |
| Tunisia | 9,454 | 84 | 100 |
| Iran | 11,883 | 74 | 888 |

Source: International Monetary Fund, Washington, 2011

using current exchange rates might suggest. Egypt, for example, has a PPP per capita GNP figure of $6,417 compared to an actual figure of $2,808. For Syria the PPP figure is $5,126 compared with an actual figure of $2,823. If PPP figures are used none of the countries cited fall into the World Bank's and United Nations low-income category for developing countries. Most are in the middle-income bracket, apart from the Gulf economies and Israel, which have per capita gross national product figures comparable to developed industrial countries. If PPP comparisons are taken, the remarks made above about the relative poverty of the Middle East in relation to the industrialised world may need considerable qualification.

Table 3.2 shows the nine poorest states in the Middle East, with Sudan having the lowest GDP per capita figure. The data for Sudan includes the south, which became a separate state in 2011, and has to be considered as part of sub-Saharan Africa rather than the Middle East. As much of Sudan's oil is in the south the remaining part of the country in the north has fewer resources and diminished development prospects, and hence is likely to remain the Middle East's poorest state. From the table it is also clear how far oil-rich Iraq has declined, partly as a consequence of misrule by Saddam Hussein, and the disastrous aftermath of the Anglo-American invasion and the accompanying sectarian strife. Syria can also be classified as a failed state, not just politically under the legacy of Hafez al-Assad and his son, but also economically in terms of its regional development ranking and poor living standards.

**Nominal and real income**

When examining changes over time in GNP or GDP it is necessary to allow for the effect of price changes. Nominal rises mean little if economies are subject to substantial inflationary pressures, as has often been the case in the Middle East. All countries in the region compile price indices, but the coverage of these is often restricted, which means their usefulness as gross national product deflators must be open to question. The most inflation-prone economies, Turkey in the past and Iran today, construct fairly sophisticated retail and wholesale price indices. Israel, which had high rates of inflation until the late 1980s, used its indices for wage indexing, though there were some moves to reduce the inflationary bias by moving away from this.[5] Turkey's inflation has fluctuated considerably, the rate rising from 38.8 per cent in 1987 to 75.4 per cent the following year before falling back to 63.8 per cent in 1990.[6] Its average inflation rate over the 2004–10 period was much lower at around 9 per cent, compared to just over 2 per cent for Israel, 17 per cent for Iran and 14 per cent in the case of Egypt.

The difficulty with such high and volatile rates of inflation is that different commodities can be affected in markedly dissimilar ways over even quite short periods of time. Prices of imported goods may increase with a lag following depreciation, for example, but depreciation may be far from a smooth continuous process. Domestically produced goods may rise in price after wage settlements, but these are usually annual or biannual rather than monthly or quarterly, even in high-inflation countries such as Iran. Given inflation differentials between commodities one problem that arises is which weights to assign to each component of the GNP deflator and when to weight. There are two standard methods, either the use of a base weighted index, the Laspeyre approach, or a current weighted index, the Paasche approach. The problem with the former is that the weights become outdated and irrelevant. In the latter case reindexing is necessary for each new period, but the problem is then consistency over time. In the Middle East it is the Laspeyre approach that is most commonly used so the appropriateness of the weighting must be open to question.

There are also distribution issues that arise when deflating GNP. Price indices in the Middle East are based on urban rather than rural prices. As a result the impact of inflation on agriculture and the countryside may be over- or under-estimated. In practice the value of urban and manufacturing production is usually exaggerated by a higher average rate of inflation in cities and major towns. Even the decline in the share of agricultural in GNP may be partly attributed to a pricing miscalculation.

## The wealth of nations

Per capita GNP only measures current income but reveals little about the underlying wealth of nations. The literature on national accounting stresses the importance of the wealth stock as well as the income flows. Countries such as Japan have a high gross national product per capita, but the accumulated wealth in the private housing stock does not compare with the United Kingdom, a country with a similar level of income, but a much richer capital endowment for its citizens to enjoy. In mature industrial nations the problem is to generate sufficient income to maintain the existing capital stock. Any additions are a welcome bonus.

How do the Middle Eastern countries compare in international income and wealth relatively? Natural calamities such as earthquakes are a problem in some countries of the region, notably Turkey and Iran, but even the worst quake has not destroyed more than 1 per cent of the capital stock of any single country. It is common practice to provide steel frames for buildings and reinforce concrete with metal rods, but this is not a major expense. The climate, despite the extremes of temperature, is kind as far as buildings and infrastructure are concerned, and storm or flood damage is less of a problem than in many parts of the world. No country in the region faces problems like those of Bangladesh, where capital accumulation seems futile given the annual problems of typhoons, tidal waves and monsoon-induced flooding.

The Middle East has a rich cultural and architectural inheritance, which is reflected in the magnificence of some of the mosques and other public buildings. These represent only a minute proportion of the building stock, however, and the more modern buildings financed by government are at best nondescript, and at worst vertical slums. The peak public building period in Egypt, Syria and Iraq was the secularist era of Arab socialism of the 1950s and 1960s when the inspiration was the tower blocks of Eastern Europe. The contribution to the wealth stock of these high-rise buildings is extremely debatable. Indeed many in the Middle East regard such blocks as liabilities rather than assets. These were never suitable for Arab lifestyles, given the desire for family privacy and space for male and female separation within the household. Additional space was also needed to accommodate several generations together, given the preference for extended family structures.

There is considerable variation in the quality of both the housing stock and infrastructure in the Middle East. Maintenance has often been poor and conservation neglected. The mud brick houses of the Nile valley and delta may not have contributed much to the value of Egypt's capital stock, but they are cheap to maintain and rebuilt. The more expensive high-rise buildings constructed during the last three decades require much more maintenance and are likely to prove a greater drain on current income. There are some architectural masterpieces in the oil-rich states of the Gulf, but these buildings are the exception rather than the rule. Most buildings are as shoddy and mediocre in the Gulf as in the poorer states of the region, and unfortunately the generation of the oil boom has bequeathed a dismal inheritance for their children.

The wealth stock has implications for national income accounting. Replacement investment is needed as machinery and equipment come to the end of their productive lives, and even buildings and plant have to be replaced eventually. An allowance for depreciation has to be built into investment calculations. At the national income level net national product refers to the value of a nation's annual output less the capital consumption experienced in producing that output. In other words, net national product equals GDP minus depreciation.[7]

In the Middle East, given the poor quality of much of the capital stock and inexperience in the maintenance of modern plant, depreciation can be extremely rapid. GNP figures may therefore give a more favourable impression than is justified. Much investment is replacement investment rather than new investment. Arguably comparisons should be made using net rather than gross national product figures, but this is not done, as there are no international standards governing depreciation. In the Middle East such calculations are invariably rough and ready.

## Investment in transport and infrastructure

The communications infrastructure is good in the Middle East by Third World standards, and this is perhaps the most positive lasting development that was facilitated by the oil boom of the 1970s. With some notable exceptions, such as Tehran and Jeddah, airports compare with the best internationally. For intra-regional passenger travel, air is the preferred, and indeed usually the most common option. Airline fleets are of variable age, and most of the airlines that have modernised have purchased or leased the cheaper twin-engine aircraft, even for long-haul flights. Many national carriers would not be viable without government subsidies, but spending state money on this rather than on ground transport raises equity issues. Cross-border airline mergers could bring savings in the Middle East and produce a world-class airline but, as the experience of Gulf Air shows, this is not guaranteed. At present the tendency is more towards fragmentation. Emirates, the Dubai-based airline, has been an outstanding regional and global success. Low refuelling costs, tax-free salaries and the absence of staff unions have helped, and the quality of the product offered remains impressive despite the very rapid expansion of the airline.

Road transport has become the primary means of national communication in the Middle East as in most other parts of the world. Dependence on the internal combustion engine is perhaps quite appropriate in a major oil-exporting region, with a large proportion of global reserves. Most freight is carried by road, and the haulage business is one of the most buoyant private sector activities. Roads have been much improved during the last four decades, and the network of dual carriageways is particularly impressive in the Gulf states.

Communications have been planned on a purely national basis in the Middle East and there is no inter-state road system like that found in North America or the European Union. There is relatively little intra-regional trade and commerce in the Middle East, though the explanation for this is related more to economic structure than the transport infrastructure. It is always debatable how far the lack of inter-state highways merely reflects the low level of intra-regional trade or is itself a cause of the restricted volume. Given the willingness in the Middle East to exploit to the full even limited facilities, the latter direction of causation would appear unlikely.

Overland transport links were distorted and impeded following the creation of the state of Israel.[8] The area that constituted Palestine was at the heart of the intra-regional communications, and Israel acted as a wedge between the Arab countries of North Africa and Western Asia. Jordan was cut off from the Mediterranean, with its only access to the sea via Aqaba. As most Jordanian trade had been with Britain, and even today is with the European Union, this route was inconvenient, and added to transport costs, with shipping having to pass through the Suez Canal. Jordan has benefited considerably from the normalisation of relations with Israel, and although direct bilateral trade possibilities have proved to be limited, there have been significant benefits for transit trade and tourism.

Road communications may be more appropriate than railway links in a large, unevenly populated region such as the Middle East. There is no high-speed inter-city rail network either within countries or regionally, and the cost of such investment would be enormous. The comparatively short distance between Cairo and Alexandria has a good connection, but the quality of track between Cairo and Aswan is poor, with priority given to rolling stock. There is a modern upgraded track from Riyadh to Dammam, but elsewhere investment in the railways has been minimal. The Cairo metro system represented a substantial investment, but whether this was a justifiable priority for Egypt as a whole must be debatable, although it did help speed up urban transit times in the capital. The Dubai light railway network, the largest public transport scheme in the Middle East, has been successfully operating since 2009. The Haramain High Speed Rail Project, linking Jeddah with Medina and Mecca, will facilitate even larger numbers of pilgrims to undertake Hajj and Umrah. It will eventually link up with the proposed land-bridge rail project, linking Jeddah and Riyadh.

## The state of land and agriculture

Historically the Middle East was not only self-sufficient in most foodstuffs, but there was a substantial grain surplus for export. The region contained some of the oldest areas of settled agriculture in the world. The highlands of Yemen had elaborate terracing for its agriculture, and the Nile and Tigris-Euphrates valleys had complex irrigation systems dating back to the fourth millennium B.C. Crop rotation to prevent soil exhaustion was pioneered in the region. North Africa was the granary for much of the Roman Empire, and the Mediterranean littoral of the region was one of the first areas in the world to support fruit and vegetable production on a significant scale. The order established by the Ottomans enabled agriculture to flourish, and the security of tenure that land registration brought encouraged landowners to invest in farm improvement.

Over the last four decades the Middle East has become a substantial net importer of food, partly because of population growth and the consequent increase in demand. There have been significant rises in agricultural output, with both increased yields per acre and an expansion in the cultivated area, but the additional supply has been insufficient to overcome shortfalls. Egypt's population continues to increase by over a million every nine months, and already exceeds eighty million. In Iran the population has risen from thirty-eight million before the Islamic revolution to over seventy million in three decades. In these circumstances it is hardly surprising that both countries need to import a large proportion of their foodstuffs, despite the efforts to encourage higher levels of domestic agricultural production.

It is evident that agricultural self-sufficiency is not a realistic prospect for most economies in the Middle East. Such a goal is questionable in any case. Self-sufficiency can be virtually guaranteed at a price, but given the land resource base of the Middle East the opportunity cost may be considerable. Funds spent on land improvement reduce the budget for industrial infrastructure. Water used in agriculture could be used by manufacturing establishments. There may also be pricing distortions internally. Saudi Arabia has been able to produce a substantial grain surplus for export, but only by pricing domestically produced grain at five times the world level.[9]

For shares of sectors in national income within countries the World Bank uses GDP rather than GNP, as the concern is with production within countries. A falling share of agriculture in GDP is often viewed as a sign of development.[10] It represents part of the structural adjustment process rather than being economically detrimental. If a stages of growth approach to development is taken then in the early stages primary productive activities such as agriculture are the dominant forms of economic production. With economic growth comes the development of processing and manufacturing activity, which may result in the establishment of a significant industrial base. The role of agriculture may therefore decline as an outcome of the growth process itself, even if this is relative rather than absolute.

In the Middle East the share of agriculture in GDP has declined in countries such as Egypt and Turkey, as might be expected, with a 10 and 15 per cent fall respectively over the 1981–2010 period, as Table 3.3 shows. In Egypt and Turkey agriculture only accounts for 10 per cent of GDP, though in Turkey's case as its GDP is higher, the absolute value of agricultural production is much higher, with the country not only feeding itself, but exporting fruit, vegetables and grains to other countries in the Middle East. In contrast Egypt has to import most of the grain it consumes. The figures for the share of agriculture in GDP remain well above 5 per cent and less typical of many industrialised countries, but the gap has clearly narrowed. Even in Sudan, the least developed country of the region, the share of agriculture has fallen to

*Table 3.3* Value added in agriculture as a percentage of GDP

| Country | 1981 | 2010 |
| --- | --- | --- |
| Algeria | 9 | 11 |
| Egypt | 20 | 10 |
| Iran | 20 | 10 |
| Jordan | 6 | 3 |
| Morocco | 13 | 15 |
| Saudi Arabia | 1 | 3 |
| Sudan | 36 | 24 |
| Syria | 22 | 21 |
| Tunisia | 14 | 7 |
| Turkey | 25 | 10 |

Source: World Bank, Washington, 2011

less than one-quarter. The share in Saudi Arabia is only 3 per cent but, as already indicated, the Kingdom has increased agricultural production substantially and, given the large size of its GDP, agricultural output is comparable to that of countries such as Syria where the share of agriculture in GDP is much higher.

In the case of some states in the Middle East declines in the share of agriculture have not meant a declining dependence on primary production, but merely an increase in the share of oil. It must be debatable if the substitution of extractive primary activity for the exploitation of a renewable resource, namely agricultural land, really constitutes development. This substitution of oil for farm produce has not only occurred in the largely arid Arabian Peninsula states but also in more populous countries with historically important agricultural sectors. Though Egypt is not an OPEC state and its reserves of oil are limited, petroleum and gas have become its major exports and largest contributors to GDP. It is this that accounts for much of the relative decline in the share of its agricultural sector, not the rise of manufacturing or even the growth of services.

For some countries great care has to be taken in interpreting figures for the value of agricultural output, as not all production may be recorded.[11] Often only marketed output is accounted for in official statistics, and in some cases merely produce sold through government agencies rather than private merchants. The latter often constitute part of the informal sector where economic activity is not enumerated, rather than the so-called formal modern sector. Subsistence agricultural production is also invariably excluded from the official figures for farm output. In the Middle East many rural families grew a significant proportion of the food they consumed themselves, a practice that continues even today. When cash crop production is substituted for subsistence output the contribution of the agricultural sector might be interpreted as rising, when this may not in fact be the case.

The major constraint on agriculture in the Middle East is the region's limited water resources. Rather than further depleting the water resources of the Arabian Peninsula the GCC countries are looking to invest in agriculture in other regions of the world to ensure food security. In return for receiving investment from countries such as Saudi Arabia and Qatar, recipient countries will be expected to give supply preferences to the investor nations. Such schemes are potentially controversial as although the investment inflows will benefit the supplying countries and hopefully increase their levels of agricultural production, smallholders and tenants could be displaced by the agro-industrial projects. The schemes could result in increasing inequalities in the rural economies of the host countries and even cause food shortages while priority is given to supplying the much more affluent countries of the Gulf.[12]

## Industrialisation and development

Since the reign of Muhammad Ali in the first half of the nineteenth century in Egypt, there has been an interest in the Middle East in establishing modern industries. Muhammad Ali was very conscious of the successful experience of industrialisation in northern Europe and the United Kingdom in particular, and wanted his country to follow the same path. Egypt was an increasingly important producer of cotton, but most of the raw produce was sent to Lancashire in England for manufacture into textiles rather than being processed locally. It seemed ironic that cotton textiles were actually imported into Egypt, from a country that could not itself grow cotton. Muhammad Ali thought a modest step forward would be to establish textile factories in Egypt to produce substitutes for these imports, but it was realised that the "infant industry" would need tariff protection until it became properly established.[13]

Many development economists see industrialisation as the key to development, as manufacturing can act as a leading sector and serve as a stimulus to growth through linkages to other parts of an economy.[14] Development may involve structural transformation as the share of primary extractive and agricultural activity declines in relation to gross domestic product and the share of secondary manufacturing rises. At the same time industrialisation not only involves physical investment but also, perhaps more importantly, human capital formation. The acquisition of industrial skills can be a crucial learning process, which may be a prerequisite for development. Often the Japanese experience is cited as proof of just how significant the human skill element can be.

The motivation for the establishment of modern factories in Egypt by Muhammad Ali was not primarily related to development objectives as they are understood in the West today. Indeed this could not have been possible, as the notion of developed and underdeveloped countries only emerged in the twentieth century, largely as a result of the relatively long periods of growth enjoyed by some industrialising countries. Muhammad Ali wanted to industrialise to make Egypt more independent, and increase his freedom of manoeuvre. The objective was basically nationalistic, a desire not so much to emulate Britain and the West, but rather to detach Egypt from the imperial powers.

Military strength appeared to come from industrial success, and it was this that attracted Muhammad Ali and later Middle Eastern political leaders. The question of raising living standards for ordinary Egyptian families was of much less, if any, concern. What mattered was national economic power and the consequent political prestige, not the welfare of individuals. Saddam Hussein of Iraq, although a very different type of figure to Mohammad Ali, was very much in this tradition, with his vision of a strong ruler leading a mighty army and nation.

Given such objectives it is hardly surprising that nationalism and industrialisation became linked in the Middle East, with the state rather than the private sector taking the lead. This was the case in Ataturk's Turkey, Nasser's Egypt and even Iran under the Shah. This explains why industrialisation has been pursued with a disregard for financial objectives, as profit has not been a major or even a significant motivation. It also explains why the populations of Middle Eastern states have often been much less enthusiastic about industrialisation than the political leadership.

The industrialisation programmes of the early reformists may seem old fashioned and inappropriate when viewed with the benefit of hindsight, but they have to be judged in relation to the norms of their times. The stress was on the establishment of basic heavy industries such as steel making, following to varying degrees the Soviet model of industrial development. In Turkey under Ataturk in the 1920s the state played the leading role in the establishment of such plants, which were seen as development imperatives irrespective of the country's factor endowment of available resources.[15] In fact Turkey had both coal and iron ore, so domestic circumstances were not unfavourable for industries such as steel making, and there was clearly a market for reinforcing steel rods in particular, given the requirements of the construction industry in an earthquake-prone country.

In the case of Egypt conditions were much less favourable for the heavy industry established under Nasser in the 1950s and 1960s. The Helwan steel plant was dependent on coking coal from Poland and imported iron ore, and used dated Soviet technology that was environmentally disastrous.[16] It is this type of plant that was closed down in Eastern Europe, but in Egypt such a closure with its resultant lay-offs would be politically unacceptable. The country is therefore burdened with a lame duck industry that requires both protection from international competition by quotas and continuing financial subsidies. The aluminium smelter was more up to date, but the rationale for such a plant in a country with only limited oil and gas supplies was never very clear. The main advantage for such plants in the Gulf is the cheap and abundant feedstock, but in Egypt the opportunity cost of providing cheap energy is arguably much higher.

The comparative advantage of the more populous Middle Eastern states might be expected to be in labour-intensive activities such as textiles. There was a more obvious rationale for what Muhammad Ali was trying to achieve than with Nasser's industrialisation efforts. The textile mills could at least use local cotton, and employ relatively low-cost indigenous labour.[17] This was also the thinking in Iran in the 1930s when the first modern textile mills were set up in Isfahan, though in its case the international advantage continued to be in traditional craft activities such as the manufacture of hand-knotted carpets. These were of unique design, and the weaving was a highly skilled operation, though admittedly the main skills were managerial. It was those who oversaw the intricate production that were the creative or artistic force; the weaving itself was a very repetitive task often undertaken by women and children who merely followed detailed instructions.

Now that the heavy industrialisation efforts can be viewed from an historical perspective, in some cases more than a century after, it is clear that the plants have mostly not been a success, either in financial or economic terms. The financial costs might have been justified had there been spin-offs and linkages to other industries. In practice there was no "big push" into self-sustaining growth; instead they appear to be dead-end industries. The plants have survived because of political sensitivities and their monopolistic position, but there can

*Table 3.4* Value added in manufacturing as a percentage of GDP

| Country | 1981 | 2010 |
|---|---|---|
| Algeria | 11 | 6 |
| Egypt | 13 | 14 |
| Iran | 8 | 11 |
| Jordan | 14 | 19 |
| Morocco | 18 | 16 |
| Saudi Arabia | 5 | 10 |
| Sudan | 7 | 6 |
| Syria | 12 | 13 |
| Tunisia | 12 | 15 |
| Turkey | 20 | 17 |

Source: World Bank, Washington, 2011

be no real future. In contrast traditional industries are enjoying a revival. Their market advantage derives from the differentiated nature of the products, reflecting their unique designs and the skills of the production managers. They do not need artificial protection like the import substitute heavy industries. Their profits come partly from a natural rent reflecting a real scarcity in management skills, not a monopoly rent resulting from government protection and the exclusion of competitors.

Table 3.4 shows the changes in the share of manufacturing in GDP over the 1981–2010 period for those Middle Eastern states that have made the greatest efforts to industrialise. Primary extractive industry is excluded, as this would severely distort the picture for major oil exporting states such as Saudi Arabia. Petrochemicals dominate the manufacturing scene in Saudi Arabia, but there are also a number of smaller import substitution ventures. Turkey has clearly a much more substantial manufacturing base than the other states of the region, but the figures demonstrates just how far the Maghreb states have progressed. Tunisia and Morocco have many small garments manufacturing establishments, usually undertaking sub-contracting work for French companies.

## The contribution of services to economic activity

The stages of an economic growth approach to development, as outlined in the previous chapter, suggests that the share of services in GDP tends to grow in post-industrial societies. As economies mature there is a move away from basic heavy industry towards more specialised manufacturing, and much of the ancillary support gets hived off to other businesses, especially service companies. Demand- as well as supply-side theories also support an increasing role for services. With rising income the demand for services tends to increase while the demand for foodstuffs and basic manufactured products stagnates. In other words, the income elasticity of demand for services is higher, as fewer services fall into the category of inferior goods. Spending on education, health, travel and leisure can be virtually limitless, but there are often self-imposed limits on trading up in clothing, footwear, housing and even consumer durables.

In the Middle East the share of services in GDP has been rising in all countries, and extremely rapidly in some. Throughout the region the services sector accounts for the largest single proportion of GDP, and in some countries such as Egypt and Syria around half of the total. Many find the dominance of services surprising in Egypt given the size of its population, its rich land resource in the Nile Valley and the long-established industrial base. In the cases of smaller economies such as Jordan and Lebanon, where services account for over two-thirds of GDP, the position is perhaps less surprising, as Jordan was a significant transit route for Iraq,[18] and Lebanon, before its disastrous civil war, was a financial centre for the whole region.[19]

In the OPEC states of the Middle East services account for a slightly lower proportion of GDP, the share being 43 per cent in Kuwait and the United Arab Emirates, 45 per cent in Libya and 41 per cent in Saudi Arabia. To a large extent this reflects the dominance of oil in GDP. The national accounting ratios can in fact be misleading. Services are likely on economic grounds to be more rather than less dominant in oil-exporting states given their rentier nature. Such economies can finance high levels of both current expenditure from oil revenues by government and consumer expenditure. Consumer goods tend to be imported, but most services demanded fall into the non-tradable category. These include government provided services, such as education or health, the income elasticity of demand for which can be very high. There may also be a buoyant demand for private sector services, especially in transportation and distribution, with positive multiplier effects on the domestic non-tradable sector.

Trading activity was of course of paramount importance in the OPEC oil exporting states of the Middle East long before the oil boom of the 1970s. The Arabian Peninsula states were to a large extent merchant economies, and the cities of the region developed as trading centres. Oil production increasingly dominated GDP from the 1940s onward, but the role of the traders was enhanced rather than reduced. Oil acted as a stimulus, and presented new opportunities. The migrant workers attracted by the oil boom became clients of the merchants, and the increased ability to finance imports encouraged buoyant trading conditions. As only the value of imports rather than the retail prices were recorded, there tended to be an underestimation of the value added by the trading sector, and hence its contribution to GDP.

Despite the oil boom, the economies of the Middle East have often suffered the effects of falling asset values, particularly real estate, which has dampened consumer spending. Not surprisingly this has adversely affected services, especially trading. Actual conflicts and threats to regional security have resulted in increased military expenditure, which has meant a squeeze on government current spending on education and health. Hence services have experienced a double blow. Nevertheless the sector as a whole has proved remarkably resilient, perhaps reflecting its deepseated economic strengths and historical experience. The natural caution of the merchants has helped their position. Most stock was self-financed rather than acquired through bank borrowing. Premises are usually owned rather than rented. Employees are often family members, and are willing to accept lower remuneration in hard times. In such circumstances cash flow becomes less critical and low sales and turnover can be more easily accommodated. There is a flexibility to business cycles that traders in the West might well envy.

## Economic structure and development

With development the share of agriculture in gross domestic product is expected to fall and that of industry to rise. That at least has been the experience of most of today's industrialised countries and many developing countries. The position of services is more ambiguous. Traditional services such as domestic servants have tended to decline, but modern services such as finance, insurance, consultancy and the media have all grown. There appears to be an ever-increasing role for services in so-called "post-industrial" societies, although there is often a classification problem between industry and services. White-collar workers in industrial enterprises contribute to industrial GDP. If their jobs are contracted out to management consultants, external accountants or computer software firms, this output is then recorded under services. Rises in the share of services and observed declines in manufacturing may reflect such practices, but this is merely a consequence of the method of measurement. Appearances may be deceptive.

In the Middle East the position is even more confused. There is of course the effect of the oil sector on GDP accounting already discussed in the previous section. Even allowing for this, however, it is not clear whether the economies are jumping a stage, from agriculture and other primary activity to services, leaving out the intermediate manufacturing stage. Can economies move to the post-industrial phase without ever establishing a substantial manufacturing base? Is an emphasis on industrialisation merely old fashioned, given the negative image of much heavy industry and the poor record of much of what has been established in the Middle East? Should governments and populations be aspiring for an alternative to industrialisation in the Middle East, and what form should that alternative take?

The stages of development approach advanced by the economic historian Walt Rostow includes the notion of "take-off", a concept which implies that economies reach a certain stage where self-sustaining growth occurs.[20] Countries then proceed automatically along a growth path that leads to the establishment of a modern industrial state. There is much doubt about the validity of these assertions, and evidence from many parts of the world suggests that often there is no definitive transition to growth being a continuous process. Indeed the early stages of industrialisation appear to be fraught with difficulties, and growth is often fragile.

The Latin American experience demonstrates just how fragile growth can be, with significant reversals rather than mere recessions in Mexico, Brazil and Argentina in the 1980s. Admittedly the problems of these economies were exacerbated by their debt crises. Other experiences lend more support to the Rostow thesis. In East and South East Asia, economies such as South Korea, Taiwan, Hong Kong and Singapore, the so-called "gang of four", appear to have taken off into self-sustaining economic growth as discussed in the previous chapter. Malaysia and Thailand seem to be following in the same direction and even very large populous states such as Indonesia show signs of heading in a similar direction, while China has become a global economic powerhouse.

Compared to these states the economies of the Middle East must be regarded as poor performers if Rostow's criteria are used. Only Turkey could be regarded as an economy that has taken off, with the turning point being the early 1980s. There were arguably very special circumstances that permitted Turkey's rapid advance during the last three decades, and many continue to express doubts about how self-sustaining its growth will be in the long run. There was significant under-utilisation of industrial capacity in Turkey during the chaotic 1970s, but greater demand stability in the 1980s meant this capacity could be brought into production. The country arguably benefited from the Iraq–Iran war in the short term, by being a significant exporter and re-exporter to both states. The oil-for-consumer-goods barter with Iraq was especially advantageous. At the same time, earnings from tourism increased enormously, underpinning the balance of payments position.[21]

For the Gulf states it could of course be argued that 1974 represented the year of take-off, as the quadrupling of oil prices enabled them to embark on large infrastructure expenditures that created the basic facilities needed for modern industries. The Riyadh Government directly financed petrochemical diversification through the Saudi Basic Industries Corporation, while generous assistance was made available through the Saudi Industrial Development Fund to support the electricity industry and import substitute ventures.

Whether all these efforts and the huge funding have really placed the Gulf economies on a path of self-sustaining growth must be debatable. Dependence on crude oil export earnings remains, and much of the diversification has been in petroleum-related fields. The new industries are largely manned by expatriate workers rather than local citizens, and although the level of education and skills amongst Gulf nationals has improved remarkably it will inevitably be a long time before these countries have a capable indigenous industrial workforce.[22] Indeed it is doubtful that these states will be able to emulate the rapidly industrialising states of South East Asia, even if they wanted to. The culture is quite different in West Asia to East Asia, and this is reflected in employee attitudes to work. Social commitments affect work patterns in the Middle East, and work for material reward may not be the highest priority. The region will certainly develop along different lines to other parts of the world, but the challenge is to identify what the patterns are, and predict how they will evolve.

## Leading sectors and unbalanced growth

There has been considerable debate amongst development economists about the relative merits of balanced versus unbalanced growth. Writers such as Ragnar Nurkse[23] and Paul Rosenstein-Rodan[24] who advocate a "big push" approach argue that countries have to develop a wide range of industries simultaneously if they are to succeed in achieving sustainable growth. This prevents bottlenecks occurring, as one industry can supply another. An integrated industrial base can be established with strong input–output relationships between the firms involved. Favourable externalities result, with the revenues generated by one expanding business feeding through to others. Domestic multiplier effects are maximised, with minimal leakages abroad through imports of supplies and capital equipment.

Other development economists such as Albert Hirschman argue that balanced growth is unrealistic, and that countries need to concentrate their efforts on particular sectors or even just a few industries.[25] Once the leading sector gets established then backward and forward linkages may build up with other industries and stimulate their development. Backward linkages will encourage the emergence of local suppliers and sub-contractors. Forward linkages will stimulate distributors and encourage more final processing. Both will result in increasing domestic value added. Uneven development must come first, however, and only then can the benefits of growth be spread out more widely.

The Middle Eastern economies would appear to be excellent examples of unbalanced development. Have the linkages that Hirschman identifies started to appear? Would more even development along the lines suggested by Nurkse and Rosenstein-Rodan be preferable? Government advisers in the Middle East were certainly aware of these differing approaches to development. The basic industries such as iron and steel making were established in order to provide building blocks for further industrialisation. The Helwan steel plant in Egypt, an example that has already been referred to, manufactured girders and reinforcing rods for the construction industry, and in addition provided sheet steel for the country's car assembly plant. The plant was designed with linkages in mind, the aim being to set up an integrated industrial complex in the greater Cairo area.

This strategy of integrated industrial development worked as long as the government was prepared to finance on very favourable terms the initial capital investment, subsidise the plants concerned once they started production and keep out competing foreign goods through tariffs, quotas and other measures. The downstream companies were obliged to purchase domestically produced steel products, but in order to prevent monopolistic overcharging, prices were set by government. Industry managers argued these were too low to cover costs, hence justifying the call for state subsidies.

The consequences of the policy were distorted prices, ever-increasing government spending and little discretion and choice for state sector management. It was similar rigidities that lead to the collapse of socialist planning in Eastern Europe. Linkages were created, but these were forced by government, and in many respects were highly artificial. They did not arise as a natural outcome of market forces, rather such forces were repressed. In the Middle East Turkey, Egypt, Iran and even Syria have all moved away from such policies towards a re-emphasis on markets, although the commitment to market reform can be questioned. Powerful lobbies have been created as a result of the state-sponsored industrialisation, and there are many in government who seek to protect the interests of state sector managers.[26]

The establishment of an integrated industrial base should not be confused with even development. Hirschman was correct in stressing that such policies were more likely to be associated with unbalanced growth. The whole modern industrial sector represented an enclave economy, with substantial intra-sectorial linkages, but few inter-sectorial linkages. Commerce and trade with the traditional economy was minimal. Indeed the latter suffered, as government finances were directed to the enclave sector, but it was the traditional sector that was the main source of government revenue, both directly through taxes and indirectly as marketing was directed through state controlled channels. The prices paid to cotton producers in Egypt and Sudan, for example, were well below the prices at which the crop was sold in international markets by the state marketing monopolies.[27]

The OPEC economies of the Middle East also exhibit the characteristics of unbalanced growth. The oil sector exists in an enclave of its own, with few productive linkages to the rest of the economy. It is of course a source of revenue for the government, and through government spending the major stimulus of economic activity. The links with other sectors are at the macro rather than the micro level, financial rather than involving the real economy. Only a small proportion of the workforce is actually employed in the oil industry, and in the Arabian Peninsula states most of these are expatriates. Most oil industry output is exported, and its inputs are imported. The linkages are worldwide rather than local.

Efforts have been made to build up integrated industrial activity around the oil industry, diversifying out of crude oil and increasing domestic value added. Initially these involved refining, but later diversification into petro-chemicals. Other notable efforts have included the utilisation of hitherto flared off gas for liquefaction and export, and as an input into energy intensive industries such as aluminium smelting. As with the steel industry in Egypt and Turkey, a considerable amount of intra-industry linkages have been established in OPEC states such as Saudi Arabia, but within a very narrow sector of the economy.[28] The enclave remains. It has merely become more diversified within itself and expanded marginally. At least market prices have not been as distorted as much as in the countries that established industrial bases earlier. There are only minimal opportunity costs in the low feedstock prices paid by the petrochemical industry, as where oil is the feedstock, it could not have been sold off in any case due to OPEC quotas. In the case of gas, where the alternative is flaring, the opportunity cost is zero, indeed there is an environmental benefit, a positive externality.

## Modernisation and structural transformation

Development is often seen in terms of the modernisation of economic activity.[29] Subsistence agriculture is replaced with cash cropping, with prices determining production and sales, and marketing geared to national or even international markets. In manufacturing, small handicraft activities are replaced by large mechanised and automated plants, textiles, clothing and household furnishings being amongst the first activities to be modernised. Even labour intensive services can be updated, modern commercial banks replacing traditional money-lenders and money-changers, and supermarkets being substituted for small *bazaar* or *souk* trading establishments.

In the Middle East modernisation has occurred, but traditional economic activity continues to exist alongside the new industries. It is by no means clear that the modern sector will replace traditional activities entirely, even in the long term. Subsistence agriculture, handicrafts and informal financial intermediation have existed for millennia in the Middle East, and are one of the region's economic strengths. There has been a relative decline in the proportion of GDP accounted for by traditional activities, even allowing for measurement underestimation. In absolute terms, however, traditional economic activities continue to expand, and in some cases are proving more resilient than the modern industries established at such huge expense.

It is interesting to speculate whether the growth of the modern sector has damaged traditional economic activities, or if it has actually been beneficial. In a stronger form the question is whether the modern sector is a substitute for traditional activity, or if the two sectors complement each other.[30] Both clearly compete for resources, which involves factors of production and inputs. As the labour market is fragmented in the Middle East, with only limited inter-sectorial mobility, competition for workers is limited. Nevertheless in Iran under the Shah a shortage of labour arose in the *bazaar* sector because young people stayed on in education and entered modern industries. It was the modern sector that offered higher wages and salaries, though these were not justified by the sector's productivity, which remained low.

These new manufacturing facilities were protected from international competition and received generous state funding. Foreign exchange was freely available to much of the modern sector, while imports for the *bazaar* merchants were subject to stringent controls. Yet it was the traditional sector that accounted for most of Iran's non-oil exports, while the modern industries struggled to produce goods that were barely acceptable in the domestic market. The Shah's technocrats were expensive to support, and in the end contributed little to the viability of the Iranian economy. It was, however, the *bazaar* sector which paid the price for modern development, with quality craft goods such as traditional hand-woven carpets going into significant decline. The full opportunity cost of modern industry was never apparent under the Shah; it was only after the Islamic revolution that the extent of previous economic mismanagement became highly visible.[31]

On the other side of the Gulf in Saudi Arabia and the smaller Arab states the oil boom years were the best ever period for the traditional sector. Government expenditure financed from petroleum revenue helped stimulate traditional trading; indeed many of the merchant families became extremely wealthy. Imports flowed in, but these represented new goods to distribute and sell; they were not a substitute for domestically produced supplies, as in the case of Iran. Modern industries were created, but in non-traditional areas such as petrochemicals which did not threaten the traditional economy. Of course there was relatively little traditional manufacturing to replace, unlike in the more populous and historically more developed countries of the region. Nevertheless, the fact that much of the modern sector was export rather than domestically oriented meant inter-sectorial conflict between the old and the new was avoided.

The fundamental question must remain whether modernisation has really improved the economic situation of the Middle East. It can be argued that second-rate modernisation does not bring an improvement if menial production-line jobs are created to replace traditional craft and skills. A region such as the Middle East may move into areas where it lacks any comparative advantage, and consequently it may for the foreseeable future always lag behind both the advanced industrialised world and the dynamic emergent economies of Asia and Latin America.[32] Modernisation may cause frustration, loss of respect, and even a sense of failure if the process remains incomplete and the new activities are poorly organised and executed. Rather than making craft goods that rank amongst the best in the world, the modern output may be shoddy and defective. Is this where development is leading the economies of the Middle East? The chapters that follow should shed further light on this issue, starting with the next chapter, which is concerned with the human dimension of development.

# 4   Population growth and employment

The relationship between population growth and economic development has been subject to much debate in both the western world and the Middle East, but as with so much else in economics, no generally accepted conclusions have been reached. There is not even agreement on the fundamental issues of what determines population growth and if there are universal trends. Many development economists believe that the rate of population growth reflects the stage of economic development a country has reached, with a tendency for the rate to decline as an outcome of the development process.[1] Others assert that population growth reflects family preferences, and is determined by cultural and social factors.[2] The trends in the western world towards falling rates of population growth may therefore not be followed in a region such as the Middle East where Islamic values prevail.

## The demographic transition

Figures for population increase represent the difference between birth rates and death rates. High rates of population growth may occur as a "once off" result of a demographic transition, when death rates decline, in particular infant mortality rates, but there is a lag before birth rates fall. Several arguments are advanced for this assertion. One is that when infant mortality rates are high, couples have more children so that there is at least a chance of some surviving. Such arguments are based on expectations, probabilities and risk. The demographic transition is a period when expectations are adapted or adjusted, but this takes time.[3]

There are real economic as well as human benefits associated with lower infant mortality. Family lands can be passed on to children when the parents become old. They then assume economic responsibility for their aged parents. There are diminishing returns to labour in relation to fixed family land holdings, however, and excessive numbers of offspring only add to the consumption burden without contributing much to production. It is this type of constraint that may encourage couples to limit family size.

How relevant are these arguments in the Middle East? Infant mortality rates declined rapidly in all countries of the region between 1981 and 2010,

*Table 4.1* Infant mortality rates in the Middle East (infant deaths per 1,000 live births)

| Country | 1981 | 2010 |
|---|---|---|
| Algeria | 84 | 31 |
| Egypt | 108 | 19 |
| Iran | 72 | 22 |
| Israel | 15 | 4 |
| Jordan | 46 | 18 |
| Kuwait | 27 | 10 |
| Morocco | 91 | 30 |
| Saudi Arabia | 62 | 15 |
| Sudan | 87 | 66 |
| Syria | 52 | 14 |
| Tunisia | 65 | 14 |
| Turkey | 99 | 14 |
| UAE | 33 | 6 |
| Yemen | 125 | 57 |

Source: World Bank, Washington, 2011

although the rates remain high in comparison with western figures of 8 per thousand births and less. In Egypt the fall was from 108 per thousand to 19, in Iran from 72 to 22 and in Turkey from 99 to 14. In some of the Gulf States such as Kuwait the infant mortality rate had fallen to 10 by 2010 while in the UAE the rate was below most western countries and almost on a par with Israel's rate, as Table 4.1 shows.[4]

The countries of the Middle East have experienced a dramatic fall in fertility rates over the last four decades and this has accelerated during the last decade. The rate for a stable population is around 2.2, a rate that countries such as Iran, Turkey, Tunisia and the UAE all fall below, the implication being that these countries will shrink in terms of population size. With women spending longer at school and university and postponing marriage, family sizes have fallen considerably in a single generation. High levels of divorce are also reducing family size, notably in the UAE, Kuwait and Saudi Arabia. It is only in high infant mortality rate countries such as Yemen and the Sudan that the fertility rate remains high, as Table 4.2 shows.

There are some notable exceptions to the overall demographic trends, notably Israel, which has the lowest infant mortality rate in the region, but a stable fertility rate of 3.0, which indicates its population will continue to rise. Neighbouring Jordan has an even higher fertility rate, although this has steadily fallen over the last four decades. Syria, despite its sluggish and underperforming economy, has a lower infant mortality rate than Jordan, and a fertility rate comparable to that of Israel.

Although fertility rates have fallen dramatically there are social factors that may prevent the collapse that some southern and eastern European countries have experienced. First, there may be a preference for children rather than material commodities, with children conferring status. Second, it is easier to bring up children when several generations live under one roof and grandparents can

Although B.R. is falling, there's 2 cultural battles @ play. 1 culture women are waiting to get married & going to school second culture children are valued more then material things same w/ Birth Control

*Table 4.2* Fertility rates in the Middle East (births per woman)

| Country | 1981 | 2010 |
| --- | --- | --- |
| Algeria | 6.8 | 2.3 |
| Egypt | 5.3 | 2.8 |
| Iran | 6.5 | 1.7 |
| Israel | 3.2 | 3.0 |
| Jordan | 7.2 | 3.8 |
| Kuwait | 5.4 | 2.3 |
| Morocco | 5.5 | 2.3 |
| Saudi Arabia | 7.1 | 2.9 |
| Sudan | 6.4 | 4.5 |
| Syria | 7.0 | 3.0 |
| Tunisia | 5.2 | 2.1 |
| Turkey | 4.3 | 2.1 |
| UAE | 5.3 | 1.8 |
| Yemen | 9.1 | 5.3 |

Source: World Bank, Washington, 2011

help look after the offspring, although this contributes to high divorce rates in the Gulf. Third, the sexual segregation in Muslim society encourages family-minded women to influence each other. Given the desire for at least one son, many women continue having children until that goal is achieved.[5]

Government policy in the past may also have encouraged large families. The provision of free schooling meant that education was not a burden on families, but this is changing due to state financing constraints. Subsidies on housing and low rentals also resulted in the costs of families accruing to the state, or in other words being a public rather than a private cost, but again this has changed with housing becoming more expensive. Controlled food prices and subsidies to agriculture reduced the cost of feeding additional family members, but subsidies have been, or are being, phased out. In societies where family meals are cooked using fresh produce rather than merely assembled from pre-prepared ingredients, the cost of feeding additional mouths is minimal. There are economies of scale in cooking for an extended family, whereas the packaged foodstuffs or take away-meals consumed by many in western societies have a constant marginal cost. However, even in the Middle East the trend towards convenience foods increases food costs, including those of feeding additional children.

With the possible exception of Egypt, the Middle Eastern countries are not highly populated by East Asian or European standards, and though food imports are increasing, it would be incorrect to suggest that population pressure is resulting in a real squeeze on resources. There were those doomsday pundits in Europe who worried about the population on the southern shore of the Mediterranean exceeding that on the northern shore, but apart from their own bigotry or Euro-ethnocentric view of the world, it is not clear why this should have been a concern. In Islamic writing there is no generally agreed position on birth control, with Muslim scholars arguing both that it is permitted and against. There are few who would actively encourage such a policy, however, the general feeling being it is a private matter for the individual.[6]

The evidence suggests that there has been little exceptionalism in the Middle East to the demographic trends experienced worldwide. Indeed the current youth bulge of school leavers and young adults will disappear over the coming decades and the baby boomers will age. For the next two or three decades the Middle East will enjoy a demographic advantage with a young workforce but a reduced child dependence. Eventually, as in Europe and East Asia, the problem of aged dependence will arise. The frustrations associated with the Arab Spring demonstrate that the region is not taking advantage of its youth and a demographic opportunity is being wasted.

## Education and human capital formation

There have been remarkable changes in the level of educational attainment in the Middle East over the last fifty years. As early as 1970 the majority of the population of primary school age were in school, with the notable exceptions of Oman, Sudan and Yemen. Now there are very high rates of literacy and numeracy amongst the young, and Oman has caught up with the other Gulf States. The major expansion in recent years has been in secondary and higher education. Enrolment ratios in relation to the relevant age groups at secondary level exceed 80 per cent in Egypt, Israel, Jordan and the states of the Gulf. Elsewhere in Iran, Turkey and Saudi Arabia the proportion exceeds 50 per cent.

Table 4.3 shows the education index for the Middle East calculated by the United Nations on the basis of primary, secondary and tertiary enrolment,

*Table 4.3* Education index for the Middle East

| Country | 1980 | 2010 |
| --- | --- | --- |
| Algeria | 0.253 | 0.652 |
| Egypt | 0.262 | 0.560 |
| Iraq | 0.260 | 0.491 |
| Iran | 0.279 | 0.640 |
| Israel | 0.731 | 0.907 |
| Jordan | 0.404 | 0.710 |
| Kuwait | 0.459 | 0.577 |
| Libya | 0.353 | 0.731 |
| Morocco | 0.181 | 0.447 |
| Saudi Arabia | 0.493 | 0.689 |
| Sudan | 0.120 | 0.247 |
| Syria | 0.331 | 0.534 |
| Tunisia | 0.270 | 0.645 |
| Turkey | 0.298 | 0.583 |
| UAE | 0.343 | 0.741 |
| Yemen | 0.033 | 0.310 |

Source: UN Human Development Report, New York, 2011

pupil teacher ratios and the level of teacher training. The higher the number the better the educational provision.

Israel is the highest ranked in the education index amongst Middle East countries followed by the UAE and perhaps surprisingly Libya. Despite its many faults, the Gaddafi regime devoted substantial resources to education at all levels, resulting in the country rising dramatically from its very poor position in 1980 to become, with the UAE, the most improved state. The improvement in Jordan, a country without oil, is also impressive. In contrast oil-rich Kuwait seems to have fared relatively less well and by 2010 was overtaken by Saudi Arabia. Unsurprisingly, Sudan and Yemen were bottom ranked.

Only limited data is available on expenditure per student at different levels of education, as Table 4.4 shows. The data highlights the underspending by Kuwait in comparison with Saudi Arabia. Arguably some countries allocate excessive resources to tertiary and secondary education at the expense of primary education, Morocco being a clear example, although the figures should be treated with caution.

Ultimately what matters in education are results, one measure of this being literacy rates. As Table 4.5 shows, these are very high in Kuwait despite its relative underspending on education and the rates in Jordan, Libya and Turkey are impressive, with universal literacy amongst those under 40. Saudi Arabia and Iran also have high rates of literacy. Unsurprisingly, the second lowest rate is found in Yemen, but Sudan, despite its meagre resources, fares better than its northern neighbour, Egypt, although there most of the illiterate are old. Morocco has the least literacy, perhaps a consequence of the misallocation of the education budget away from primary schooling.

At university level there are more graduates from Egyptian universities than from those in Britain. Some countries in the Middle East have the highest enrolment rates for tertiary education in the developing world, notably Lebanon, where the university population represents over one-quarter of the age group and Jordan, where the proportion exceeds one-fifth. Israel, which is not included in the statistics for developing countries because of its level of development, has the highest number of doctoral degrees per thousand population in the world.

*Table 4.4* Expenditure per student as a percentage of GDP per capita

| Country | Primary | Secondary | Tertiary |
|---|---|---|---|
| Iran | 15.1 | 21.0 | 22.2 |
| Israel | 19.5 | 20.4 | 21.3 |
| Jordan | 12.1 | 15.6 | N/A |
| Kuwait | 10.9 | 14.9 | N/A |
| Morocco | 16.1 | 38.7 | 71.1 |
| Saudi Arabia | 18.4 | 18.3 | N/A |
| Syria | 18.3 | 15.5 | N/A |

Source: World Bank, Washington, 2011

*Table 4.5* Literacy rates, percentage of people aged 15 and above

| Country | Year | Rate |
| --- | --- | --- |
| Algeria | 2006 | 73 |
| Egypt | 2006 | 66 |
| Iran | 2008 | 85 |
| Iraq | 2009 | 78 |
| Jordan | 2007 | 92 |
| Kuwait | 2008 | 94 |
| Libya | 2009 | 89 |
| Morocco | 2009 | 56 |
| Saudi Arabia | 2009 | 86 |
| Sudan | 2009 | 70 |
| Syria | 2009 | 84 |
| Tunisia | 2008 | 78 |
| Turkey | 2009 | 91 |
| Yemen | 2009 | 62 |

Source: World Bank, Washington, 2011

Education is of course an end in itself as well as a means of human advancement and development. Economists regard it as both a consumption and an investment good. Evaluating the contribution of education to development in the Middle East is far from straightforward. It is not clear whether education is a fruit of development or a prerequisite for economic growth. Traditionally education was associated with the religious establishment, the *ulamã*, rather than the state, the main emphasis being on learning to read and recite the *Qur'an*.[7] The aim was to please *Allah* by understanding his teaching, not to use educational skills to promote material advancement. This was considered unimportant in comparison to spiritual matters.

The modern education system in the Middle East has been heavily influenced by the western model, and covers a much wider breadth of knowledge than traditional religious education. It exists in parallel with traditional religious education, but in practice for most school children in the region, the latter has been virtually superseded. Even in Iran, the Islamic revolution did not bring a return to traditional education. The modern, essentially secular, approach to education remained, but with major changes to the curriculum in subjects such as history. Nevertheless it would be incorrect to view education provision in the Middle East as a mere western clone. The cultural characteristics that define Arabic and the other languages of the region have an impact, as the means of instruction inevitably determine the output.

Undoubtedly the major development inheritance from the Nasser period in Egyptian history has been the system of education. This has not only affected the impart of knowledge and skills in Egypt, but throughout the Arab world, as Egyptian teachers have taken up positions in many neighbouring countries. From Libya to the Gulf it is Egyptian teachers who dominated the educational establishment in the 1970s and 1980s, and Egyptian television programmes and films that provided entertainment for the Arab masses.[8] Not surprisingly, it is also Egyptian attitudes and values that have been a major influence for much of the region. There is respect for the old and experienced, suspicion of impatient youth, scepticism about government and politicians and perhaps an over-obsession with form rather than substance. Of course it is always dangerous to generalise, and casual observation can be no substitute for solid anthropological enquiry. It is important that economists interested in development are aware of the wider social context, however, and not merely the quantitative indicators.

Under Nasser great efforts were made to educate girls as well as boys, as universal female literacy was seen as a highly desirable social and development objective. The traditional *Quranic* schools were restricted to males, but many felt that female education was essential for modern societies and economies. The proportion of girls of primary school age who were in education was already 57 per cent by 1970 in Egypt, and the percentage rose to 93 by 1991 and has since become universal. In the Gulf there have been very striking advances in female education. Saudi Arabia had only 29 per cent of its female population of primary school age in education in 1970, but by 1991 the proportion had risen to 72 per cent and now all females of school age are being educated.

Female school children and many female students are educated separately from males throughout the Gulf, which some educationalists argue is an advantage as they are not crowded out by more aggressive males. Interestingly the examination results appear to be better for females up to university level in the Gulf. A much higher proportion of males attend overseas universities, however, especially at master's degree level and beyond. The good results for females within the Middle East at this level may reflect the fact that the more able who could enter foreign universities are obliged to stay at universities near their homes.

Perhaps surprisingly, it has been in Iran since the Islamic revolution where female education has made its greatest advance. Despite the lip service that the Shah's regime paid to the education of girls and the stress on elimination of illiteracy, only half of the female population of primary school age were in education in 1970. By the 1990s there was universal primary education for girls, and an increasing number, even from the poorest homes, were proceeding to secondary school and university. As in Japan there is a recognition that even where women remain at home and leave formal employment after marriage, they have a crucial role in the informal education of their children. Education not only takes place in the classroom, but at home. Schooling for the mothers of tomorrow may be the best way of ensuring the spread of skills and knowledge in Muslim societies where the family is the key social unit.

The type of educational provision and the standard attained may have implications for development. Rapid expansion of education has meant large classes at all levels, with little possibility of individual attention. Shortages of books and teaching materials means that student-centred learning is impracticable, with reliance on teaching methods largely involving instruction to whole classes rather than small group and team learning. Even in universities tutorial and seminars are rare, most undergraduate teaching consisting of lecturing to large groups, with the emphasis on dictation and taking good notes to avoid the expense of purchasing textbooks. There is a liberal arts bias, though in Egypt subjects such as engineering and agronomy are highly respected, but there are poor facilities for experimental and practical work. Management education is in its infancy, but there are large schools of administrative studies in most countries of the region.

Standards of education are often criticised by academics from the West, but in a situation of scarce resources the choice has been whether to provide high-quality, individually tailored education to a few or more basic education to many. If an important part of development is seen as the widening of opportunities for the masses then the policy pursued in the Middle East has been remarkably successful. If, however, a highly educated elite playing a leadership role is seen as essential for development then the region has failed, but so arguably has the West, where intellectuals seldom occupy key positions. There is always the risk of a brain drain from a region such as the Middle East. Many of Iran's intelligentsia left the country in the years following the Islamic Revolution. Some of the world's leading medical scientists are Egyptian, but most of them practise in the West. Israel has been unable to provide suitable employment for its highly educated population, and the absorption of well-qualified Russian Jewish immigrants has proved a major headache.

Science education is often felt to be more relevant to development needs than a liberal arts education, although these issues arouse fierce controversy amongst educationalists. Relatively low proportions of those in schools and universities study science in the Gulf States, Sudan and Egypt, perhaps reflecting a liberal arts bias. In Iran and some of the Maghreb states the proportion is high, even by western standards, perhaps indicating that these states can more easily cope with transferred technology. However, the transfer can be two-way. Those with science knowledge and skills can more easily find employment abroad than law or arts graduates, with more national or cultural specific educational attainments.

The merit of having a high proportion of students studying abroad can also be questioned. This may mean that students from developing countries have access to the often better education systems and facilities of the western countries. It is not only oil-exporting states such as the UAE that have a high proportion of students abroad; so, too, do some of the poorest countries in the Middle East, including Sudan and Yemen. A large proportion of these students stay abroad if they have the opportunity, given the limited opportunities at home and much more attractive pay rates in the West. This also applies in Jordan, where educational aspirations and attainment are high but domestic employment opportunities limited. Many of the Jordanians at university in the United States and other western countries never return, apart from when visiting their relatives.

## Manpower planning and career choice

It can of course be argued that much of the huge public funding which has gone into education in the Middle East has been wasted, if the newly qualified cannot find jobs. In the past the case has been made for manpower planning that attempts to tailor education provision to the type of jobs on offer.[10] Manpower planning has met with little success in those countries in the Middle East such as Egypt, Syria and Iraq where it has been attempted, admittedly only to a limited extent.[11] The basic problem is that students are educated for a working life that can extend beyond forty years, but it is impossible to predict what the employment pattern will be that far into the future. The horizon for development planning seldom exceeds five years, and many argue that even this is too long.

A more fundamental issue is whether the use of manpower planning in determining education priorities is desirable in any case if choices are taken away from students and their parents. It is presumptuous to assume that unelected planners can make the optimal decisions on behalf of those whose interests they purport to represent. A contrary argument is that planners have better access to information, and possess the necessary tools and knowledge to make good use of that information. Nevertheless, those who are making decisions for themselves and their offspring are more highly motivated to make the best choices to suit their individual circumstances. Planners lack knowledge at this level, and even if their decisions are socially motivated, the outcomes may conflict with the individual wishes of those being educated and their parents.

Manpower planning is essentially quantitative, but qualitative factors, or in other words the question of standards, are of course vital in education. The quality of the inputs – those who do the teaching – will determine the productivity and effectiveness of the outputs – those who have been educated. In the Middle East teacher training could be much improved, and arguably resources devoted to this would ultimately yield high returns. Such issues have been ignored by manpower planners in the region.

Another neglected issue is that of educational deepening, which is arguably a major factor in economic advance. By this is meant people with more schooling taking over jobs that were previously carried out by those with fewer qualifications and less formal training and knowledge. Accountancy and banking in many western countries have become careers for university graduates, for example, rather than school leavers. In the Middle East similar trends are occurring, with the civil service increasingly filled with graduates, potential company managers recruited from universities and even many of those in industries such as tourism increasingly well educated with language degrees or hotel and catering qualifications.

The question of private versus social choice that arises in manpower planning is related to who pays for education. In the Middle East it is the state that pays for the most part, as at schools and universities tuition is usually free. Arguably, government should have some say in provision if it is the taxpayers as a whole that are meeting the bill. In practice much government spending in the Middle East, including that on education, is financed from oil revenues. This makes governments less accountable to their own citizens, and means there is little lobbying over value for money in education. The major debate has been over how Islamic the curriculum should be.

There is nevertheless a large private subsidy by families for education. There is no system of student grants apart from at post-graduate level in the Middle East, and no formalised government loan schemes. Families have to support their offspring in education, the expectation being that the beneficiaries will pay for the upkeep of younger brothers and sisters or even cousins when they are fortunate enough to find employment. The extended family system has important financial implications for education in a region such as the Middle East. This should be taken into account in any calculations involving private and social costs and benefits in education.

## Labour surplus models

The modern literature on employment in developing countries often takes as its starting point the Lewis model of labour surplus economies, even though many question the assumptions of the model.[12] Lewis assumes that the marginal productivity of labour in agriculture is zero, and therefore transferring labour from the traditional agricultural sector to the modern industrial sector will not result in a loss of food output. At the same time, the surplus of labour limits wage payments in industry, and means the value of output exceeds the cost of the labour inputs. Hence when labour is re-deployed from the traditional sector to the more productive modern sector, a surplus or profit results, which can be used to finance investment.

Growth becomes self-sustaining as long as rural labour is mobile and the surplus labour remains, keeping down wage rates in the modern sector. This neo-Ricardian two-sector model is consistent with the notion that labour-abundant developing countries should concentrate on the development of labour-intensive activities. It is in these that their comparative advantage lies, reflecting low marginal wage costs. This will be pursued further in Chapter 8, where the role of the Middle East in international trade is examined.

How applicable is the Lewis labour sector model in the Middle East? In the case of the Gulf States, at least in the 1970s, it appeared irrelevant, as local labour was comparatively scarce and expensive, and a substantial proportion of the workforce was accounted for by expatriate migrant labour. With population increase and oil price falls, the situation in the Gulf has changed in the 1980s and 1990s, but the Lewis model assumes that industrialisation requires large amounts of labour, which has clearly not been the pattern in the Gulf.

For the more populous states of the region with substantial agricultural labour forces such as Egypt, Iran and Turkey the Lewis model arguably has more validity. However, empirical studies of Egypt and other states in the region indicate that the marginal productivity of labour in agriculture is positive, and that rural–urban migration is a much more complicated affair than Lewis suggests.[13] There is an opportunity cost involved in searching for employment as wages are forgone. In rural areas employment is often seasonal, but so are the vacancies. Job search is necessary but employment seekers may have to spend time on this during periods when alternative work is available rather than when they are seasonally unemployed.

The expectation of finding a job may influence the decision to leave employment in the countryside. The Harris and Todaro model may well have relevance in the Middle East, as it includes employment probability as a factor explaining migration.[14] Domestic labour markets are imperfect and segmented, but information about potential vacancies circulates through informal family networks, and if opportunities arise potential applicants can usually be found. There is often only a limited response to wage differentials, but this does not indicate that markets are not working. Rather, it shows that wage offers on recruitment are only one factor interesting job seekers. In the Middle East workers often take a longer-term view than those in the West. What concerns them is job security and employment prospects. Employer attitudes also matter. Those who help their employees in time of need by settling debts or making interest-free loans are more likely to win the loyalty of their employees in Muslim societies.

There is some evidence to suggest that improved education has increased occupational mobility in the Middle East and reduced social stratification.[15] This has arguably increased the efficiency of labour markets, though not necessarily their competitiveness. Loyalty by both employers and employees is highly valued in the Middle East. Employers will not simply dismiss their workers and hire others prepared to work for lower wages. The employer assumes a social commitment to the employee and his family, and will not attempt to bargain down wages merely because there is a reserve army of unemployed. For his part the labourer will also stay loyal, and will not desert his post for better-paid employment during periods when labour may be scarce. In the *bazaar* economy there is a tradition of lifetime employment. This may be less true for unskilled agricultural labour, and at the other end of the spectrum amongst the well-educated professional classes. Nevertheless there is a tendency for these groups not to shift about from job to job, but rather seek stability of employment.

In agriculture, work is often a family endeavour. Men carry out heavy irrigation work and planting, but women and children do much of the harvesting. Remuneration for the latter two groups is lower, and during harvest time wages fall. Men however seldom undertake these tasks, and wage differentials in rural areas often relate to different groups of workers for particular seasons.[16] The unemployed will not be taken on if the families of those employed on a regular basis are looking for work. Family preferences and nepotism is accepted at all levels. Indeed it is regarded as more socially acceptable to employ a family member rather than a stranger. Perhaps it is also more efficient if some of the family members are accustomed to working as a team.

## Unemployment and underemployment

Although birth rates have fallen, record numbers are seeking to enter the workforce, a legacy of the higher birth rates two decades ago. Every year in Egypt, Turkey and Iran over half a million new entrants come onto each country's job market. Can these economies generate sufficient employment to clear the market? Are job seekers prepared to accept lower salaries than those paid to people in employment? How flexible are the young in taking what is on offer, rather than waiting for employment for which they believe they are qualified? What role, if any, can government usefully play in employment creation?

There is a major employment problem across the Middle East, even in the oil-exporting states of the Gulf. Jobs are scarce, not only for primary and secondary school leavers, but also for university graduates. Indeed the more highly qualified the job seeker, the more difficult it is to secure employment. Much of the unemployment is disguised, the costs borne not by the state but by the job seeker's family. There is no system of unemployment insurance or state benefits for the unemployed in the Middle East, and in these circumstances there is no point in registering as unemployed. Any unemployment statistics that are published in the region are meaningless, even those reported to the International Labour Organisation. Increasingly it is the difficulty of finding a job that induces the young to stay on in education. Their families would have to support them in any case, and tuition, as already indicated, is mostly free or at relatively low cost.

The ability of governments to generate employment has reached its limits in most of the Middle East. Under Nasser there was a guarantee of a job for every Egyptian graduate as public sector industries and the civil service were obliged to increase the number of employees on their payrolls each year, with the government setting the target in relation to the anticipated supply of graduates.[17] Industries would indicate their employment requirements and the planners would take these into account, as well as the size of the existing workforce in the firm or plant. Usually the allocation was made as a percentage of the existing workforce, the numbers exceeding those requested by the industries. The result was poor individual supervision on graduate training programmes, and increasing underemployment at the white-collar level throughout the state sector. Underemployment occurs where employees are engaged on a full-time basis, but in practice only have enough work to keep themselves usefully occupied for less than twenty hours per week.

Nasser's guarantee of a job for every Egyptian graduate was politically popular with the middle classes and the urban elite, but was not sustainable in the long run, economically and financially. The policy had to be abandoned by Sadat, and under Mubarak considerable efforts were made to curtail public sector spending, partly by limiting employment expansion in the civil service and state industries. Public sector pay has been frozen for long periods, making government employment much less attractive than the private sector.

Underemployment remains, but in practice employees receive what amounts to part-time pay for part-time work, though that is not the official job description. Many public servants work for the government from eight in the morning until two in the afternoon, the official working day, but then have a second informal job in the evening. Typical "moonlighting" occupations include taxi driving and retailing, with the *souk* offering numerous opportunities for part-time, occasional and always flexible employment.

The public sector has been subject to similar strains in Turkey and Iran in recent years to those in Egypt. In the past it was the less educated who were subject to the rigours of the labour market while university graduates enjoyed the protection of government. Now, however, all job seekers are in the same uncertain position, so at least there is an equality of insecurity. In the Gulf, where there was much less financial strain, the creation of employment in the bureaucracy was much easier in the 1970s and early 1980s. Since then even these governments have had to exercise considerable spending constraint. This is particularly frustrating for many graduates and school leavers, as they are usually better qualified than those who hold the type of employment that they seek. Most current public sector employees in the Gulf were recruited when labour market conditions were much tighter, and qualified local nationals were unavailable.

## Urbanisation and population distribution

Throughout the developing world the population is becoming more urbanised and this trend is apparent in all the economies of the Middle East. Cities and towns have always been important as trading centres, and the deserts of the region have never been able to support large populations. In most of the Arabian Peninsula the urban centres were more economically significant than their hinterlands, and even before the oil boom and the rise of the modern city state in the Gulf, the sheikhdoms and emirates could be described as town, if not city, states with economies based on fishing and pearling. The region contains some of the world's oldest centres of settled agriculture, such as the Nile and Tigris-Euphrates valleys, but even in these areas the populations were housed in large and small settlements rather than isolated farms and homesteads on the European and North American pattern.

The move to urban living is perhaps less traumatic for those who have always lived in communities rather than in detached surroundings as the change is a question of scale rather than reorganisation and reorientation. Greater Cairo may have become a city of almost twenty million inhabitants, but socially it is structured like a series of contiguous villages. Most inhabitants identify with their own neighbourhoods in the first instance rather than the wider metropolis. This makes living in Africa's largest city less intimidating, especially as the strong social fabric of Middle Eastern societies means that serious crime is comparatively rare. The cities of the region may appear chaotic, but their inhabitants do not suffer the same risk of random crime as those in the urban jungles of the West.

Egypt, Syria and the Maghreb states have around half of their populations living in major urban centres with populations exceeding 100,000. In Iran the proportion is just below 60 per cent, and in Turkey and Jordan the urban percentage is just above this figure. Israel, despite the agricultural orientation of its early settlers, has over 90 per cent of its population living in urban areas, making it almost comparable with Kuwait and Bahrain. It is only in Sudan and Yemen where less than one-quarter of the population is urbanised, though there has been a significant rise in urbanisation in recent years in the latter.[18]

There is a positive relationship between urbanisation and gross domestic product per capita in the Middle East. Those countries with higher levels of per capita income appear to be more urbanised, as might be expected, but with the exception of Israel, all the states in the high-income category owe much of their prosperity to oil. Agriculture is of only limited significance in these higher income countries, but interestingly the relationship between industrialisation and urbanisation is also weak in the Middle East. Services are, however, more developed in the more urbanised countries. The standard literature on economic development tends to stress the advantages of agglomeration to industry in urban areas and the presence of external economies through inter-industry linkages.[19] Much less attention is paid to services, though in the Middle East the primary activity in urban centres has always been trading, not manufacturing.

## Emigration and migration

Historically there has always been considerable movements of population in the Middle East, as the deserts served as routes for trade and commerce rather than representing barriers to economic exchange. The nomadic tradition encouraged travel, and the *bazaars* and *souks* often had merchants from many parts of the region. Nationality or ethnic group was not a bar to migration, as peoples could move comparatively freely throughout the Ottoman Empire. In the past the main barriers to movement were economic rather than administrative. It was the cost of travel, and the opportunity cost of remuneration forgone, that kept people near their home base. Since political independence and the rise of the nation state in the region, it has been immigration laws, passport controls and work and residence permits that have hindered the mobility of workers and their dependants.

Many countries in the region have become more ethnically and religiously homogenous since the rise of the modern Middle Eastern nation state. Turkey, for example, is predominately Muslim, most of the Armenian and Greek Christians having left Asia Minor following the early years of independence. In Egypt the substantial Greek Orthodox community left Alexandria, although the Christian Copts remain, an indigenous minority numbering at least eight million. Israel being a Jewish state may have preferred religious homogeneity, but the Arab Muslims and Christians within its borders have risen in both absolute and relative numbers in recent years. If the populations of the occupied territories are included, less than 60 per cent of the total inhabitants are Jewish.

The permanent ethnic and religious mixing within the Ottoman Empire has been replaced by a more temporary migration of workers. There have been two major destinations for migrants, the OPEC states of the Gulf and Libya, which have attracted workers from the poorer Arab states, and the European Union, which has imported labour from Turkey and the Maghreb. In addition, since the Israeli occupation of the West Bank and Gaza in 1967 there has been daily and weekly commuting from the territories into Israel to work. This involved both Palestinian Arab workers and Jewish settlers in the territories, although the Palestinian uprising and more recent events in Gaza have restricted these labour flows.

A considerable amount has been written on the labour migrations of the 1970s and 1980s in the Middle East, most notably the study by Birks *et al.*[20] In some respects the area has displayed more of the characteristics of a common market than a free trade area, as the mobility of factors of production such as labour and capital has been much more economically significant than the movement of traded goods. Whether from a historical perspective the labour migration has any lasting impact compared to the population movements of the early centuries of Islam or the Ottoman period must be more debatable.

The migration to the Gulf and Libya of Egyptians and Palestinians appears to be even more transitory than that of Turks to Germany or Maghreb nationals to France. Non-nationals in the Gulf are only given work permits of fixed duration and they are not allowed to acquire property in these OPEC states. In contrast, many Turkish migrants have taken their families to Germany, and after going through the German school system, most prefer to remain and seek employment.[21] Despite the considerable ethnic, religious and cultural differences between Turkey and central and Western Europe, the migrants increasingly identify with their country of residence. In contrast in Libya and the Gulf, the migrants may be Arabs in Arab and Islamic countries, but they seldom see a long-term future for themselves as expatriates, and in most cases there is no desire to be absorbed with local nationals.

There has been a decline in the number of Arab migrant workers in the Gulf and Libya since the peak of the early 1980s when there were almost two million Arab migrants in Saudi Arabia, one million in Kuwait and 200,000 in Libya.[22] The decline is due to three factors. First, the fall in oil prices during the mid 1980s resulted in a squeeze on government spending and economic activity generally. Second, there was an increasing tendency to employ workers from the Indian sub-continent, who accepted lower wages, and workers from the Far East, who were recruited directly by companies from their own countries which won contracts in the OPEC states. Third, there was social and political resistance to employing Arabs from outside the Gulf. The expulsion of Palestinians from Kuwait following its liberation from Iraqi occupation was the most striking instance of this. Many paid a heavy price for staying at their place of employment during the occupation, and for the actions of the few who collaborated with the Iraqi authorities.

## The economic effects of international labour mobility

The effects of labour migration can be evaluated from the points of view of the sending and recipient countries, and from a private and social perspective. The scale of migration in the Middle East in the 1970s and 1980s demonstrates that wage differentials between states are important, and that workers are more than willing to move in response to these price signals. Controls through work permits and visa administration prevent labour mobility reducing wage differentials to the point where there would be a regional equilibrium, with no national oversupply or excess demand.

The private benefits of labour migration are simply the additional wages that the worker can earn in Saudi Arabia or the Gulf compared with those in Egypt or Jordan. Migrants may be permitted to purchase consumer goods, including cars, in their country of work and import these goods on preferential terms into their countries of origin. There is also the value of the job training that they receive in countries where there is more modern and sophisticated equipment and plant. This applies to some extent in the Gulf, but is with certainty the case with Turkish workers in Germany. Private costs include the immeasurable anxiety associated with leaving friends and family, and the costs of visits to home, though these will often be covered by the employer in the host country.

Social costs and benefits are even more difficult to evaluate.[23] The balance of payments of the sending country is helped by the inflow of remittances. Such transfers made a major contribution to small economies such as that of Jordan from the 1970s onwards,[24] and even for larger economies such as Egypt the benefit from the remittances was considerable.[25] Repatriated earnings were used to fund housing improvements, health care for ageing relatives and private education and overseas tuition for the young. As well as bringing private benefits, there are social spin-offs from such expenditure by reducing the burden of families on the state. Remittances used for house-building help create local employment in the construction sector, with positive multiplier effects as building workers in turn spend their wages. Education funded through remittances can bring positive social externalities if the beneficiaries use their newly acquired skills and knowledge to good effect by being more competent managers or expert users of high technology.

There will be less benefit for the labour supplying country if the remittances are merely used to purchase imported consumer durables such as household appliances. The local distributors of imported electrical goods will nevertheless gain their margin from the remittances being spent, and the government may directly benefit from import duties. On the negative side, in so far as the government has borne the cost of educating the emigrant, there is a national loss as the skills and knowledge acquired are not used in the sending country. There is a brain drain if those with higher education, who have been subsidised the most by their countries of origin, become migrant workers or perhaps more permanent emigrants.[26] The Coptic Christians from Egypt who have emigrated to Australia and North America often fall into the latter category, as do the thousands of technocrats from Iran who left following the Islamic revolution.

As migrants, unlike emigrants, return to their home countries, it can be argued that the work experience and training they have received abroad can be put to good use in their countries of origin. In practice in the Middle East there are few instances of such benefits. The Turkish workers in Germany, who have been increasingly displaced by immigrants from Eastern Europe, find the high technology skills they have acquired are of little use when they come home. Many former car workers drive taxis or set up their own small retail establishments. There appears to be a preference for self-employment, and a reluctance to work in Turkish manufacturing given the low level of wages in relation to those in Germany. Pride and self-regard appear to be as crucial to the work decisions of former migrants as economic and financial considerations.

In the Maghreb countries of Jordan and Egypt similar considerations apply. Egyptians who taught in schools and universities in the Gulf are reluctant to take up employment in the local educational system. Medical doctors have preferred to move on from the Gulf to North America or Europe rather than return to Egypt and Jordan. Often migrants who return retire prematurely, with no ambition to continue a career beyond the age of fifty. They live off their past savings, or from the rental income from property they have acquired with their remittances. Whole apartment buildings in Cairo have been acquired by Egyptians resident in the Gulf.

Those who have supported younger family members often feel that it is their turn to be helped financially. As a consequence there are large social groups who are consumers rather than producers, and as a result economies such as Jordan or the West Bank and Gaza can increasingly be depicted as rentier economies. The term was often used with reference to the Gulf oil states, but in the 1990s it is perhaps more applicable to those states that have become dependent on remittances and other financial transfers rather than the export of commodities or visible goods.

The scale and financial impact of migration is illustrated in Table 4.6. Saudi Arabia has almost 7.3 million migrant workers who remit over $27 billion per year to their home countries. The UAE and Kuwait also host large numbers of economic migrants, in the case of the latter remitting over $11 billion annually, but no figures are available for the UAE. Not surprisingly Egypt receives the largest remittance inflows, worth almost $8 billion annually. Morocco and Jordan are also significant recipient nations. The large numbers of migrants in Jordan and Syria are mostly political refugees from neighbouring countries, mainly Iraq and Palestine. The figure for Iran refers to refugees from Afghanistan. Israel's migrants are partly Eastern Europeans brought in to work following the Palestinian uprising and the displacement of Palestinian workers. Others come from as far away as the Philippines, but are not being integrated into Israeli society.

*Table 4.6* Inward remittances $ million

| Country | Migrant stock | Outward remittances $ million | Inward remittances |
|---|---|---|---|
| Algeria | 242,324 | 46 | 2,044 |
| Egypt | 244,714 | 255 | 7,725 |
| Iran | 2,128,685 | N/A | 1,181 |
| Israel | 2,940,494 | 3,739 | 1,411 |
| Jordan | 2,972,983 | 495 | 3,640 |
| Kuwait | 2,097,527 | 11,385 | N/A |
| Morocco | 49,098 | 62 | 6,422 |
| Saudi Arabia | 7,288,900 | 27,069 | 236 |
| Sudan | 753,447 | 1 | 1,974 |
| Syria | 2,205,847 | 214 | 1,646 |
| Tunisia | 33,591 | 13 | 1,970 |
| Turkey | 1,410,947 | 175 | 874 |
| UAE | 3,293,264 | N/A | N/A |
| Yemen | 517,926 | 336 | 1,240 |

Source: World Bank, Washington, 2011

## Social costs and benefits of migration for the host country

From the point of view of the host countries the benefits of labour migration should be more clear cut, as presumably the foreign workers would not be hired if they were not needed. Conflicts of interest may arise within the host country however, as the experience of Egyptian migration to Saudi Arabia showed. There is clearly a private benefit to the employers as the imported labour is employed productively. The foreign workers often have skills that local labour lack and they may be prepared to work for lower wages. This may prove controversial if it reduces local wage levels.

There are of course benefits to the host country if it is able to gain from the knowledge and skills of the migrant workers while it has not incurred the cost of their education. When the highly educated and skilled leave Egypt and Jordan for the Gulf or Libya there is a hidden subsidy from the poorer states to the richer countries of the region. The cost of this publicly funded education subsidy is arguably greater than the aid transfers from the OPEC countries to their fellow Arab and Muslim states. This may also apply in the case of Turkish and German financial relations and those between France and the Maghreb.

On the negative side the disadvantage of host country dependence on imported labour may be both economic and social. The learning experience may be ultimately the most important benefit from an industrialisation programme such as that instigated by the Saudi Basic Industries Corporation (SABIC). These wider economic gains may justify the investment even when the financial returns are disappointing. It is, in other words, the externalities that are important, but these will be reduced from the national point of view if the workforce is foreign, and if expatriates hold all the key technical positions. Socially, relations between the foreign workforce and local labour may be strained. At the workplace this may inhibit skill transfers and hinder on-the-job training for local nationals. In the wider society it can produce political tensions, especially if the immigrants are from more radical states, and are less willing to accept the conservative social norms of the Gulf states.

Such factors have resulted in a reduction in the work permits issued to Arabs in the Gulf states, and the substitution of South Asian and South East Asian labour for Egyptians and Palestinians, as already indicated. There were concerns that at least some of the latter might subvert the local population with their ideas. There was also a worry that the migrants might wish to become permanent residents. In the case of non-Arab labour in the Gulf this is unlikely, as most only come for the money and wish to return to their home states as soon as possible once their work is finished.[27] They have no desire to establish roots in the Gulf, and are uninterested in the domestic political scene. The workers from South Asia speak little Arabic, and those from South East Asia usually speak none, so communication with the local population is limited. Most live in special accommodation with other migrants, which is separate from local residential districts. Social mixing is rare, and even in the workplace there is the bare minimum of contact.

The prospects for future labour mobility both within and from the Middle East are poor. To some extent the opportunity of migration to the Gulf served as a safety valve for Palestinians from Jordan and the occupied territories in the 1970s and early 1980s. It provided welcome opportunities for educated Egyptians who could not be absorbed into lucrative employment at home. Germany was an attractive employment destination for both skilled and unskilled Turkish workers, and France played the same role in relation to the Maghreb countries, especially for the non-Arab Berbers of Algeria who faced an uncertain future following the departure of the French colonists in the early 1960s.[28]

If labour is likely to be more tied to within national boundaries in the Middle East in the years ahead there will be more pressures to create suitable employment opportunities locally. With rapidly increasing populations this is likely to prove extremely difficult. Substantial investment will clearly be needed, but this raises the question of finance. It is these issues that are addressed in the next chapter on capital markets and savings.

# 5   Capital markets, savings and investment

Finance is regarded as a major constraint on development in most regions of the developing world. There is often insufficient money available to finance worthwhile projects and the price of loanable funds is usually high, reflecting the shortage of savings. In low-income economies it is not surprising that savings rates are low, as most disposable income has to be used to purchase the necessities for everyday living, and many families simply cannot afford to make financial provision for the future, even though this leaves them insecure and vulnerable.[1]

The Middle East is different from other developing areas, as although there are shortages of financial capital in individual countries, for the region as a whole the revenue generated from oil exports produced a healthy surplus since the 1970s despite some downturns when oil prices were temporarily low. This surplus benefited not only the major oil exporting countries but, through government-to-government transfers and remittances, it also aided the poorer countries of the region. Although by the 1990s the surpluses were much reduced, the oil price rises of 1973–74 and 1979 brought the greatest ever boost to capital formation throughout the region and resulted in the beneficial infrastructure improvements described in Chapter 3. In comparison to most other areas of the Third World, the Middle East can therefore be considered well-endowed with both financial and physical capital.

Favourable financial circumstances are not sufficient in themselves to ensure economic development occurs. Much depends on the efficiency of the capital market and the effectiveness of the commercial banks and other financial institutions as intermediaries.[2] In the Middle East the position is complicated by the fact that oil revenues accrue to governments, and part of the role of financial intermediaries is to ensure that this revenue gets distributed to those sectors of the economy where it can be harnessed most effectively. State financial institutions play a key part in this process, but there is still a significant role for commercial banks as government spending finds its way into private businesses and the pockets of individual families and from there into bank accounts.[3]

As well as the market for loanable funds, which involves the commercial banks, there is also the issue of risk capital, and the need for equity markets.

These are underdeveloped in the Middle East, but the question that must be asked is whether this really matters. Would development have been more rapid if the state had played less of a role in the financial system of the Middle East, with equity and loan finance dominant as in most Western economies? Market efficiency depends on prices acting as an allocative mechanism and market participants being able to read the pricing signals. Have interest rates been allowed to bring the demand and supply of loanable funds into equilibrium in the Middle East? Is there evidence of financial repression with interest rates being held below equilibrium levels, and the state determining how credit is rationed?[4] These issues will be addressed in this chapter, and an attempt made to find answers in the light of the evidence from the region.

## Domestic savings ratios

The national account figures detailing consumption and savings as a proportion of gross domestic product are a useful starting point when considering the economic growth potential of any group of countries. High levels of savings might be expected for oil-exporting countries, and as Table 5.1 shows this indeed appears to be the case in the Middle East, with a 59 per cent savings ratio for Kuwait in relation to GDP and ratios of 47 per cent for Algeria and 33 per cent for Saudi Arabia. In Kuwait's case there is a large discrepancy between the gross savings ration and that for fixed capital formation. This is because much of the oil revenue is used to acquire overseas financial assets rather than being channelled into domestic investment. Although it could be argued that such a policy handicaps national economic development, in the long term there is a strong case for the strategy as earnings from overseas assets will continue to accrue to Kuwait once oil is depleted or is replaced by alternative sources of power. The worldwide assets controlled by the Kuwait Investment Authority are regarded as a fund for future generations. Investing the funds locally would only result in much lower economic returns and

*Table 5.1* Gross savings and fixed capital formation as a percentage GDP

| Country | Savings | Fixed capital formation |
| --- | --- | --- |
| Algeria | 47 | 33 |
| Egypt | 17 | 19 |
| Israel | 18 | 17 |
| Jordan | 10 | 15 |
| Kuwait | 59 | 14 |
| Morocco | 30 | 31 |
| Saudi Arabia | 33 | 21 |
| Sudan | 18 | 20 |
| Syria | 14 | 19 |
| Tunisia | 21 | 24 |
| Turkey | 15 | 19 |

Source: World Bank, Washington, 2011

increase the numbers of migrant workers, skewing the population balance away from Kuwaiti nationals.

⌐ Saudi Arabia is in a similar position to Kuwait, although as it has a larger local population and is trying, with difficulty, to increase employment opportunities for local nationals in the private sector, there has been substantial expenditure on infrastructure with contracts increasingly offered to local companies. Algeria also has a high savings ratio but a relatively higher rate of fixed capital formation than other countries in the region. Some of this is accounted for by the high investment costs associated with gas extraction. These yield a high return, but the returns from investment in industry and agriculture to diversify the Algerian economy have proved disappointing, partly because of political uncertainties and the difficulty in accessing and competing in foreign markets apart from those for oil and gas.

Deficiencies between savings and investment can of course be met by inflows of capital from abroad to bridge the gap. Where there is foreign aid, international borrowing, investment flows and remittances, the level of investment can exceed savings. In Table 5.1 Egypt, Jordan, Syria, Tunisia and Turkey all have rates of fixed capital formation in excess of the domestic savings ratio. In the cases of Egypt, Jordan and Syria the earnings of their own citizens working in the Gulf have facilitated a level of investment well beyond what the capacity of the domestic economy could support.[5]

In Israel the savings level has risen in recent years and easily covers fixed capital formation. This has reduced economic dependency on the United States, which has historically been a major source for capital investment in the country. Israel is trying to diversify its economic relations and build links with India and China, economies growing much faster than the United States.

## Financial intermediation and development

There has been much debate amongst development economists about whether financial intermediation is a prerequisite for economic development, or if the development of banks and other financial institutions is a mere outcome of the development process.[6] The limited role of financial intermediaries and the inefficiency of some of the banks themselves may explain the poor performance of the Middle East in relation to East and South East Asia.

The development of financial intermediation has a qualitative as well as a quantitative impact on economic activity. It is the judgemental skills of the economic historian that are needed to make this assessment and not merely the computational skills of the applied economist. In the Middle East the pattern of banking development in the nineteenth century followed the standard colonial model, but during the twentieth century there were a wealth of different experiences that makes the region of particular interest to the financial historian. Developments in banking reflect the ideology and circumstances of particular Middle Eastern countries, but the causality is two-way, as the systems of banking have some impact on economic outcomes.

All the early banks active in the region were European owned, the most widely represented, the Ottoman Bank, being a joint Anglo-French company that was quoted on both the London stock market and the Paris *bourse*. Both the National Bank of Egypt and the Imperial Bank of Iran were British owned in spite of their names. These institutions were largely involved in trade finance, arranging letters of credit and issuing bills of exchange, usually on behalf of European companies that were active in the Middle East.[7] Their commercial banking activity had a minimal impact on local merchants as they continued to use the services of money-lenders and money-changers whom they knew and understood rather than institutions run by foreigners mostly on behalf of foreigners.

Given their access to and knowledge of European financial markets these new banks were well placed to raise funds externally on behalf of Middle Eastern governments. As the Ottoman, Egyptian and Iranian authorities were constantly in need of funds, it was only natural that they should come to rely on the new institutions for assistance. The arranging of sovereign loans and the management of bond issues for Middle Eastern governments became a major activity,[8] and despite their commercial nature the banks played a double role by performing some of the functions of central banks. This role continued until central banks were established in the 1920s in Turkey and Iran and until the early 1950s in the case of Egypt. Central banks were set up for nationalistic reasons, as state dependence on foreign-owned banks was regarded as politically unacceptable.

In practice the new central banks lacked experience of international capital markets and also had few external banking contacts. As just another arm of the state bureaucracy they were not able to play much of a role in raising international funding on behalf of their governments. This would have mattered less if there were indigenous capital markets for government stock. The absence of adequate markets severely constrains the fiscal stance of Middle Eastern governments because although treasury bills can be off-loaded onto the commercial banks to a limited degree they lack the ability to fund longer-term debt through bond issues. There are very small domestic markets in Turkish, Iranian, Egyptian and more recently Saudi Arabian government paper, but these lack both width and depth, the major participants being the commercial banks of each country. On any given day it is often quite difficult to sell the government bills and bonds, which means the liquidity of the assets must be questioned.

## The spread of indigenous banks

The rise of locally owned banks dates from the 1920s in Turkey, Iran and Egypt, and the late 1930s in Palestine and Saudi Arabia, and as late as the 1960s in some of the Gulf States.[9] In Turkey the first indigenous commercial banks included Turkiye Tutunculer Bankasi (1924), Turkiye is Bankasi (1925), Denizli Iktisat Bankasi (1927) and Turkiye Imar Bankasi (1928).

These banks were established to challenge the monopoly of the Anglo-French owned Ottoman Bank and to fill the gap left by the exodus of Greek and Armenian private bankers, money-lenders and money-changers from Anatolia as a result of the inter-ethnic tensions that accompanied the founding of the modern Turkish state.

In Iran Bank Melli was established in 1928 as a national institution to act as central bank, and to challenge the dominance of the British owned Imperial Bank of Iran. Bank Melli was owned by the government, which gave it a significant amount of state financial business, largely at the expense of the Imperial Bank. Unlike in Iran, the initiative in Egypt to establish an indigenous bank came from a group of local wealthy merchants and landowners. There as in Iran it was British owned banks that dominated, particularly the National Bank of Egypt and Barclays, with the latter financing much of the Alexandria cotton trade. Banque Misr, the first locally owned financial institution, was established as a bank to help Arab and Muslim traders specifically, and to finance the development of the textile industry. It was to be a very effective institution, playing a major role in the industrialisation of Egypt in the 1930s.[10]

It was not until 1930 that a locally owned bank was established in British administered Palestine, the Arab Bank, which opened in Jerusalem. It was founded by a Palestinian business entrepreneur, Abdel Majid Shoman, who had emigrated to New York in 1920, and learnt at first-hand how American banks operated by working as an accountant with a textile firm. He returned to Jerusalem with the ambition to found a bank, and won the backing of a group of Arab merchants in Jerusalem to realise this ambition. Following the foundation of the state of Israel in 1948 the bank moved its headquarters to Amman and became the largest bank in Jordan. To this day it remains the main bank serving the Palestinian community worldwide, with branches almost everywhere Palestinians live. It became the first truly international Arab bank, though this was largely by force of circumstances rather than by design.

In Saudi Arabia there was much resistance to the introduction of modern banking, partly from Islamic fundamentalists who regarded all dealings in *riba* or interest as unacceptable and associated banks with the *infidel* or unbelievers. Most of the local money-lenders and money-changers wanted the King to exclude foreign banks from his Kingdom, as they argued that they could provide virtually the same services as banks, but using means which were Islamically acceptable. Eventually, however, two of the largest money-changers of the Hijaz, Salim Bin Mahfouz and the Kaki brothers, lobbied the King for permission to establish a licensed bank. As the King knew these money-changers were devout Moslems, the licence was granted, while at the same time Banque Misr was excluded, and later Citibank of America was to be refused access. The National Commercial Bank that Bin Mahfouz and the Kaki families founded in 1938 was to enjoy a monopoly of banking in Saudi Arabia, which enabled it to become eventually the largest bank in the Middle East in terms of its assets.[11]

## Nationalisation of banking

The moves to nationalise banks were motivated by patriotism, and a desire to take over the assets of the former imperial powers, rather than because of any ideological commitment to state ownership, or a desire to impose government control over the commanding heights of the economy. Mosadeq in Iran was to make the first moves in 1952 as part of a package of measures that accompanied the nationalisation of the Iranian oil industry. Then came the Suez Crisis of 1956, when Britain and France invaded Egypt to retake the Suez Canal which Nasser had nationalised. In the aftermath of this Nasser retaliated by seizing British and French assets, including the National Bank of Egypt, Barclays, which was renamed Bank of Alexandria, and Banque du Caire. Egypt ended up by having just four state owned banks, as Banque Misr was also nationalised to reduce the power of the landowners and merchants.

In Syria all the foreign owned banks were merged, and a new state owned institution created, the Commercial Bank of Syria. Following the Iraqi revolution in 1958 the Baghdad government adopted a similar policy, and the Raifidain Bank was granted a monopoly of all domestic and foreign banking transactions.[12] Algeria, following the expulsion of the French, was to take the same position, with Banque Nationale d'Algerie taking over most commercial banking business in 1966, while another state owned institution, Credit Populaire d'Algeria, was founded to manage the business of the smaller credit banks.

Elsewhere in the Middle East governments were less keen to be involved in the ownership of commercial banking, except where private capital was not forthcoming. Even then there was more willingness to contemplate more flexible arrangements such as partnership in ownership through joint ventures. In Kuwait, for example, there were strong pressures after independence from the merchant community to ensure that all banks were under local ownership. The merchants were more interested in investment opportunities for themselves, however, not state ownership. Hence a law was passed stating that all banks should be owned by local citizens. Those few shares in the National Bank of Kuwait owned by foreigners were sold to local investors. The Gulf, Al Ahli and Commercial Banks were established with purely local capital. In the case of the British Bank of the Middle East, however, the British owned stake was sold to the Kuwait government, and local shareholders were brought in to take 51 per cent of the shares, which gave them effective control. The Kuwait government was content to act as facilitator, maintaining a 49 per cent stake.

In Saudi Arabia the government only injected capital into the Riyadh Bank, the second largest bank in the kingdom, when it ran into difficulties. As it was only founded in 1957, it always had problems competing with the National Commercial Bank which had almost a 20-year lead. Eventually when lending difficulties in the 1960s resulted in liquidity problems, the Saudi Arabian Monetary Agency took a 38 per cent stake. The motive was to provide a much-needed capital injection to help the merchant sheikhs who continued to own most of the bank and maintained control. In Saudi Arabia, as in Kuwait, there was pressures by the 1970s to curtail the foreign owned banks, which as a result of United States government lobbying had been allowed to gain a minor foothold in the Kingdom in the 1950s and 1960s to serve the western partners in the Arabian American Oil Company, ARAMCO.

Citibank's Saudi operations were Saudised in 1979, which resulted in the founding of the Saudi American Bank. This was 40 per cent owned by Citibank, but the other 60 per cent of the capital was sold to Saudi citizens. The idea was to combine Saudi Arabian private investment with American bank management expertise for the benefit of all parties. The Saudi British, Saudi French and Saudi Dutch Banks were created under similar arrangements, bringing real competition in banking services to the Kingdom.

## Banking regulation

The ownership of commercial banks arguably matters less than their effective regulation. At least some of the shortcomings of the operation of financial intermediaries in the Middle East may be due to the ineffectiveness of the central banks in the region. No central bank in the Middle East enjoys independence from government, so there is no question of independent monetary policies being pursued, but all have the regulation of the banking sector within their remit. The problem is the extent to which even the regulation of the banking system is subject to political interference on the one hand, and lobbying from the commercial banks themselves on the other. There is little doubt that the freedom of manoeuvre of central banks in the Middle East is very limited, and it is only in Israel that the central bank could be said to have reasonable independence over regulatory matters, and more limited independence on monetary issues.

In Saudi Arabia and Bahrain there was not even a formally constituted central bank, both countries having monetary agencies with much weaker powers, although this changed in Bahrain in 2002 when the Central Bank was established. The failure to regulate the Riyadh Bank in the 1950s almost led to its collapse, and more recently in the late 1980s the debt problems facing the Kingdom's largest bank were allowed to mount up, without proper provisions being made. These problems were sorted out with the re-capitalisation of the bank, but there was a three-year period when there was a reluctance to act, not least because some leading Saudi Arabian merchants and members of the royal family were involved. In the 1980s there was the debate over whether the money-changers, Al Rajhi, should be given a banking licence. By 1986 they were granted the licence because of political pressures, but the regulatory regime differs from that applied to the other banks.

In Egypt the joint ventures between foreign banks and the nationalised Egyptian banks have been subject to lax regulation. These banks are largely involved in import finance, for which they levy high charges, largely reflecting their privileged position in the banking system, and the lack of competition. These banks do little to help with export finance, which arguably would help the Egyptian economy more. The numerous investment companies in Egypt have been left to their own devices, and some have solicited for deposits, marketing themselves as a more lucrative alternative to the state owned banks. Yet when the largest investment company, Al Rayan, became bankrupt, many investors of very modest means lost their savings, and the Central Bank of Egypt did nothing to help.

The largely Abu Dhabi owned Bank of Credit and Commerce International (BCCI) was regulated from Luxembourg rather than from the United Arab Emirates. Its collapse caused substantial damage to many Arab commercial banks because of cross-holdings, including the National Commercial Bank of Saudi Arabia, but no efforts were made to avert the eventual bankruptcy, even though it was evident to most bankers in the Emirates from 1985 onward that BCCI was a flawed and corrupt institution.

## Financial penetration

The depth of banking development can be measured by the number of accounts per 1,000 adults. Unfortunately data is more limited for the Middle East than for other regions of the developing world; indeed, perhaps surprisingly, in some economies where banking is well developed, such as those of the Gulf, there is no data. This does not reflect the absence of banking data, as data is available from both the central banks and leading commercial banks, but rather the issue of how to measure population size, and whether to include or exclude foreign migratory workers from the total. Virtually all local adult Gulf nationals, and indeed local children, have bank accounts. Amongst expatriates, however, only the higher paid have bank accounts, as most of the foreign labour in lower paid, less skilled jobs rely on cash and use exchange agents rather than banks for their remittances.

Table 5.2 shows the number of deposit and loan accounts per 1,000 adults for those states in the Middle East that report on this data. Israel has the highest number of deposit accounts with virtually every household having at least one account. Turkey is also highly banked, with most families using bank accounts for their everyday transactions, mainly by debit and credit cards, with their salaries credited each month to their banks rather than being paid in cash. In contrast in Syria and Yemen few have bank accounts, indeed in the case of the former the value of its entire banking sector is lower than that of neighbouring Jordan, a much smaller country. This partly reflects the absence of modern banking facilities in Syria and the former virtual monopoly of the state owned Commercial Bank of Syria. There seems to be no correlation between interest rates paid on deposits and the proportion of accounts held. The negative real deposit rates in Algeria reflect its high inflation.

From a developmental perspective, bank deposits matter as they represent funds that are harnessed for bank lending. If funds are merely hoarded they will not contribute to economic activity. If they are passed on to family members this may not represent the most efficient allocation. In contrast banks can potentially allocate funds to the most efficient use. Those

*Table 5.2* Financial penetration

| Country | Deposit accounts per 1,000 adults | Deposit real interest rates % | Loan accounts per 1,000 adults | Credit depth of information |
|---|---|---|---|---|
| Algeria | 683 | −4.2 | N/A | 2 |
| Egypt | N/A | 0.8 | N/A | 6 |
| Iran | N/A | 11.3 | N/A | 4 |
| Israel | 2,254 | 3.4 | 1,055 | 5 |
| Jordan | 814 | 2.6 | 160 | 2 |
| Kuwait | N/A | 2.5 | N/A | 4 |
| Morocco | 277 | N/A | N/A | 5 |
| Syria | 157 | 3.5 | 23 | 2 |
| Tunisia | 672 | N/A | 176 | 5 |
| Turkey | 1,851 | N/A | 315 | 5 |
| Yemen | 106 | −2.0 | 6 | 2 |

Source: World Bank, Washington, 2011
Note: Credit depth of information: 1 = low, 6 = high

businesses with the best prospects will receive the funding they need while even consumer credit will stimulate the economy through creating greater demand for goods and services produced or distributed by local businesses.

Data on loan accounts is limited in the Middle East as Table 5.2 shows, with Israel having by far the largest number per 1,000 people of those countries reporting this statistic and Turkey in second place. All the countries cited report on the depth of information of their loan recipients. Perhaps surprisingly the figure is highest for Egypt, followed by Israel, Morocco, Tunisia and Turkey. The lowest scores for credit information are recorded by Algeria, Syria and Yemen.

It would be expected that there should be a negative relationship between high proportions of non-performing loans and poor credit information. Table 5.3, however, shows that this is not necessarily the case as, for example, Algeria has a relatively low ratio of non-performing loans to total loans in spite of its low depth of credit information. This may be explained by many of the loans being to state sector entities that are unlikely to default rather than the private sector. There is an especially high ratio of non-performing loans to total loans in Turkey despite the favourable score for depth of credit information. Most bank lending in Turkey is either to consumers or small and medium sized businesses. The high number of non-performing loans indicates poor risk appraisal by Turkish banks despite the otherwise healthy state of the economy in recent years. Not all the lessons may have been learnt from the banking crisis of 2002 in Turkey, although its banks are well capitalised, and should be able to survive any future financial shocks. Tunisia and Iran also have relatively high default ratios in spite of reporting favourable depth of credit information.

Table 5.3 also shows bank credit to GDP ratios that indicate the depth of the banking sector and its role in financing. They also provide a measure of

*Table 5.3* Banking indicators (per cent)

| Country | Bank credit/GDP | Non-performing loans/total loans | Capital to assets ratio |
|---|---|---|---|
| Algeria | N/A | 1.8 | N/A |
| Egypt | 69.4 | 6.5 | 6.4 |
| Iran | 37.2 | 13.1 | N/A |
| Israel | 87.5 | 1.1 | 6.0 |
| Jordan | 96.0 | 4.9 | 11.0 |
| Kuwait | 84.0 | 2.8 | 12.1 |
| Morocco | 102.7 | 3.8 | 8.0 |
| Saudi Arabia | N/A | 3.3 | 13.3 |
| Sudan | 20.5 | N/A | N/A |
| Syria | 47.7 | 6.4 | N/A |
| Tunisia | 73.7 | 13.2 | N/A |
| Turkey | 69.2 | 17.6 | 13.4 |
| UAE | 114.5 | 5.7 | N/A |
| Yemen | 19.3 | 10.7 | N/A |

Source: World Bank, Washington, 2011

private indebtedness that can be viewed more negatively. The ratio is especially high in the UAE and Morocco, with much of the lending in these two economies being for real estate lending, both to developers and property purchasers. As the real estate bubble in Dubai showed, such lending can be risky, even though the ratio of non-performing loans in the UAE was fairly modest. The low figure for bank credit to GDP in Yemen reflects the under-development of its banking system and the reliance of the private sector on informal credit, usually from money-lenders.

## Currency standards and exchange

As markets develop and widen, currency is needed to facilitate transactions, as barter is really only appropriate for simple economies based on bilateral exchanges. The Middle East was the first region of the world where coins were used to facilitate trade, and from the time of the ancient Babylonians in Iraq, the Pharaohs of Egypt, and the early recorded history of the biblical lands, there is evidence of currency being issued. Coins made out of both gold and silver were used in the days of the Prophet Mohammed and there was much discussion of appropriate rates of exchange between the two mediums, as the price of silver, then as now, seldom moved in line with the price of gold.

Bimetallism was to continue up until Ottoman times, with the silver *akche* circulating alongside gold, though eventually a paper currency was issued, the *kurush*, which was backed by treasury bills (*kaimeh*), as well as both metals.[13] It was only in 1880 that the Ottoman Empire was to adopt the gold standard, but silver coins continued to circulate internally, and their price varied in terms of the gold-backed currency issue. As the economies of the Middle East became increasingly dominated by the European powers in the nineteenth century, European currencies were substituted for local money. In Egypt sterling became the main medium of exchange from the 1880s onward, and the French franc was legal tender in Algeria from 1851 onwards and in Tunisia from 1891.

With increasing economic independence the economies of the Middle East issued their own paper currencies, but those states tied to a particular European power could not freely convert their currency, apart from into that of the colonial country. The Egyptian pound was tied to sterling, for example, which facilitated trade with the British Empire, but not with third parties. The same applied to the Maghreb states and Syria, which were part of the French franc currency area. With political independence the links with the former colonial currencies were broken, but Middle Eastern currencies were then completely inconvertible. This enabled governments to insulate their economies more fully from the outside world. In economic terms it meant that the currency issue merely facilitated internal exchange and the operation of the domestic market. Wider international exchange reverted to being conducted on a barter basis, as with inconvertibility, there was no medium of exchange to facilitate external transactions. Increasingly the United States dollar was used to fill this gap, but this in fact meant a return to a dual currency standard, with the high transactions costs which that implies.

The Gulf states have fully convertible currencies unlike the other economies of the Middle East, though some such as Turkey have made important moves in that direction with the encouragement of the International Monetary Fund.[14] It is oil earnings and the substantial holdings of foreign assets that have enabled the Gulf states to maintain convertibility, not only for payments for traded goods, but also for capital flows. This has encouraged outward and inward investment by both Gulf nationals and foreigners, and reduced the transactions costs with international trade. Choice of imported goods has been maintained, unlike in those countries where inconvertibility has necessitated barter, often referred to as countertrade, especially where elaborate deals involving three or more parties are involved.

Historically the Gulf states have always been trading economies and currency inconvertibility would be politically unacceptable, especially to the powerful merchant classes. There was resistance to the introduction of paper currency into Saudi Arabia by King Abdul Aziz himself back in the 1940s, as the silver riyal was preferred, but pilgrim receipts were to eventually form the basis of the new paper currency.[15] Suspicion about money whose value can be affected by government economic policy remains, however, and there is a concern that tampering with a currency standard may conflict with the ideals of Islam.

Inflation is a very sensitive issue, as price rises have consequences for income distribution and justice in trading. Those in debt may benefit from inflation if the service charge on debt does not rise with inflation, but those providing credit may lose through no fault of their own. If debt servicing charges or interest rates rise with inflation, this results in worries over *riba* or usury, which is prohibited under the *shari'ah* Islamic law. In Saudi Arabia Islamic concerns over monetary management have resulted in resistance to the establishment of a fully fledged central bank. The Kingdom still has only a monetary agency to oversee its financial system, and monetary instruments such as interest rates have never been used in pursuance of economic policy. Inflation is held at as low a level as possible, and there was considerable concern after the oil price rises of 1973–74 when inflation rose to double-digit levels. Swift cuts in government expenditure were implemented, which reduced economic growth, but this was felt to be the lesser evil.

## International borrowing and government debt

As a result of the underdeveloped nature of local capital markets, Middle Eastern governments whose expenditure exceeds tax and other receipts are forced to borrow internationally. This imposes burdens which do not arise in the case of internal debt. The borrowing is usually dollar denominated, which increases the cost of debt servicing and repayments in local currency terms with devaluation and depreciation. If the interest rates on the debt are variable, and related to euro-dollar rates over which Middle East governments have no control, this introduces an additional element of uncertainty and potential vulnerability.

Of greatest concern in the Middle East have been the political costs of borrowing. The governments of the region have in fact relatively little indebtedness to the commercial euro-dollar markets. Much of their borrowing has been from western governments, the World Bank and the International Monetary Fund.[16] The latter have imposed structural adjustment programmes as part of their lending conditionality which many politically active groups on both the secular left and the Islamist right have opposed. These policies have included the phasing out of subsidies to reduce government deficits, liberalisation of imports and regulations on foreign capital, privatisation and exchange rate devaluation which has caused inflationary pressures.

## Financial flows and the financing gap

In the literature on economic development much attention has been paid to the notion of a dual gap, the difference between investment and savings on the one hand, and between balance of payments receipts and outgoings on the other.[17] Financial inflows can fill the external gap, at least for a few years, until debt servicing obligations build up. In the Middle East, however, inflows have also been required to cover a third gap, that between government expenditure and receipts. In so far as it is the state which is the major investor, and most saving is of a compulsory nature through taxation, the government deficit may correspond to the internal gap between savings and investment.

Fewer foreign financial inflows would be needed if taxation receipts were higher or if government spending was lower. An alternative, which is much favoured by officials of the International Monetary Fund, is to have a slimmer government, with more investment undertaken by the private sector, financed by personal and corporate savings. This may not solve the gap problem, however, as investment goods may be largely imported, and contribute to the foreign exchange gap. Nevertheless, the economies of the Middle East are being nudged in the direction of leaner government and enhanced private financing, partly by international pressures, but also by internal dissent over the outcomes of past interventionist policies. Are the domestic banking and financial systems within Middle Eastern economies fit to cope with the demands of increasingly free enterprise economies? It is to this question that we must now turn.

Reference has already been made to the overbanked nature of some Middle Eastern economies, and the underbanked nature of others. What are the institutional arrangements associated with each of these conditions? Are there any general patterns to emerge or conclusions to draw? The Middle East provides some interesting contrasts, with indigenous banks replacing foreign banks in the early post-independence period and moves towards state ownership with bank nationalisation in some states, but not in others. More recently there have been changes in direction with financial liberalisation and deregulation, a process that is on-going, and which is still only in its early stages. Each of these developments will be reviewed here, but the specific regional issue of the Islamisation of banking will be left to Chapter 6, as it is perhaps best considered in the context of more fundamental Muslim economic issues.

## Offshore banking

The action by revolutionary governments against individuals with substantial private wealth inevitably resulted in attempts at evasion. Capital transfers were made through unofficial black market transactions that, though illegal, were nevertheless substantial in Egypt, Syria and Iraq in the 1950s and 1960s. At the same time, the restrictions on the operation of foreign banks, and the outright bank nationalisations, created a vacuum as there were many businessmen and wealthy private individuals who were unhappy about dealing with state owned or controlled banks, as they did not wish to disclose to governments full details of all their financial dealings.

It was this market that Beirut's private bankers sought to exploit, as unlike other Middle Eastern governments, the Lebanese authorities adopted a laissez-faire attitude to banking, and openly welcomed foreign banks. In 1956 a bank secrecy law was passed modelled on the Swiss legislation that permitted depositors to open numbered bank accounts to provide anonymity. As a result substantial amounts were deposited in the Lebanese banking system, mainly in hard currency, especially in United States dollars. By the mid-1960s Beirut had become the major financial centre for the region, providing highly personalised banking services for wealthy Middle Eastern businessmen on the Swiss model. In addition to Lebanese banks, major foreign banks were also involved, including Citibank of New York and leading French and British banks. Lebanese nationals were employed by these banks, however, so arguably the foreign banks brought prosperity to Beirut, and the quality names brought business that might not have come to local banks which were inevitably regarded as less secure. Local Lebanese banks offered higher deposit rates, however, so clients had a classic choice between risks and returns.

The Lebanese civil war which started in 1975 effectively finished Beirut as a financial centre, as personal banking by its nature implies frequent client consultation, but the wealthy were reluctant to risk visiting Beirut, and once communications links were cut, with the periodic closure of the airport, the international banks started to pull out. Though by the early 1990s a degree of law and order was restored to Beirut, it is unlikely to regain its pre-eminent role in Middle Eastern finance. There are several reasons for this. First, there is no need to transit through Beirut with non-stop flights to Europe and North America from the Gulf. Second, clients from Saudi Arabia and other Gulf states have got used to travelling to London, or in dealing through Bahrain to some extent as outlined below if they need personal contacts closer to home. Finally, the telecommunications revolution also means less need for centres such as Beirut.

Beirut's demise left a gap that Bahrain was to fill from the late 1970s onward following the enactment of offshore banking legislation in 1975. Like Lebanon and unlike neighbouring Saudi Arabia, Bahrain welcomed foreign banks, provided they confined their dealings to non-residents.[18] The Bahrain authorities saw that there was the opportunity to make their island the dominant financial centre in the Gulf, creating much needed high-paid employment, which the country with its meagre oil reserves found highly appealing. This policy was to prove highly successful, as by the early 1980s over 100 leading international banks maintained offshore banking units in Bahrain, largely aimed at attracting deposits from Saudi Arabian clients, usually in dollars, but also in riyals, which earned higher interest than was paid onshore because of the Islamic concerns over *riba*.

As with Beirut, conflict and uncertainty were to contribute to Bahrain's demise, especially the Iraq–Iran War and the Gulf War, although the unrest in Bahrain associated with the Arab Spring has inevitably proved to be the major factor. Increasingly with modern telecommunications and computer links bankers and wealthy private businessmen are able to deal directly with European financial markets, especially with London. At the same time, the retail banks in Saudi Arabia have become more sophisticated, and themselves maintain a presence in Europe and the United States. The need for regional banking centres is less clear, given these developments.

This is illustrated by the case of Cyprus, which passed offshore banking legislation in 1982. No major Gulf banks have established a presence in Limassol or Nicosia, the only regional banks represented being the Arab and Jordan National Bank.[19] Lebanese banks transferred operations to Cyprus when conditions were particularly difficult in Beirut in the 1980s, but most of this business subsequently returned to Lebanon. The main offshore banks attracted to Cyprus from the 1990s have been from co-religionist Orthodox countries, especially Russia and Serbia, as the latter's foreign trade financing activities from Belgrade were curtailed by United Nations sanctions. However, as Serbia's situation was normalised this business has returned to the Balkans, illustrating the fragility of offshore centres and the reversibility of the funding inflows given the footloose nature of financial capital. There are clearly lessons for any future aspiring offshore centres in the Middle East.

## Stock market development and equity finance

Modern business enterprises raise much of their funding requirements through equity markets rather than by bank borrowings. If risk capital can be utilised, this arguably reduces risks for the business enterprises as there are not the debt servicing and repayments commitments. The complete absence until the 1990s of any major public companies in the Middle East, and the fact that there are no multinational corporations with their headquarters in the region, reflected the underdeveloped nature of the area's equity markets until the last decade.

Other parts of the Third World, such as South and South East Asia, are the bases for increasingly important multinational enterprises, yet the Middle East, despite its substantial oil wealth, remains dependent on multinationals based elsewhere, with little corporate loyalty or affiliation with the region. Most large manufacturing companies in the Middle East are state owned, but this means they take a narrow nationalistic view, which is constrained by the small economic size of the states in which they are based. Some may argue that this identification of corporate with state interests is desirable, but it has resulted in local manufacturing being subject to domestic political pressures, and being at a disadvantage in relation to the much freer multinational companies based in the industrialised world.

The Alexandria Stock Exchange predated many markets in Europe and East Asia, as it was established in 1863, with investment companies and transport undertakings quoted and traded. The growth of the market was constrained by the limited size of the economy and the fact that most of the modern sector was foreign owned and financed. Commercial banks, for example, are usually amongst the first shares to be quoted on young stock exchanges, but the National Bank of Egypt, as already indicated, was British owned. As there was no industrial base following the collapse of Mohammed Ali's textile mills, there were no manufacturing companies seeking quotations. Most of the local trading concerns were family businesses. It was only the enterprises serving the cotton trade which were quoted companies as these were more substantial in size. Even in the transport infrastructure sphere, the largest project of all, the Suez Canal, was an Anglo-French venture, financed from London and Paris.

This experience illustrates that without a demand for local equity finance there is unlikely to be a supply. It was less a case of foreign investment filling a domestic savings gap, but rather the equity market being seen as a source of funding for left-over projects that were too small to merit international funding, and where local knowledge was crucial. Equity markets cannot in themselves promote development, instead they are reactive, though the presence of an active market may encourage entrepreneurs to take risks with expansion secure in the knowledge that the risks can be shared. The Egyptian market throughout its 150-year history has never been very active, its heyday being the 1930s and 1940s before the young officers' coup of 1952. In Egypt financiers had always been in the habit of looking abroad, and the main reaction to the events of 1952 and the Suez Crisis of 1956 was a flight of capital overseas, both legally and illegally. It was this that drove Nasser to look to the state to fund his industrialisation drive, as he despaired of Egypt's entrepreneurs. The nationalisation measures of the 1950s and 1960s were motivated by pragmatism rather than ideology.

Under Sadat there was increased interest in private finance but the main reliance was on foreign capital through the "Open Door Policy" introduced in 1974, not the revival of the Egyptian stock exchange that had been virtually moribund during Nasser's period of nationalisations. By the late 1980s the stock market had revived, largely without government encouragement, and the number of companies quoted more than doubled to 582 by 1991, with a total market capitalisation of over $907 million.[20] This, however, was less than one-fortieth of the capitalisation of Singapore, and less than 0.1 per cent of that of the London Stock Exchange at that time.

Furthermore, over 60 per cent of the equity values on the Egyptian exchange represented closed companies rather than joint stock companies which are open to the public. The attraction of closed companies is that the capital cannot be diluted by new share issues to the general public, which might undermine equity prices. Rights issues to existing shareholders are permitted, but the limitation on wider issues forces companies to rely more on debt finance. Following a re-organisation of the Egyptian stock market the closed companies were de-listed, resulting in 211 companies remaining.

This feature of the Cairo stock exchange was not found in other markets in the Middle East, though these remain equally underdeveloped. There has been a revival of dealings on the Tehran stock market after the ending of the Iraq–Iran War, a development encouraged by President Rafsanjani. Though foreign investment is permitted again, foreign companies, most of which are now Chinese, are restricted to a 49 per cent non-controlling interest in Iranian companies. Local equity capital is seen as a better alternative for risk capital, though the need for foreign expertise in manufacturing is once again recognised. The stock market remains smaller than that of Cairo, however, whereas the Istanbul exchange has developed rapidly since the mid-1980s. The other Middle Eastern countries with very active markets are Israel, Kuwait, Turkey and Saudi Arabia, the latter being far the largest market as Table 5.4 shows.

In Saudi Arabia the most actively traded stocks are shares in the so-called Saudi-ised banks such as the Saudi American bank, and holdings in government enterprises that have been part-privatised such as the Saudi Basic Industries Corporation (SABIC). Most private businesses, including the large trading companies with import franchises, remain in private hands. There is a reluctance

*Table 5.4* Stock market development

| Country | Market capitalisation of listed companies, $US billion | Market capitalisation of listed companies, % GDP | Listed companies | Stock turnover ratio % |
|---|---|---|---|---|
| Bahrain | 20.4 | 82.2 | 44 | 1.5 |
| Egypt | 82.4 | 37.7 | 211 | 43.0 |
| Iran | 86.6 | 19.1 | 341 | 22.9 |
| Israel | 218.1 | 100.3 | 596 | 66.7 |
| Jordan | 30.9 | 111.9 | 277 | 30.1 |
| Kuwait | 119.6 | 87.6 | 215 | 38.8 |
| Morocco | 69.1 | 75.8 | 73 | 16.3 |
| Oman | 20.2 | 36.9 | 120 | 18.2 |
| Qatar | 123.6 | 89.4 | 43 | 17.3 |
| Saudi Arabia | 353.4 | 81.3 | 146 | 60.5 |
| Tunisia | 10.6 | 24.1 | 54 | 17.2 |
| Turkey | 306.7 | 41.7 | 337 | 158.4 |
| UAE | 104.7 | 47.6 | 101 | 25.6 |

Source: World Bank, Washington, 2011

to "go public" and launch equity issues as this would result in the dilution or perhaps even the end of family control. Despite the size of the oil rich Saudi economy, a small business mentality predominates that limits the potential for equity market development. Nevertheless, during the last decade the market has enjoyed considerable growth although investors have mostly suffered capital losses since the market peaked in 2007.

Kuwait had a much larger equity market than Saudi Arabia prior to the Gulf War, but its exchange has a chequered history.[21] The greatest boom period was the early 1980s, when dealings were buoyant not only on the official market, but on the unofficial *souk al manakh*. Companies whose shares were traded on the latter did not produce audited accounts, and in some cases disclosed little information on their activities. The market was highly speculative, more like a casino, where fortunes were won and lost. In the end, as in all such markets the bubble burst, leaving a mountain of debt the effects of which were felt for most of the 1980s. Such markets are arguably detrimental for development rather than beneficial.

The Middle East appears to have largely lost out in the boom in emerging financial markets in the 1990s.[22] Yet as will be seen in the next chapter on Islamic models of economic development, there is a strong potential role for equity finance on a profit sharing basis rather than loan finance involving interest.

## Foreign investment flows

A distinction must be made between direct foreign investment flows, usually undertaken by multinational companies, and portfolio flows, usually involving institutional investors. The aim of foreign direct investment is to secure ownership and control through concentration whereas the aim of portfolio

*Table 5.5* Foreign investment flows

| Country | Inflows/ GDP % | Outflows/ GDP % | Inflows $ million | Portfolio investment flows $ million |
|---|---|---|---|---|
| Egypt | 3 | 0 | 6,385 | 393 |
| Israel | 2 | 4 | 5,152 | −612 |
| Jordan | 6 | 0 | 1,701 | −20 |
| Kuwait | 0 | 8 | 80 | −815 |
| Morocco | 1 | 1 | 1,241 | 131 |
| Saudi Arabia | 5 | 1 | 21,560 | 0 |
| Sudan | 5 | 0 | 2,894 | 0 |
| Tunisia | 3 | 0 | 1,512 | −88 |
| Turkey | 1 | 0 | 9,278 | 3,468 |
| UAE | 2 | 0 | 3,948 | 0 |

Source: World Bank, Washington, 2011

investment is risk diversification through acquiring a wide range of equities or other assets. Inflows and outward flows of private portfolio investment reflect stock market conditions and expectations and tend to be short to medium term. In contrast direct investment is largely illiquid and implies a long-term commitment to the country hosting the investment.

Table 5.5 shows inflows and outflows of foreign direct investment as a proportion of GDP in the Middle East as well as the value of foreign direct investment inflows in United States dollars. Saudi Arabia receives more foreign direct investment than all the other Arab countries combined, most of which is in industrial activities associated with its oil sector. The Kingdom has pursued active policies to attract foreign investment by offering fast track licensing through the Saudi Arabia General Investment Authority (SAGIA), 100 per cent foreign ownership including of property, no restriction on repatriation of capital and the ability to sponsor foreign employees.[23] There are in addition generous financial incentives including no income tax and a corporation tax rate of only 20 per cent. It is, however, the energy resources that have attracted most foreign investors, although some have established joint ventures with Saudi Arabian partners to serve the local market, which is the largest in the Arab world.

Turkey is the second largest recipient of foreign direct investment in the region, ahead of Egypt and Israel as Table 5.5 shows. Like Saudi Arabia it has a 20 per cent corporate tax rate but income tax rates that increase progressively from 15 to 35 per cent. There are guarantees of repatriation of capital and free access to the European Union market for exports.[24] These together with the strong industrial and service culture have attracted much investment from Europe. Egypt matches the Turkish financial incentives, but the industrial and service culture is more problematic, although this may improve with the new political climate following the Arab Spring and the greater transparency and reduction in corruption. Kuwait in contrast does not attempt to attract foreign investment as it has more than enough domestic capital, the stress being on capital exports with outflows representing 8 per cent of GDP in 2010.

As Table 5.5 shows, Turkey attracts significant portfolio investment from abroad given the emerging market status of the Istanbul Stock Exchange. In contrast Saudi Arabia is a closed market reserved for domestic investors with the only access by foreigners being through managed funds regulated in the Kingdom. Egypt receives modest inflows of foreign portfolio investment, just over one-tenth of that of Turkey in 2010. These subsequently collapsed in 2011 as a result of the uncertainties after the uprising. Most of the other countries cited in Table 5.5 are net exporters of portfolio investment.

Having reviewed capital markets and the banking sector from a development perspective in the Middle East the next chapter will consider the implications of Islamic beliefs and culture for the region, especially given Islam's increasing political and aspirational significance.

# 6  An Islamic model for economic development

The countries of the Middle East all have Muslim majority populations, many of whom are devout in their religious beliefs, and all of whom have been affected to a greater or lesser extent by Islam. These beliefs have determined the prevailing value systems of the societies throughout the region, and any study of development has to take these into account. It should not be assumed that development objectives are universal; they may relate to the value systems of the groups involved.[1] How these objectives are achieved may also raise moral issues, which Muslims cannot ignore if they are sincere in their beliefs.

For many, perhaps most, western trained economists the objective of development is usually identified in terms of increasing material prosperity for individuals, with many economists also concerned with how the increasing income is distributed. Although the latter may involve moral issues of equity and fairness, the concern is essentially materialistic. Furthermore the emphasis is on outcomes, rather than on the moral legitimacy of the means through which the material results are delivered. The approach is supposedly "positive", which means value free, but what this actually means is debatable. Positive is interpreted as scientific in the sense that economic theories rest on logical deductions and the construction of models that can be empirically tested. It is possible to define utility functions to take account of preferences between work and leisure, as well as the consumption of material goods. In practice, however, most economists stress the link between commodities and services and utility, any other possible dimensions being ignored.

For devout Muslims, as with many other religious believers, personal and even social material considerations are secondary.[2] The consumption of goods and services is a means, not an end. The term Muslim refers to submission to the will of *Allah*. It is this submission that brings the real rewards, the satisfaction from being faithful and of living as *Allah* wishes. Believers do not have to be wealthy to obtain these rewards; indeed they are unrelated to personal income or a country's level of development.

Faith in *Allah* represents a spiritual rather than a material dimension, and western trained secular economists, including those of Middle East origin, may feel uncomfortable with this. Yet the issue of belief should perhaps be faced by all students of Muslim economies, even non-believers. Recognition of the value systems of Middle Eastern Muslim societies means asking funda-mental questions. What is the purpose of development? Will it bring believers closer to their goal of submission to *Allah*? Does increasing individual and social prosperity facilitate living according to the will of *Allah*, or is it morally corrupting?

Secular economists who regard themselves as "modernisers" often view Islam, and to varying degrees other religions, as a negative influence on development. Rewards in the next life are seen as a distraction from the tribulations of earthly life, indeed perhaps a factor that undermines material incentives. The teaching in the *Qur'an*, which dates back over 1,400 years to a pre-industrial society, is not thought to be relevant to developing economies. The cities of Mecca and Medina in the Hejaz at the time of the Prophet Mohammed, in what is now the western region of Saudi Arabia, are thought of as static economies with no means of, or potential for, growth. Islam in other words is seen as backward rather than forward looking, with little relevance for the present day. Indeed some even attribute the low level of development in the Middle East to the population's adherence to Islamic beliefs.[3] Secularisation, if not westernisation, is seen as the key to development, with religion viewed as an obstacle to be overcome, if not actively discouraged.

## The position of Islamic economists

Needless to say there are few in the Middle East who take this view, and any who do are an unrepresentative minority. Political demands are increasingly expressed in the language of Islam, and much of the political momentum now comes from the Islamists rather than the secularist left. These developments have been reflected in the economic sphere by the growth of interest in Islamic economics.[4] Funding from Saudi Arabian sources has of course encouraged research in this field, but the growth of interest in Islamic economics has more to do with politics than simply finance. The Iranian revolution in 1979 was the most dramatic manifestation of the desire to bring Islam into the political and economic sphere, but there are continuing indications of popular support for Islamic policies throughout the region. In Algeria the Islamic parties won the first round of the 1992 elections, which prompted the secularist government to cancel the second round. In Egypt many of the poor and low-income earners looked to local Muslim activists rather than the governments of Sadat and Mubarak, and the trend towards stricter religious adherence is apparent even amongst the highly educated youth in the universities. Islamic parties are well represented in the Jordanian parliament, although they suffered a setback in the 1992 elections.

These political developments have been accompanied by a parallel growth of interest in Islamic writings by academic economists.[5] Much of the initial work and discussions were amongst economists in universities in Pakistan, most of whom had completed higher degrees in Britain. Pakistan had of course been created as a specifically Muslim state in 1948, as it was the religious factor rather than ethnic or linguistic differences that distinguished the country from neighbouring India. In such circumstances the search for specifically Islamic economic policies could be viewed as part of the quest for a distinct national identity.

In the Middle East there was not the same coincidence of religious and nationalistic forces, as national identity could be defined in ethnic and linguistic terms. This was as much the case for Nasser's Arab "nation" as it was for Ataturk's Turkey. In such a context secularist economic policies were quite acceptable. There was, nevertheless, a desire for an alternative to the capitalist economic system, which was associated by many in the Middle East with colonialism and imperialism. For some in government and academic circles a socialist planned economy was viewed as the best alternative, although not necessarily a communist system, which outside Iraq and Yemen had few adherents in the Middle East. Even those who rejected western economics in the 1950s and 1960s were secularised themselves in their economic thinking. There was little awareness, and no desire, to try to rediscover Islamic economic ideas, at least amongst the intellegencia and the ruling classes.

In most Middle East states the modern secularised education system existed side-by-side with traditional *Quranic* schools, but over time the latter were increasingly marginalised as resources were directed to state education. Even at university level religious education tended to be segregated from the new main-stream, with teachers at traditional religious universities such as Al Azhar in Cairo largely isolated and neglected. The Egyptian government tried to bring the latter under its control and influence, much to the dismay of many Islamists, the term which is sometimes used to describe those who support the application of Islamic teaching in the political and economic sphere. Teaching and research on Islamic commercial practice was left to lawyers, with little interest in development, rather than economists. Most academic economists in Egypt were found in institutions such as the private American University, or the state financed Cairo and Ain Shams Universities. Few of these had much knowledge of or interest in Islamic economics. Those who were devout Muslims tended to separate their professional interests from their religious beliefs, partly because they were given no encouragement to do otherwise.

It is only during the last three decades that Islamic economics has started to be treated as a discipline in its own right, with courses being offered in some state institutions. Part of the revival has been aided through private funding from Gulf sources, as already mentioned, such as the assistance from the Al Baraka Islamic financial group for the Centre of Islamic Economics in the King Abdul Aziz University in Jeddah and the Islamic Foundation in Leicester, England. Both these centres promote research in Islamic economics and development. There has also been encouragement from the Islamic Development Bank in Jeddah, which has helped to bring together Pakistani and Arab economists interested in this area. Needless to say, in Iran since the Islamic revolution there has been a proliferation of courses in Islamic economics in universities throughout the country, although the research effort is arguably weaker.

## The methodology of western and Islamic economics

It would be incorrect to believe that it is only Islamic economists who deal with broader ethical questions. Early western philosophers and economic thinkers were concerned with moral issues, notably Thomas Aquinas in the thirteenth century and Nicholas Oresme in the fourteenth century.[6] Both writers criticised the accumulation of material goods for their own sake, and commercial and money-lending practices that compromised people's spiritual lives. Adam Smith regarded himself as a moral philosopher as much as an economist, indeed he did not really distinguish between the two.

With Ricardo classical economics became a more specialised discipline, and the increasing technical complexity meant that students wishing to progress to the highest levels of the subject had to devote all their time to it. Discourse with other disciplines such as philosophy or theology became minimal, a trend that was reinforced still further with the marginal revolution in the nineteenth century and the advent of neo-classical economics. This process was perhaps inevitable as the methodology of economics became more refined, but it meant the subject became increasingly abstract and cut off from its moral roots.

Modern neo-classical economists pride themselves on being positive, meaning value free. What they have to offer is a well-developed and tested box of tools to apply to any problem that is presented. Economists in their professional capacity do not make moral judgements. They may have private views, but these are best kept to themselves in case they interfere with pro-fessional advice. Economists can use their models to demonstrate outcomes given particular sets of circumstances, and show how these change when the assumptions are altered. Moral judgements are left to decision makers who take not only their advice into account, but also those of other specialists, including political advisors. The moral decisions are therefore avoided by economists; the buck is passed on to a higher authority.

Islamic economists, because of their religious beliefs, cannot duck their moral responsibilities in this way. This is why the subject is viewed as normative rather than positive, as Islamic economists do not wish to attempt to give value-free advice. It is not merely the outcomes that matter, but the legitimacy of the means to reach desirable objectives. How such concerns are handled raises important methodological issues. One way is to adopt almost a polemic approach, urging that policy makers follow a particular line because it is morally right, almost regardless of the economic arguments, or indeed the economic costs. Economic theory is then adapted to fit the moral arguments, rather than any moral compromises being made, as it is the morality which is of paramount importance. This approach is interdisciplinary in the sense that economics is regarded as part of moral philosophy, even if those involved are working in a particular specialised area.

An alternative methodological approach is to construct a completely Islamic economic paradigm from first principles, drawing on the writings of early Islamic economic thinkers such as Zaid bin Ali and Abu Yusuf in the eighth century and later scholars such as Abu Ubaid, Ibn Khaldun and Jamaluddin al-Afghani.[7] Some followers of this approach ignore or even reject the conventional western neo-classical literature and instead build up models that tend to be historical and legalistic in nature, with some parallels in institutional economics.

Other modern Islamic economists, perhaps the majority, draw on the writings of earlier Muslim scholars, but at the same time recognise the value of the tools and methods of western economists. Their approach is more in the mainstream of modern economics, at least with regard to method and style, but is nevertheless distinct in starting from different axioms.[8] Some Islamic economists are even more mainstream in approach, accepting the basic premises of western theories, but modifying certain assumptions to make them acceptable to Muslims. For those who follow this approach, the task is to validate what is acceptable in classical and neo-classical theory, and weed out and suggest alternatives for what is not.

## Sources of Islamic economic philosophy

In order to understand the principles of Islamic economics and their significance for development thinking, it is important to know something about the sources. Western neo-classical economics makes little or no reference to biblical teaching, but the ultimate source of inspiration for Islamic economics is the holy *Qur'an*. The Prophet Mohammed as a leader and ruler was specifically concerned with economic justice and rights, and his experience as a trader meant he had a practical knowledge of commerce and the procedures involved in economic transactions. Hence the *Qur'an* is very explicit in its economic teaching, as is the *Hadith*, the sayings and the deeds of the Prophet Mohammed as recorded in the *Sunnah* holy writings. These represent another important source of authority for Muslims, especially for the majority *Sunni* sect, who dominate in the Middle East with the exception of Iran and Iraq.

There is much more space in the *Qur'an* devoted to economic matters than in the Bible. Over 1,400 of the 6,226 verses refer to economic issues, as the *Qur'an* provides comprehensive guidance for all aspects of life, material as well as spiritual. It is quite specific about the duties and obligations of believers, as well as their economic rights and entitlements. On inheritance, for example, it is stated:

> A male shall inherit a portion equal to that of two females ... for parents one sixth to each if the deceased left children ... in what ye (the man) leaves (his wife's) share is a fourth if they die childless but if ye leave children, (your wife) gets an eighth after payment of legacies and debts.[9]

Under this formula a married man who leaves a widow, a son and a daughter, but whose parents are dead, will have his estate divided in the following manner.

Widow's share = 1/8
Son's share = (1 − 1/8) × 2/3 = 7/12
Daughter's share = (1 − 1/8) × 1/3 = 7/24

This contrasts with the usual situation in the West where, in the absence of specific instructions in the will of the deceased, a widow inherits all of her husband's estate, which then gets passed on to each of the children, in equal proportions regardless of sex, on her death.

The Muslim inheritance laws, as with much of the guidance provided by the *Qur'an*, are enacted in the *shari'ah*, the Islamic religious laws. These cover most aspects of economic activity and commercial life, as well as criminal justice and other matters. In states such as Saudi Arabia and Iran, the *shari'ah* law is the ultimate legal authority, but even in those states which have enacted western commercial codes such as Egypt, Syria, Turkey and the Maghreb countries, many believers still look to religious laws rather than the secular. These states have in fact incorporated Islamic inheritance laws into their legal systems, but not Muslim commercial codes. *Shari'ah* courts hear cases concerning commercial matters in the Gulf States and Iran, but even in the more secular countries in the Middle East, with civil courts, many of the local businessmen may prefer to have the religious authorities arbitrate in disputes between Muslims. In those states where there is not a formal parallel *shari'ah* court system, there is in practice an informal network, which looks after most everyday commercial affairs.

The other source of authority for commercial transactions in Muslim states is the *fiqh*, which refers to Islamic jurisprudence. This is the science or philosophy of Muslim law, especially the necessary knowledge for its interpretation. The *fuqaha* are the jurists who give opinions on various legal issues in the light of the *Qur'an* and the *sunnah*, and these opinions are included in the *fiqh*. On most fundamental matters there is a consensus amongst Muslim jurists which is referred to as *ijma*. As this has been reached by general agreement it is much respected. For many commercial and economic matters, especially those reflecting modern developments, it is the *ijtihãd* which is important, the effort to derive juristic opinions.

Those most qualified to give such opinions are the *ulamã*, the religious scholars who are fully conversant with the *Qur'an* and the *sunnah*. In the past such scholars tended to be often removed from the everyday realities of the commercial world, and had great religious knowledge, but little economic awareness. This is changing today as more widely educated and travelled Muslims are accepted into the *ulamã*, although amongst the highest Islamic legal authorities there remains more of an emphasis on scholarly work than on practical dealings.

## Islamic views on trade and commercial activity

Economic activities are classified as productive and unproductive by both western classical and Islamic economists. Adam Smith viewed manufacturing as productive, as it made a positive contribution to the wealth of nations, but trading and distribution were seen as unproductive as they did not add value. Islamic economists have always taken a rather different view, as trading is held to be as important as manufacturing. Without distribution and sales, production would be worthless. This is more in line with modern western economic thinking that draws no distinction between physical goods and services. What is classified as unproductive by Islamic economists is any task which requires no effort, yet is rewarded. It is those who work that will benefit.

> Those who patiently persevere will truly receive a reward without measure.[10]

Interest as a reward for deferring consumption is, for example, seen as unjust as the return comes from mere waiting, not from effort.

There are many passages where trading is singled out for praise in the *Qur'an* as a worthy occupation. Exchange is viewed as mutually beneficial, and preferable to keeping exclusive control over personal property.

> O ye who believe, eat not up your property among yourselves in vanities: but let there be amongst you traffic and trade by mutual goodwill.[11]

Another passage in the *Qur'an* speaks of the:

> Hope for a commerce that will never fail.[12]

Buying and selling can corrupt, however, and, as indicated in Chapter 1, fraudulent and dishonest trading practices are condemned. Competition in the accumulation of material possessions is seen as especially harmful.

> The mutual rivalry for piling up the good things of this world diverts you from more serious things.[13]

In other words, material accumulation in order to show off to others or even keep up with their consumption levels can be a harmful distraction from more important spiritual concerns. As in the bible, in the *Qur'an* the coveting of a neighbour's goods is explicitly condemned:

> And in no wise covet those things in which God hath bestowed his gifts more freely on some of you than on others: to men is allocated what they earn and to women what they earn.[14]

The prophet Mohammed himself had first-hand experience of trading in camels following his marriage to Khadija. Later, as the ruler of Medina at the commercial heart of the Hejaz, he was frequently called upon to arbitrate in disputes between buyers and sellers. Disagreements over weights and measures were common, as were differences over exactly what bargain had been struck and the nature of the goods being covered. Honesty in trade is stressed in the *Qur'an*, and any attempt to deceive or cheat in transactions is condemned:

> Give full measure when ye measure, and weigh with a balance which is straight: that is the most fitting and the most advantageous in the final determination.[15]

With agricultural products freshness was often an issue in a region with a hot summer climate and no technology to preserve fresh produce. Mohammed was concerned that proper contracts should be drawn up for trade, and that there should be transparency in all transactions and trading practices. People should not attempt to get involved in dealings in areas in which they have little knowledge:

> And pursue not that of which thou hast no knowledge; for every act of hearing or of seeing will be enquired into (on the day of reckoning).[16]

Traders are respected as knowledgeable throughout the Middle East, and they are seen as playing a key role in the dissemination of knowledge. These attitudes owe much to traditional Islamic teaching and writings. Such attitudes can be helpful for development in modern societies, however, if the marketing matters as much as mere production.

The international advantage of Islamic economies arguably lies in efficient information transmission through a well-developed trading system. This may act to the advantage of the Middle East in coming decades, as links between smaller firms become more important and production is scaled down, with greater emphasis on flexibility and diversity. The obsession with large-scale production under both the capitalist and the communist systems and the downgrading of mercantilism was ill suited to Islamic societies. If the next stage of development is the emergence of a new form of mercantilism, the Islamic world will be in a much better relative position.

## Just rewards in an Islamic economy

Western economists and development theorists have always been deeply concerned with questions of income distribution both within and between nations, and modern welfare economics attempts to show how a redistribution of income and wealth can bring about an improvement in utility or satisfaction for society as a whole. Islamic economists are also concerned with these issues, but their interest is not merely with the outcomes, but how material rewards can be justified. Merchants and traders, for example, earn their rewards through conveying information and taking risks. This is a justifiable reason for remuneration as it implies effort. Rewards on such a basis are always legitimate, whereas windfall gains as a result of gambling or the exploitation of others are viewed as unjust.

There are nine passages in the *Qur'an* that specifically deal with rewards. Muslims get their rewards from *Allah* both in their worldly life and in the hereafter, the latter being more important. All believers have a right to a basic entitlement during their lives, as without this, they would be unable to realise their human potential. The position is set out clearly in the *Qur'an*:

> It is God who has created you; further he has provided you with your sustenance.[17]

The amount of entitlement is not important, the emphasis being on needs rather than the situation of one Muslim relative to another.

> God may reward them according to the best of their deeds, and add even more for them out of his grace: for God doth provide for those whom he will without measure.[18]

There may be a minimum reward, but there is no maximum. In an economic policy context this could be interpreted as support for the notion of a minimum wage, so that all Muslims can live with dignity, but not for a programme of compulsory redistribution of income and wealth that takes from the rich to give to the poor. Such policies create resentments, and redistribution under duress from the secular authorities is regarded as undesirable in contrast to voluntary giving of alms which is viewed as part of a believer's duty in serving God. Riches bring responsibilities, including the responsibility to give:

> Your riches and your children may be but a trial: but in the presence of God is the highest reward. So fear God as much as ye can; listen and obey; and spend in charity for the benefit of your own soul and those saved from the covetousness of their own souls … If you loan to God a beautiful loan, he will double it to your credit.[19]

The real reward of wealth is the ability to be generous. Wealth is only a means of serving God, not an end in itself.

Striving for material possessions may result in earthly rewards, but these are not important in the long run; indeed materialism may bring ruin:

> If any do wish for the transitory things of this life we readily grant them – such things as we will to such persons as we will … (but) … in the end we have provided hell for them.[20]

In contrast, those that strive in the service of God for a place in the hereafter will be blessed. It is not the material possessions that are condemned, however; what matters is how they were acquired. People should not become obsessed with the amount of goods that others have; God's bounty is for all believers, but

not necessarily equally. What is important is that everyone should have sufficient, not that all believers should have the same:

> God has bestowed his gifts of sustenance more freely on some of you than
> on others: those more favoured are not going to throw back their gifts to
> those whom their right hands possess, so as to be equal in that respect.[21]

In other words, income and wealth distribution in this world are not important
issues, as believers are promised so much more in the hereafter. It is submission
to *Allah* during life on earth that brings fulfilment, but the fruits of this are
enjoyed in the afterlife. Given such beliefs, concern over worldly goods are
inevitably secondary.

## Incentives and aspirations in Muslim society

Economists who emphasise constraints on the supply side as an impediment
to development often stress the importance of incentives for the individual businessman, entrepreneur or capitalist as the key to faster growth. How important
are such material incentives in Islamic societies? Can a value system that
condemns the individual pursuit of material self-interest be conducive to
economic development? Does the downgrading of economic differentiation as
defined by living standards impede material advance?

For many in Iran it is the Ayatollahs, Mullahs and other members of the
*ulamā*, the religious scholars, who are the most highly respected members of
society. Business leaders, and even the government and lay members of the
*majilis*, the Iranian parliament, do not command the same respect. The authority of the religious leadership comes from their knowledge of the *Qur'an* and the
holy writings, and their ability to interpret the *shari'ah* religious laws. An
Ayatollah is able to recite the entire *Qur'an* without referring to the written
text, a remarkable feat of memory that few can achieve. Many regard those
who can manage this task as inspired by *Allah*.

The religious leaders are respected for their piety, not their possessions, as
they have little personal material wealth, and no need or desire for worldly
goods beyond what is necessary for sustenance so that they can perform their
religious duties. Ayatollah Khomeini had little interest in economics; indeed
he is credited with saying that economics is a donkey. The donkey is the servant
of man, who is in turn the servant of God. This places economics in a very low
position. Development for Khomeini was a tool, a means, but not an end. The
objective of development was to strengthen the community of believers, the
*ummah*, the true Muslim nation. Only then could they confront the *infidel*,
the unbelievers, including the great Satan, the leadership of the United States
who wallowed in their materialistic decadence, and repeatedly tried to corrupt
the Muslim faithful.

Such views may sound extreme to many in the West, but in Iran where the
CIA was credited with overthrowing the Mosaddeq government in the 1950s

and reinforcing the power of the corrupt governments under the Shah, the rhetoric still strikes a popular chord. Elsewhere in the Middle East, especially in the Arab world, similar sentiments bring popular approval, and explain why the mourning for President Sadat of Egypt, when he was assassinated by extremists, was so muted. Mubarak was regarded by a significant element of the Muslim masses in Egypt as a tool of the United States and its agent, the much-despised International Monetary Fund, which has dictated so much of economic policy in Egypt as a result of the government's indebtedness.

The mix of religious conviction and the politics of populist rebellion has proved a powerful force in the Middle East, which has somewhat sidelined economic debate in recent years. Against this background reforms that try to reduce the role of the state through privatisation or the reduction of regulation are seen as peripheral. It is not that Islamists are opposed to such policies, but rather the fact that they believe that most Arab governments were incapable of carrying out any worthwhile policy because of their moral corruption. The United States and the western economies are not seen as role models which the Islamic economies should aspire to follow in any case, and therefore any western economic policies which they pursue are at best inappropriate and perhaps *haram*, forbidden to the faithful.

Private ownership of property is respected in Islam; indeed, as already indicated, there are detailed rules governing its inheritance. The accumulation of property is not viewed as an end in itself or an incentive mechanism, rather private ownership is regarded as the natural state of affairs. Aggressive take-over activity is frowned upon in the Islamic world, as is any attempt to monopolise a market by driving competitors out of business. Believers should not deal with their fellow believers in such a manner. God is realistic about the aggressive nature of man, but although human conflict may be inevitable, it is important that this should not result in injustice. In the *Qur'an* there are several passages dealing with the distribution of the spoils of war:

> And know that out of all the booty that ye may acquire in war a fifth share is assigned to God, – and to the Apostle, and to near relatives, orphans, the needy and the wayfarer.[22]

It can of course be debated whether this ruling should apply to take-over battles in business, but the implied business ethics make some sense. In the *Qur'an* and other Islamic holy writings, there is always balance. The writings may be concerned with spiritual matters, but that does not mean they are out of touch with everyday economic realities.

## The prohibition of *riba*

One of the most well-known *Quranic* injunctions in the economics sphere is the prohibition of *riba* or interest. This has been much debated in writings by Muslim economists, including the question of what is meant by *riba*, the alternatives to *riba*-based finance and the implications for the relationship between Islamic and western economies.

The definition of *riba* has itself been a contentious matter, complicated by the difficulty of the precise interpretation of meaning from classical Arabic, the language of the *Qur'an*, to English, the language of most western economic writing and international commerce. Even the interpretation of classical Arabic in terms of modern colloquial Arabic used by bankers and businessmen can present problems; hence it is hardly surprising that much confusion and misunderstanding has arisen. *Riba* can be interpreted as the addition to a principal sum advanced through a loan, which accrues to the lender and is paid by the borrower. One *shari'ah* court in the United Arab Emirates interpreted the addition as being compound interest, with the prohibition of *riba* not applying to simple interest. Most Islamic scholars reject this view, however, and see simple interest as an additional levy.

There is general agreement that usury, meaning exploitive interest charged by a lender to a borrower, constitutes *riba*. Such exploitative practices are morally dubious, and the case for a prohibition on moral grounds appears convincing, especially if the lender is a wealthy individual or institution such as a bank, and the borrower is poor, and in need of funds. In such circumstances interest charges represent a redistributive flow from the poor to the rich, which can be regarded as regressive, a move worsening income and ultimately wealth inequalities. The *Qur'an* is explicit in condemning usury, which is compared unfavourably with rewards from desirable activities such as trade.

They say that trade is like usury, but God hath permitted trade and forbidden usury.[23]

Debtors should be treated with leniency rather than exploited:

If the debtor is in a difficulty, grant him time till it is easy for him to repay. If ye remit it by way of charity, that is best for you if ye only knew.[24]

In other words, debt rescheduling is desirable, and debt forgiveness especially worthy.

In developing countries, including the economies of the Middle East, the charges levied by money-lenders are often regarded as usury. They advance funds to those who do not qualify for bank lending, either because they are perceived as too risky, or because the amounts required are small, and the transactions costs in processing the loan are large in relation to the potential returns. These can only be recovered by charging high rates to the borrower, either through interest, or some other means. Whether such charges are actually exploitative usury must be open to question, given that the borrower has no other access to funds. Islamic economists recognise that such charges have to be recouped if lending is to continue, the issue then being how the charges are calculated and levied.

The question of whether all interest constitutes *riba* is further complicated by the distinctions between real and nominal interest. Should interest charges be allowed to compensate for inflation? This would imply zero real interest, but a nominal interest rate equal to the rate of price increase. As inflation rates vary from month to month, this means frequent variations in savings and lending rates if real interest is to be avoided. Yet such variations could be unfair, as not all savers and borrowers will be affected equally by inflation. If, for example, inflation reflects rising food prices, this may hurt the poor more. Yet as price indices include many non-food items which may be less prone to inflation, they may not adequately reflect the burden of inflation for those on low incomes.

The seasonal variations in the prices of fresh foodstuffs introduce additional difficulties. Are lending and borrowing rates to vary according to whether it is harvest or planting time? If so then rates would presumably fall at harvest time when food is plentiful, but rise during planting when the last seasons produce is running out. Yet in the rural communities of the Middle East it is during the planting season that farmers are seeking credit for seeds and fertilisers.

One of the injustices of interest transactions from the perspective of Islamic economics is the failure to distinguish between microeconomic and macroeconomic considerations. In western economies interest is used as an instrument of monetary policy to control the level of aggregate economic activity. Interest rates are raised to curtail borrowing by consumers and investors, to reduce short-term inflationary pressures. Rates of interest may also be raised when government deficits are increasing, in order to encourage the commercial banks and the public to purchase government securities. Such interest rate rises penalise existing borrowers whose loans are subject to variable interest, including those who have taken out long-term mortgages to purchase housing. Existing bond holders are also penalised as the value of their securities falls, reflecting its unattractiveness in comparison to the newer higher yielding government issues.

These macroeconomic developments are the responsibility of government, and have nothing to do with the borrowing by individuals and firms at the microeconomic level. The latter may suffer as a result of policies they were not consulted about, and indeed often could not have anticipated when they entered their agreements to borrow. Islamic economics is therefore concerned to separate the microeconomic from the macroeconomic, but this does not mean it deals only with the former. Indeed in some respects the ideas of Keynesian macroeconomics are anticipated in the *Qur'an*. There is, for example, a realisation that hoarding is undesirable as it removes funds from the circulation, reduces economic activity, and causes suffering and hardship.

> And there are those who bury gold and silver and spend it not in the way of God: announce unto them a most grievous penalty.[25]

As *riba* encourages the abstinence from consumption and the removal of funds from circulation, it is seen as unjust and inappropriate.

## Charity versus lending

In western neo-classical economics interest is regarded as a reward for deferring consumption. Muslims, however, are not encouraged to hoard in a selfish fashion, but to spend and use the bounties which *Allah* has provided for the benefit of his followers.

O ye who believe, spend out of the bounties we have provided for you.[26]

Believers are urged to be generous rather than miserly, and to share their earnings with the less fortunate:

Give of the good things which ye have honourably earned, and of the fruits of the earth which we have produced. ... And whatever ye spend in charity or devotion, be sure God knows it all.[27]

The faithful who are discrete in their giving are especially praised.

If ye disclose acts of charity, even so it is well, but if ye conceal them, and make them reach those really in need, that is best for you.[28]

Throughout the sections of the *Qur'an* dealing with *riba* the contrast is made between the evil of seeking such rewards, and the blessings which will be bestowed upon those who give freely. The prohibition of *riba* should not be viewed negatively, as it is not just the lending for interest which will lead believers astray, but there is also the lost opportunity of alms giving. It is this that represents the opportunity cost, as the generous rather than the miserly money-lenders reap the real rewards.

The parable of those who spend their substance in the way of God is that of a grain of corn: it groweth seven ears, and each ear hath a hundred grains.[29]

Another verse contains a similar appealing message:

And the likeness of those who spend their substance seeking to please God and to strengthen their souls is a garden high and fertile: heavy rain falls on it but makes it yield a double increase of harvest, and if it receives not heavy rain, light moisture sufficeth it. God seethe well whatever ye do.[30]

It is not the monetary value of the charity that matters, but the act of giving itself, and the spirit in which donations are made.

## Islamic profit sharing

In western economies the rate of interest serves as a pricing mechanism to bring the demand for loanable funds into equilibrium with the supply of savings. If the demand exceeds the supply, interest rates rise, encouraging savings but deterring borrowers. For business borrowers, the returns on the projects for which they are seeking funding may be insufficient to justify the increased costs of borrowing. Some economists in the Islamic world believe that the prohibition of *riba* only applies to personal loans and not business finance, where interest can continue to act as a rationing mechanism to determine how loanable funds are allocated. Most Muslim economists reject this thinking, asserting that it would be inconsistent to permit some transactions based on interest, but not others.[31]

The Islamic alternative to *riba* finance is based on the concept of profit sharing between those who provide the funds and those using the finance. This type of financing has two variants, *mudaraba* and *musharaka*, with the business manager investing in the partnership in the case of the latter, but not in the case of the former where the investors supply all the capital.[32] The return for the financier is related to the income from the use of the funds after costs have been covered. This implies a variable return that cannot be fixed in advance.[33] The financier's return is justified by the risk taken, as there will always be uncertainty over future returns. If there are no profits then the financier will obtain no return. This contrasts with fixed interest lending, where the borrower has to service the debt regardless of the level of profit or losses. When western businesses get into difficulty, it is often the banks that foreclose. Bankruptcy is less likely with Islamic financing, where loan servicing obligations are eliminated when there is no profit. Under some circumstances losses can even be shared, although the provider of the funds has discretion in this matter and there is no question of unlimited liability for either party.

With western *riba* based finance there are of course risks, the major risk being that of default by the borrower. For this reason collateral or some form of guarantee from a third party is often required before funds are advanced. This reduces the lender's risk. There can also be uncertainty over the return if the loan is contracted at variable interest, but in such cases the variability will depend on government monetary policy and macroeconomic conditions, not on the return from the project at the microeconomic level. Islamic finance is by nature participatory in the sense that the provider of the finance shares in the project risk with the businessman undertaking the venture. Indeed it can almost be regarded as a type of venture capital financing, especially when small businesses are the recipients.

Within an Islamic financial system the role of banks is clearly different from that of conventional commercial banks as the banks tend to be more closely involved with both their depositors and those being funded. Nevertheless, Islamic banks aim to provide a similar range of services to western banks. Depositors are offered current accounts for their everyday transactions, and are issued with cheque books and cash cards for use in automatic telling machines. No interest is offered on such accounts, but clients are usually expected to open current accounts if they are to qualify for bank funding. Overdrafts are not usually permitted by Islamic banks, although if a client accidentally goes into the red, the bank may at its discretion honour the cheque. A charge will not normally be levied in such circumstances, but the bank will write to the client seeking an explanation. The automatic telling machines are programmed to issue funds only to clients with credit balances.

Savings facilities are offered by Islamic banks on a *mudaraba* profit sharing basis with depositors sharing in the bank's profits. Such deposits are often designated as being in investment accounts, and are regarded as long-term precautionary balances rather than funds required for immediate transactions. There are often minimum periods required for notice of withdrawals from investment accounts, varying from one month to a year.[34] The longer the minimum period of notice for withdrawal, the larger the depositor's share in the bank's profit. Investment accounts are run in perpetuity, and are therefore different from time deposits which have to be renewed at regular intervals.

If a bank makes losses the depositors get no profit share, but the value of their deposits is guaranteed, and they have first call on the bank's assets in the case of liquidation. This puts them in a different category to shareholders, who can make capital losses as well as gains, and in the event of insolvency lose their investments. Shareholders are paid dividends based on the banks' profits, but these are discretionary rather than being formula based as with investment account holders.

For individuals with substantial funds to invest, Islamic banks can act as intermediaries between the investor and the fund user. In such cases the investor shares directly in the profit from the project being funded rather than the bank's profit. This of course may, and usually does, involve a higher risk for the investor. The bank charges the investor an arrangement fee for setting up such financing and a management fee for looking after the on-going distribution of the profits. The recipient is also charged fees on the same basis. As stock markets are poorly developed in the Middle East, as indicated in Chapter 4, such funding can be a substitute for equity finance.

## Islamic financing

Different types of financing are required according to the purpose for which funding is being sought and the period for which the finance is required. This applies regardless of whether the finance is provided by an Islamic or conventional bank. For example, short-term trade finance may be required by a Middle Eastern merchant to cover stockholdings of imported consumer goods until they are sold. These financing terms will be quite different from those of a manufacturer investing on a long-term basis in new premises or equipment. Once-only lump sum finance may be required, or on-going funding on a monthly, quarterly or irregular but frequent basis.

In practice in the Middle East most longer-term business finance is from ploughed back profits or borrowings from relatives rather than institutions. Governments fund large-scale investments by the large state sector businesses. This leaves the commercial banks, including the Islamic banks, mainly in the position of providing short-term trade-related financing, often to cover import purchases. Islamic banks arrange this through an interest free *murabaha* arrangement rather than through commercial lending. *Murabaha* finance involves a bank purchasing a good on behalf of a client and reselling it to the client for an agreed mark-up. The bank assumes ownership of the good until it is resold, this risk justifying its reward. In practice the bank will not take physical possession of the good, which will be in transit to the client, or in a warehouse, or even on premises owned and used by the client. The bank will, however, have legal title to the good, with all the obligations that implies.

The calculation of the *murabaha* mark-up is quite different to interest as it is related to the administrative costs of providing the finance with an additional allowance for profits, a portion of which will be shared with depositors with the financial institution. It is unrelated to interest rates as dictated by the requirements of monetary policy or the fiscal needs of government. It is also unrelated to market interest rates as determined by the demand and supply of loanable funds. In an Islamic financial system savings may be determined by current income, expected future income in relation to needs and present and past wealth, but it is not determined by interest or the price of money. Financing requirements may be determined by business needs and opportunities, including marketing considerations, but not by the price of borrowing at any particular time.

Longer-term finance for equipment and other major items of capital expenditures can be made available through *ijara* or leasing, a recognised method of Islamic finance that is becoming increasingly popular with Islamic banks and their clients.[35] Under *ijara* finance the bank maintains ownership of the equipment and the client pays an agreed rental on a monthly, quarterly or annual basis over a period of years, usually at least three but seldom exceeding five years. Rentals are fixed in advance and the bank will normally expect to more than recoup its investment in the equipment over the period of the rental. At the end of the contract, the bank may sell the equipment second hand, either to the client using it or to a third party. Under another variant, *ijara-wa-iqtina*, the client has the automatic right to acquire the equipment at the end of the contract at a price agreed when the original arrangement was made. This represents a form of hire purchase rather than a leasing arrangement.

More directly participative Islamic finance can be provided through *mudaraba* trust financing, which involves the bank taking a direct stake in the shareholding of the company. The Islamic bank then acts as the *rab-al-mal*, the beneficial owner, and is regarded as a partner with the *mudarab*, the managing trustee. The *rabb-al mal* should be regarded as more than a sleeping partner, as the bank acting in this capacity will expect to be consulted about all matters of financial policy, but the day-to-day running of the business will be left to the *mudarab*. The *rabb-al-mal* can be viewed as a non-voting shareholder but, unlike the holders of preference shares, the bank has a veto over financial dealings that it regards as imprudent or unwise. In the event of the business failing, the *mudarab* may be required to dispose of the business assets so that the *rab-al-maal* gets some compensation to pay to those whose funds it is using as trustee.

If a business wishes to get Islamic finance without unlimited liability it may prefer a *musharaka* arrangement whereby a new venture is formed between the Islamic bank providing the funding and the business seeking funding. Under this arrangement both parties share in the ownership of the new venture. If it fails, both parties lose, but the assets of the original company are not liable to be used to compensate the bank. From the bank's point of view *musharaka* investments are a greater risk, but the returns are also potentially higher, as any profits from the new venture will not be diluted by the obligations and costs of the existing business. Hence keeping the accounts of new ventures unconsolidated has powerful attractions, and it may be easier for the bank to sell its share in an unencumbered venture than disinvest from a *mudaraba* arrangement.

Islamic banks are of course commercial in nature rather than charitable agencies. Like other banks they aim to make profits for their shareholders, but in their case profits are arguably even more important as this determines the returns to those with savings and investment accounts. There is, however, provision for loans to be extended without any return to the bank through the Islamic principle of *qard hasan*, lending that is not subject to either interest charges or profit sharing. Rather than foreclose on borrowers, and then make costly provision for bad debt to correct the financial position of the bank, Islamic banks try directly to help those in difficulty. *Qard hasan* loans are only available to bank customers, funds being made available to those who have already had finance but are in business difficulties due to unforeseen circumstances such as ill health. Such loans are not intended to reduce business risk, as this might encourage unnecessary risk taking. *Qard hasan* loans are designed to help those facing unanticipated personal or family hardship due to circumstances beyond the control of those involved.

## Islamic banking development

Financial dealings in compliance with the *shari'ah* law date back to the early centuries of Islam, but these involved traditional money lending and money changing rather than commercial banking as understood today. As indicated in Chapter 4, modern commercial banking was introduced into the Middle East from Europe during the nineteenth century. The methods involved *riba* transactions, however, with no allowance made for Muslim susceptibilities.

It was only in the 1960s that serious consideration was given to how modern commercial banking could be adapted so that *riba* could be avoided. When Ahmed El Naggar, an Egyptian doctoral student, was at university in Germany he was impressed by the operation of mutual savings and loan associations. He thought that local savings banks could be organised in Egypt in a similar fashion, with savings being pooled, and distributed to members in need of funds. If a group of Muslim savers could follow this practice, there would be no need for interest. On his return to Egypt Ahmed El Naggar opened and managed a small savings bank in 1963 in the town of Mitr Ghams in the Nile delta. The venture was very successful in harnessing funds from landowners and small traders who had hitherto not used banks as they were devout Muslims who were concerned about any dealings involving *riba*. Within three years more than 60,000 Muslims had deposits with the bank.[36]

The Egyptian government was unhappy about the new Islamic bank, especially some of Nasser's more leftist ministers who were suspicious of all Islamic institutions. The senior staff of the major state owned banks and the Central Bank of Egypt were also unhappy, especially the latter as they could not monitor the bank's activities. Rather than close the bank down, which would risk causing widespread discontent, the decision was made to nationalise the bank. There was much delay and debate over this, but eventually in 1972 the Egyptian government injected LE1.4 million (more than $2 million at the then exchange rate) and effectively bought the bank. The institution was renamed the Nasser Social Bank, which survives today, but it was not encouraged to become a major financial force in the countryside as Ahmed El Nagger had envisaged. He in fact left the bank as a result of these developments, becoming eventually the Chairman of the Association of Islamic Banks.

The major move forward for Islamic banking came in the Gulf in the 1970s. In these countries there had always been support from the merchants for the principles of Islamic financing, and many businessmen refused to use conventional commercial banks. Until the 1973–74 quadrupling in oil prices these merchants lacked the resources to found any type of bank, but with the oil boom new opportunities opened up. The Dubai Islamic Bank was founded in 1975 by a group of merchants followed by the Kuwait Finance House in 1977, the Bahrain Islamic Bank in 1979 and the Qatar Islamic Bank in 1982.[37] All these banks have proved very successful in attracting depositors, and in harnessing funds from those who hitherto did not use banking services. The Kuwait Finance House accounted for almost 20 per cent of all bank deposits in the country by the late 1980s, and although the business was disrupted by the Iraqi invasion it has since recovered remarkably. It has purchased business and commercial property on behalf of its clients, who have then entered Islamic leasing and hire purchase contracts. It also offers transactions services to current account holders including the use of cash dispensers.

The oil price rises also enabled Saudi Arabian businessmen to establish Islamic banking networks throughout the Muslim world. Amongst the most notable of these was Prince Mohammed bin Faisal, who established the Faisal Islamic Banks in Egypt and the Sudan, both in 1977.[38] He also established the Geneva based Dar-al-Maal al-Islami to recycle Gulf funds Islamically into western markets, with a particular emphasis on mark-up financing involving exports to Muslim countries. The Al Baraka Investment Company, which is the Islamic Banking affiliate of Sheikh Hassan Kamel's Dallah Group, a leading Saudi Arabian trading company, has pursued a similar strategy, with branches in London, Bahrain, Tunis, Istanbul and even the Central Asian states and China. It helped the initial financing of the Jordan Islamic Bank, although this is now independent. The Al Rajhi group, which started as a money-changing business to serve pilgrims to Mecca, has now become an international Islamic investment company with offices in London, Zurich and Kuala Lumpur.

On the other side of the Gulf Islamic banking was to develop rather differently, as following the Islamic revolution in 1979 legislation was passed making it compulsory for all banks operating in Iran to conduct their business according to the *shari'ah* law.[39] This took effect in 1983, and since then all retail banking in Iran has been on an interest free basis, although discount rates are used for transactions with the central bank, and in foreign deals with *infidels*, or unbelievers, interest is still permitted. Even before the Islamic revolution there were "charity trusts" in Iran associated with the mosques which carried out some banking functions including the provision of interest free loans. These provided essential financial services to ordinary people and small merchants who did not deal with banks, and in some respects were similar to the Mitr Ghams savings bank in Egypt.

## Islamic taxation

Islamic economics not only provides a framework for private financing through a banking system free from *riba*, it also sets out the rules for public finance through taxation. The most important Islamic tax is *zakat*, a tax based on wealth, which is paid annually at a rate of one-fortieth of the value of personal or business liquid assets.[40] Property and equipment are excluded, but cash holdings and financial assets, including shares in quoted companies, are subject to the tax at the standard rate of 2.5 per cent. The payment of the tax is viewed as a religious duty, and in such circumstances there is little evasion, as this would be regarded as a moral sin.

Governments are usually responsible for *zakat* collection, although in the case of Iran before the Islamic revolution it was the *mullahs* and others working for the mosques. When the state is involved, however, it cannot treat *zakat* as general fiscal revenue, as *zakat* is regarded as a form of alms giving for worthy causes. This limits the government's discretion and means the tax cannot be used as an instrument of fiscal policy. It is often administered by a special Ministry of Religious Affairs, with revenue earmarked for transfer payments to the poor and needy. It is for example permissible to use *zakat* expenditure for health care or education for the poor, but not for military expenditure or even infrastructure work. It tends to be used for recurrent spending to meet immediate needs rather than long-term investment.

In much of the Middle East the tax base is limited, partly reflecting low incomes, apart from in the Gulf states and Libya, but also as a result of difficulty in the collection of direct taxes. Petroleum revenues and import duties are the major source of government finance. There is no income tax in the Gulf states, where *zakat* represents the major form of personal taxation. In those non-oil states that do impose income tax, it is mostly collected from the government's own employees. The value of *zakat* is that it widens the tax base, with even the less well off and those who are highly critical of governments willing to make voluntary contributions.

## Islamic insurance

Entrepreneurial activity involves taking risks, and in developing countries such as those of the Middle East an aversion to risk is often cited as a reason for business stagnation. Commercial risks cannot be covered by insurance, but risks associated with their transport and distribution can, and this represents the major form of insurance business in the Middle East. Life and endowment insurance is not regarded as legitimate, as life is in the hands of *Allah*, and if household income earners meet an untimely death, it is the duty of the *ummah*, the community of believers, to provide for the family. In closely knit societies there is less need for institutionalised support given the strong tribal and kinship support mechanisms.

Islamic law stipulates that gambling (*qimar*) is forbidden and all types of speculative activity are regarded as gambling.[41] Forward and futures dealing is prohibited in much of the Islamic world as although such markets can be used for risk avoidance, there is always the temptation to speculate, indeed speculative funds to a large extent provide the liquidity for hedging activity. Risk sharing rather than risk seeking is advocated by Islamic economists, and *murabaha* and *musharaka* are regarded as appropriate instruments for this purpose. Mutual insurance is seen as preferable to insurance through publicly quoted companies who profit from the misfortunes of others.[42] Mutual insurance funds established by the *ummah* are referred to as *takaful companies*. Unlike conventional insurance companies *takaful* undertakings are not involved in *riba* transactions, as they avoid holding long-term bonds, but may hold equities. Dar al Maal al Islami has a *takaful* insurance subsidiary, as do the Faisal Islamic Banks of Egypt and the Sudan.

## An Islamic future!

Overall it is evident how Islamic economic teaching provides a comprehensive set of principles governing commerce, banking, public finance and even insurance. Many Muslims see an Islamic economic system as an alternative to capitalism, socialism and communism. It is undoubtedly too early to judge on the economic success or failure of the newly elected Islamist political parties in Tunisia and Egypt. A significant proportion of the younger generation in the Middle East are looking to these parties for honest economic management and an end to blatant corruption. They are encouraged by the economic success of the Islamist Justice and Development Party in Turkey, but disappointed by the mediocre economic performance of the Islamic Republic of Iran, where corruption has returned (indeed, perhaps never went away). Just how these economies evolve in the coming years deserves to be studied carefully by development economists, but care is needed in the choice of criteria for evaluation. For this some knowledge of the fundamentals of Islamic economics would seem indispensable.

# 7   Oil and development

For the last eighty years oil has been of major significance for the economies of the Middle East. The region has almost one-half of the world's oil reserves and around one-quarter of global supplies of natural gas,[1] a proportion likely to rise considerably for the latter by 2030.[2] Middle East oil has been a periodic preoccupation for western governments and business, especially during the dramatic 1973–74 and 1979 oil price rises, as these had a major impact on the world economy. Within the region itself, oil production has accounted for a substantial proportion of national product, and has been the major source of government finance. The earnings generated from oil have not only contributed to development funding in the oil exporting states but have also flowed into the non-oil economies through inter-government assistance, remittances and, to a lesser extent, private investment flows.

Oil and gas exports are likely to remain crucial for the economies of the Middle East for the foreseeable future, not least because of the price rises brought about by rising and sustained demand from China, Korea, South East Asia and India since the 1990s. The price of oil has had a major impact on past development trends, and the region's economic prospects cannot be assessed without some predictions of future price changes. The determinants of oil prices are therefore of vital interest as far as Middle East development is concerned. Much of this chapter is concerned with this issue, and in particular the role of the Organization of Petroleum Exporting Countries (OPEC), in oil price determination. However, oil is more than a mere exportable commodity. It is also a resource on which an industrial strategy can be based. This issue is also addressed here, in particular the development of energy intensive manufacturing using hitherto flared gas, and the production of petrochemicals and other oil derivatives.

## The costs of oil extraction

The Gulf, Libya and Algeria are the lowest cost areas of the world for oil extraction. The cost is below $25 per barrel compared with costs of twice that amount for oil from Alaska or the North Sea. Conditions for oil extraction are extremely favourable in the Middle East with large fields, deposits easily exploited, a climate conducive to year round operations and oil of fair to high quality. When oil was first discovered it was near the surface and under pressure. As a result, when a bore hole was drilled, the oil surged out in a geyser. For the oil companies the task was largely to harness the well head supplies and arrange for the transportation of the crude to their refineries in the oil consuming countries.

As the most accessible oil has been extracted, it has been necessary to invest more to harness the oil reserves. Extraction in recent years has involved increasing the oil pressure underground artificially to ensure it flows up to the surface. The oil in the Gulf, Libya and Algeria is largely extracted by this means, with the pressure being increased by the release and compression of associated gas underground, or by water injection, including the use of sea water on coastal and offshore fields. This of course adds to costs, but the technology is well tried and tested, and the operations are almost routine.

The calculation of what should be included in costs is far from straightforward in the oil industry. As a result, any estimation of price on a cost of production plus mark-up for profits and royalties basis is more complex than first appears. The initial investment costs are very high for oil development. However, once the fixed costs have been incurred they can be virtually written off. This of course ignores the issue of the return on investment in plant and equipment. Nevertheless, where oil producers are price takers and prices are too low to cover fixed costs, the choice may be between closing down production completely, or maintaining output as long as variable costs are covered.

Economists are of course always concerned with marginal cost rather than total cost or average cost. What, however, is exactly meant by marginal cost in the oil industry? Just what additional production to include is somewhat uncertain. The costs of oil extraction vary according to the level of production from a particular field, reflecting increasing variable costs as diminishing returns set in. The cost of production also varies from field to field, the smaller and deeper outlying fields being usually more expensive to exploit than large, shallow fields on or near to which oil production operations are usually centred. Should the marginal cost refer to the cost of additional production from the central field or the marginal cost of oil output from the marginal field? There is usually much cost overlap between fields, and a considerable array of choice about where to produce the marginal barrel.[3]

## Quality, price and demand

Light oil requires less refining than heavy oil, and therefore usually commands a higher price. Most Middle Eastern oil is of light to medium quality, Libyan oil being especially light. This means it should and usually does command a price premium over rival produce. Transport costs distort the picture, however, oil from North Africa destined for Europe being naturally cheaper than oil from the Gulf.[4] The latter has either to be shipped around the Cape of Good Hope in Southern Africa on route to Europe or sent through the Suez Canal or Sumed, the Suez Mediterranean pipeline, shipments through which are subject to transit fees levied by the Egyptian government. The quality advantage may therefore be offset by a transportation disadvantage, oil from the Gulf commanding a price premium because of its quality, but a discount at the point of shipment in the Gulf, reflecting the cost of onward conveyance. In 2011, for example, Arabian light oil from Dubai was selling $6 to $10 per barrel cheaper than Forties and Brent oil from Britain's North Sea.

The demand for oil, as for any other commodity, depends on the price quoted. Oil is a normal good in the sense that at higher prices less is demanded and at lower prices demand increases. The final consumer, however, demands oil not for its own sake but as a fuel for transportation or as energy for heating or cooling. Hence the demand is derived from the demand for and use of other products, which are to considerable degree oil-dependent. If the price of oil rises quite substantially, as it did in 1973–74, the need for transportation and heating does not suddenly diminish. The increased price of the oil simply gets passed on to the final consumer, and the demand for oil is maintained. In other words, in the short run the demand for oil is inelastic with respect to price, with little response even to large price rises.

In the longer term, if the price rises are maintained the demand response will be much more elastic, partly as a result of fuel and energy consumption savings, but also as a consequence of other sources of energy being substituted for oil. As far as transportation is concerned the main savings have come through greater fuel efficiency, as there are no satisfactory substitutes for petrol or diesel powered vehicles, slow advances in battery technology limiting the potential of electric cars and vans. For aircraft there is no substitute for oil products, but modern jets have fewer, yet more powerful and fuel efficient, engines, and consume less than half the fuel per passenger mile of aircraft twenty years ago.

For electric power generation there are several viable alternatives to oil; gas, coal and nuclear energy being the main contenders. Renewable energy sources are the most attractive alternative, but only hydroelectricity has been developed on a significant scale, the experimental projects with tide and wind power only accounting for a small proportion of global electricity generation. Nuclear energy would seem to have the most promising future, despite concerns about the environmental risks and the problems of disposing of spent fuels and decommissioning older facilities. France gets four-fifths of its electricity from nuclear stations, but the proportion of electricity from nuclear generation is minimal in most developing countries, including the newly industrialising nations. A higher proportion of Middle Eastern oil and gas has been exported to these countries, partly as a result of their industrialisation, but also as at least some of the advanced industrialised countries turn increasingly to nuclear energy despite continued safety concerns heightened by the 2011 earthquake and tsunami in northern Japan.

The oil price rises of the 1970s resulted in a reappraisal of energy policy by the major oil consuming countries. The increase in the demand for oil slowed down in the United States and Japan during the 1980s, and in Germany and France the demand for oil actually fell. This was partly a result of technological advances, but also due to higher oil consumption taxes and the closure of oil powered electricity generation facilities. The question of how far tax policy was responsible for energy conservation was much debated, but demand continued to increase in the United States during the 1980s as fuel taxes remained low. In 2011 the United States still accounted for almost one-fifth of world oil consumption, compared to a 17.5 per cent share for the European Community and 8 per cent for Japan. The fastest increase in oil consumption since the 1980s has been by China, with a quadrupling as a result of its industrialisation drive. China is now the largest oil consuming nation in the world, accounting for 20.3 per cent of total consumption, with exports from the Middle East flowing increasingly eastwards rather than westwards.

For the oil exporting countries of the Middle East a major concern is whether the demand for oil will increase in the future with rising gross domestic product worldwide. In other words, what is the income elasticity of demand for oil? For countries such as France and Germany it is already negative, with rising income being associated with falls in the demand for oil imports. For the United States and the United Kingdom the income elasticity is positive but less than one. Hence with rising gross domestic product, more oil is being consumed, but proportionately less over time.[5]

It is only in the newly industrialising countries such as China where the income elasticity of demand for oil is positive and greater than one. How long this will be sustained is far from certain as China moves into a different phase of its industrialisation, with lighter, less energy-using consumer-oriented production. In some of the more mature Asian "tiger" countries such as Singapore oil imports are already starting to level out, though there is less sign of this in Taiwan and Korea, two of the more mature economies that are still classified as newly industrialising countries.

## The politics of oil supply

Oil production in the Middle East has not merely been a matter of geology or exploiting the lowest cost field. Where exploration is carried out and what fields are developed has been influenced as much by political as economic factors. Until the late 1960s oil production and exports from the region to a large extent reflected the major western oil companies' need to juggle the demands of the different governments in the Middle East, all of whom wanted to see more oil produced in their territories so that they could obtain more revenue. The oil companies were also concerned with the political stability of the regimes in the oil-exporting countries, the reliability of supply, the probability of the nationalisation of oil company facilities, demands over royalty levels and pressures to employ and train local nationals. Since then what gets produced where and exported has depended on political and economic muscle within OPEC which effectively determines country quotas.

Iran was the first country where oil was exploited in the Middle East, with trial production starting in 1903 and a major discovery in 1908.[6] Under Reza Shah the country was politically stable, and the oil concession agreement which was signed with D'Arcy in 1901 on very favourable terms was to run to 1994.[7] The Anglo-Persian Oil Company, which was later to become British Petroleum, was founded in 1909. Oil was not discovered in Iraq until 1927, but by that time Persian production was well established, and a slow growth of demand, reflecting the fragile state of the international economy at the time, meant Iraqi oil exploitation was limited in these early years.

Which oil fields were developed also reflected rivalries in Middle Eastern interests between the major western powers. With Britain, through the Anglo-Iranian Oil Company, having a virtual monopoly of exploration in Iran, the United States had little choice but to look to Saudi Arabia on the other side of the Gulf, the one area that had not come under European imperial influences. In the 1930s the oil fields of the eastern province were opened up, and the Arabian American Oil Company (ARAMCO) was formed by a consortium of leading United States oil companies.[8] It was ARAMCO that developed the Ghawar and Safaniya fields in the Dhahran area that were to prove to be the largest and most productive in the entire world. ARAMCO continues to account for most Saudi Arabian oil production and exports, though it was nationalised in the 1970s, and the role of the American associate companies is now confined to specialist support and marketing.

There was, not surprisingly, enormous resistance to attempts to take over the oil concessions awarded to western multinational oil companies. Conflicts between the oil companies and host country governments over revenues dated back to the 1920s and 1930s when oil started to be exploited in significant quantities, but it was the Iranian government that was the first to demand control of production. After Dr Musaddiq consolidated his power as prime minister in 1952 he set up the National Iran Oil Company, a state owned entity, to take over the control of Iran's oil from the Anglo-Iranian oil company.[9] This provoked a two-year boycott of purchases of Iranian oil by the major western oil companies. Purchases were only started again when Musaddiq was overthrown, and terms were agreed that were satisfactory from the point of view of the oil companies.

Meanwhile the Anglo-Iranian Oil Company had changed its name to British Petroleum. It was to concentrate on developing the oil fields of the sheikhdoms and emirates on the Arab side of the Gulf, where the rulers were much more cooperative. It was this new orientation and the cooperation with Shell, the Anglo-Dutch company, which was to result in the major developments in Kuwait, Qatar and Abu Dhabi, and eventually Oman. The increasing significance of the Arab monarchies as oil suppliers was not so much a reflection of the quality of their oil or relative cost factors. Rather what mattered was the political environment and the security of oil supplies. Iran, and subsequently Iraq, had their exploration and production curtailed because of their political intransigence. The beneficiaries were the Arabian Peninsula states that had their oil fields developed and exploited to a greater extent than might otherwise have been the case on the basis of geological decisions alone.

## OPEC control over supplies

It was the inability of the oil exporting countries to control and manage their own resources that prompted the formation of OPEC. The events surrounding Mussadiq in Iran had highlighted the conflict of interests between the western oil companies and at least some of the oil exporting countries of the Middle East over export volumes, prices and oil revenue. In these circumstances the more militant oil exporting countries felt some countervailing force was needed to take on the western oil companies and redress the balance in the oil market. When British Petroleum led a reduction in Middle East oil prices in 1959, and broke the link with United States prices, this prompted much adverse reaction from the governments of the region. This was to be the trigger for the establishment of OPEC, following a conference in Baghdad in 1960, hosted by the new revolutionary government of Iraq. The five founding members included Iran, Saudi Arabia, Kuwait, Iraq and the major non Middle Eastern exporting nation in the developing world, Venezuela. Subsequently a further eight countries were to join, four Arab nations, Algeria, Libya, the UAE and Qatar, and four non-Arab countries, Indonesia, Nigeria, Gabon and Ecuador.[10]

OPEC enjoyed little success during the 1960s in raising oil prices, largely because the United States could still supply most of its own needs, and the western oil companies were the dominant players in the international oil industry.[11] They had the exploration and production expertise, and as vertically integrated multinational companies also controlled the transportation, refining, distribution and even ultimate retail sale of petroleum and oil products. The United States multinationals acquired most Saudi Arabian output through their participation in ARAMCO, and Shell and British Petroleum (BP) accounted for much of the production in the increasingly important fields of the smaller Gulf States.

By the late 1960s the balance of economic power was starting to change, however, and the western multinationals, the so-called "seven sisters", Exxon, Mobil, Texaco, Socal, Gulf, Shell and BP, were beginning to feel threatened. First was the fact that the United States production was declining, and the country was moving from being the world's largest producer to its largest importer. Second, there was the increasing importance of independent European state oil companies such as Agip of Italy and Elf and Total of France. They wanted to break the oligopoly of the "seven sisters" by purchasing supplies directly from state companies in the producing countries such as the National Iranian Oil Company.

Third, the knowledge of how to manage and maintain oil production facilities was becoming more widespread, and the technical advantage of the "seven sisters" was steadily eroded. Technological transfers to the OPEC states had occurred, and countries such as Iran could increasingly handle all operations themselves. For highly specialised tasks they could hire in independent engineers and consultants, who were becoming less and less concerned about what the major oil companies thought of their involvement. Fourth, and perhaps most crucial at the time, was the revolution in Libya and the seizure of power by Muammar Gaddafi in 1969.[12] The new Libyan regime took a much more aggressive stance towards the oil companies, and indicated its willingness to use oil as a political weapon against the West in the context of the Arab–Israeli dispute.[13]

## OPEC as the price maker

The zenith of OPEC's power was in the mid 1970s, when it appeared to be in a position to dictate the world prices of petroleum. It is clear enough what events brought this about, but there is much disagreement over what the crucial factors were that enabled OPEC to make the running in the international oil market rather than the western oil companies as had hitherto been the case. The Arab–Israeli War of October 1973 was the catalyst for change, as the Arab members of OPEC organised a boycott of oil supplies to the United States and the Netherlands in the aftermath of the conflict.[14] Oil was to be used for the first time as a political weapon to punish the West for its alleged support for Israel. The United States was singled out as the chief ally and backer of Israel and the Netherlands was selected for its pro-Israel sympathies, which had their origin in the revulsion against the Nazi persecution of Dutch Jews back in the 1940s.[15] The Netherlands was not itself a major market for oil, but of much greater significance was its refining capacity. Rotterdam was the major refining centre for Europe, with petroleum products being sent up the Rhine to the German industrial heartland.

The boycott was ineffective as the major oil companies simply switched supply, and provided oil to both the United States and the Netherlands from non-Arab sources. The Gulf States wanted to distance themselves in any case from the hawks in the Arab League, and had already formed OAPEC, the Organisation of Arab Petroleum Exporting Countries, in anticipation of such a confrontation with the West over Israel.[16] Interestingly OAPEC included not only Saudi Arabia and Kuwait, but also Libya and Egypt. The non-Arab members of OPEC, including Iran, were less concerned about the issue of Israel; indeed, under the Shah Iran was Israel's major oil supplier. The boycott, however, resulted in considerable panic amongst western buyers, and both spot and contract prices were driven up from under $3 to over $11 per barrel, a significant amount at the time given the then value of the US dollar. Iran and Venezuela were keen to take advantage of the situation by raising the price of their oil rather than supplying extra to meet any shortfall. Therefore there was solidarity within OPEC over the new level of pricing, even though the non-Arab members did not participate in the boycott.

OPEC became very aware of the advantages of acting collectively as a result of the events of 1973–74. The actions of one member influenced the decisions of others, even when the regimes the oil ministers represented varied enormously in political complexion, from revolutionary republics such as Libya to conservative monarchies such as the Shah's Iran or Saudi Arabia. Thus when countries such as Libya and Algeria sought to get control of their own oil production through the nationalisation of foreign oil company assets, Saudi Arabia, Kuwait and Abu Dhabi were prompted to follow their example, even though there was no ideological basis for state ownership as far as the Gulf States were concerned.

The extent to which the change of ownership of oil resources was crucial for the oil price rises of 1973–74 has been much debated.[17] Ownership of course gave the producing countries control over supplies, as hitherto the oil companies could vary the amount they extracted from their concessions to suit market conditions. Their interest was in maintaining continuity of supplies and keeping prices stable and reasonably low. The western oil companies earned more from refining and distribution than production, and therefore from their point of view low prices were good for business as they encouraged oil use and expanded the long-term market for oil. Variable prices could result in users questioning the security of supply, and higher prices would deter consumption in the long run, even allowing for the short-run price inelasticity of demand. The ownership of oil resources by the western companies meant output could be expanded when conditions were buoyant and reduced in times of recession. As a result, production variations served as automatic price stabilisers.

Once the producing countries owned their own resources, they could exploit market tightness to raise prices. Whether the same result might have occurred without the transfer of ownership is by no means clear. The objectives of the oil exporting countries were, of course, different to those of the western oil companies. However, the exploration operations of the oil companies have always been regulated by concession agreements, and licensing could have been extended to cover production levels without a transfer in the asset ownership. The nationalisation, nevertheless, meant production levels could be varied on a month-to-month, or even day-to-day basis, subject to the dictates of government. This strengthened the hands of individual oil ministers in their OPEC negotiations, and there was little doubt that it was this more than any other factor that prompted the transfer of the oil industry into state ownership in the otherwise conservative oil exporting countries of the Arabian Peninsula.

## OPEC as a cartel

As the members of OPEC act collectively in announcing price and production targets, the organisation is often described as a cartel. With a cartel arrangement individual producers maintain their ownership of resources, unlike with a monopoly where ownership is pooled. There are different types of cartel, depending on the objectives of the members, and their willingness to share their resources. An extreme case is where production is based in the lowest-cost supplier within the cartel in order to maximise revenue. The cartel members then share in the revenue, including the higher-cost suppliers who may not actually produce any oil during the period in question. Such a revenue sharing cartel maximises the profits for its members over time, but it implies a high degree of trust between members.

Suppose for example Kuwait was the lowest-cost producer in OPEC, and it exploited all its oil and shared the profits with other members of the cartel. Then when its oil reserves were exhausted, oil production would shift to higher cost OPEC states such as Iraq or Iran, who would be expected in turn to share their earnings. The problem for Kuwait might be that when its turn to receive oil revenues came, the other countries might refuse to share. Kuwait, with its oil exhausted, would be in a highly vulnerable position. It is for this reason that OPEC has never been a profit sharing cartel, despite the enormous potential benefits from exploiting the lowest-cost fields fully. Instead, OPEC producers all contribute to the output of the cartel, even high-cost producers. The profit members obtain is then derived from their own sales, with no revenue sharing.

In the 1970s many viewed OPEC as a price fixing cartel, with the differentials between the members set at levels that were expected to guarantee sales of crude oil for each member of the cartel. This interpretation of OPEC's operation is, however, an extremely contentious point in the literature. If the price fixing interpretation is accepted, the implication was that the Arabian Peninsula producers' prices were set sufficiently below Libyan levels to allow for the additional transportation costs and the extra refining of the somewhat heavier crude oil. There was no attempt to impose explicit production quotas for each member of OPEC or even the cartel as a whole. By setting price differentials implicit production targets were set both for OPEC and its members, however, but there was no obligation to keep production at particular levels. Every barrel of oil that was demanded could be sold at the stipulated price without restraint. The only obligation was to maintain the price at the agreed level, and for members not to act unilaterally and cut prices before the next OPEC meeting. All price changes were to be agreed multilaterally within OPEC, with no discounting permitted that might undermine the interests of the other members.

A market sharing cartel is the main alternative to a price fixing system. OPEC started a market sharing arrangement in the 1980s with an overall production target agreed for the cartel, and shares apportioned amongst the members explicitly. The production target was set so that the overall supply of oil to the market could be restrained in order to maintain prices in a specified range. The obligation for each member was to adhere to its production quota, but it was free to obtain as high a price as it could for its oil. Such an arrangement implied the need to monitor oil flows by OPEC. This task proved far from easy, and in practice there was always the temptation for members to cheat. This was one of the factors that arguably brought about the dramatic oil price decline in 1985.

It can be argued that OPEC would not have worked had Saudi Arabia not been able to function as a swing producer. It was because it had the ability to vary its production level from four million barrels a day to over twelve million barrels a day, that OPEC had the market power to influence prices.[18] Often it did not need to exercise its market power, the mere threat was enough to influence expectations amongst oil traders. When Sheikh Yamani was at the height of his influence as Saudi Arabia's oil minister in the 1970s, the press used to eagerly report his comments at OPEC meetings, and this news could influence prices. By the 1980s, however, Saudi Arabia needed to maintain its oil production at a higher level, one factor being the requirement to maintain output of associated gas, and provide feedstock for its petrochemical industry, although the extent of this physical constraint should not be exaggerated. Arguably of greater significance were the Kingdom's increasing current revenue needs, which grew even more substantially after the Gulf War, and the resultant defence spending pressures.

By the late 1980s there were also strategic and political considerations. By maintaining oil output at a high level, prices were held in check. This curtailed Saddam Hussein's military spending as Iraq's ability to ship oil was limited given its war with Iran, and the subsequent pressures within OPEC, especially from the Gulf States. At moderate prices Saudi Arabia still had plenty of revenues for its own defence spending given a production level four times that of Iraq, before the Gulf War. After sanctions were imposed on Iraqi sales, the imbalance increased, with Saudi Arabia and later liberated Kuwait more than making up the shortfall in supplies. The lack of security following the invasion of Iraq and the demise of Saddam Hussein adversely affected Iraq's oil output, and although conditions improved in 2010 and 2011 oil output remains below its 2001 level, is lower than that of neighbouring Kuwait and is only a quarter of the Saudi Arabia production level.

## Limit pricing with OPEC as the residual supplier

The price that OPEC set as a price fixing cartel or aimed to achieve as a market sharing cartel was influenced by the behaviour of non-OPEC suppliers of oil. One result of the 1973–74 price rises was to encourage the development of oil fields well away from the Middle East. The resistance to the development of Alaska's oil on environmental grounds was less effective because United States strategic interests overrode such considerations. The higher oil prices made the development of offshore oil fields in difficult climatic conditions, such as Britain's North Sea, viable. As a consequence, the share of OPEC in world exports fell from over 87 per cent in 1973 to 62 per cent by 1983 after the second oil price shock. OPEC was increasingly forced to play the role of residual supplier, if not exactly marginalised. In 2011 OPEC accounted for 41.5 per cent of global supply, illustrating its increasing marginalisation. The increased production by Russia has helped undermine OPEC, as this has risen by 40 per cent since 2000 and now accounts for almost 13 per cent of the world total. Indeed since 2009 Russian production has exceeded that of Saudi Arabia, which had been the world's leading supplier for the previous four decades.

The cartel would have been able to continue to play a more significant role if Mexico had joined, as its oil production was becoming increasingly important in the late 1970s. There was strong pressure from the United States for Mexico not to join, and given the importance of its northern neighbour as an export market and source of investment funding it was hardly surprising that these pressures succeeded. Mexico's status in OPEC remained that of an observer. Ecuador, the only Latin American member of OPEC apart from Venezuela, actually left the organisation in 1993, the first member to quit.

## Optimal depletion and time preferences

Oil, like other extractive resources, is not renewable. As oil is extracted it contributes to national income or gross domestic product, but there is a sense in which its depletion reduces national wealth. Oil production involves the transformation of physical resources into either paper assets or manufactured products. The former may be squandered by politicians, the latter will be subject to depreciation, even when the oil revenues are used for long-term development purposes such as the building of infrastructure. Roads and bridges deteriorate over time, and the more infrastructure that is built, the more repair and replacement will be needed.

Yet leaving the oil in the ground also has its problems. Resources may be conserved for future generations, but by then technical advance may result in better alternatives being used. In the long run there may be no demand for oil and reserves will be worthless. This has already happened in the case of coal. In the 1920s and 1930s there was much concern about what would happen when world coal reserves were exhausted. Yet eighty years later demand has steadily fallen, and there are enough reserves left to meet current production levels for the next 250 years. It seems that most of the world's reserves of coal will never be mined.

In the case of the Middle East oil exporting countries, levels of reserves vary considerably. Saudi Arabia has sufficient oil for over 80 years of production at current levels, whereas Algeria has only 20 years of production remaining and Egypt, which is not a member of OPEC, a mere 13 years supply. There are clearly conflicting concerns over pricing and extraction given such differences in reserve levels. Saudi Arabia is not merely concerned with maximising revenue in the short term, but well into the next century. High prices may encourage energy saving, the development of oil substitutes and the opening up of non-OPEC fields. In the long run there may be no market for Saudi Arabian oil if OPEC pursues a high pricing strategy. This is one reason why Saudi Arabia tends to argue for price moderation in OPEC, and adopts a stance that suits the short-term interests of the consuming countries.

## Oil reserves and production

Table 7.1 shows the oil reserves of the major oil exporting countries in the Middle East plus the leading producers in the rest of the world to see the

*Table 7.1* Middle Eastern oil reserves in a global context (billion barrels)

| Country | 1980 | 1990 | 2000 | 2010 |
|---|---|---|---|---|
| Algeria | 8.2 | 9.2 | 11.3 | 12.2 |
| Libya | 20.3 | 22.8 | 36.0 | 46.4 |
| Iran | 58.3 | 92.9 | 99.5 | 137.0 |
| Iraq | 30.0 | 100.0 | 112.5 | 115.0 |
| Kuwait | 67.9 | 97.0 | 96.5 | 101.5 |
| Saudi Arabia | 168.0 | 260.1 | 262.8 | 264.5 |
| UAE | 30.4 | 98.1 | 97.8 | 97.8 |
| Kazakhstan | N/A | N/A | 25.0 | 39.8 |
| Russia | N/A | N/A | 59.0 | 77.4 |
| United States | 36.5 | 33.8 | 30.4 | 30.9 |
| Mexico | 47.2 | 50.9 | 20.2 | 11.4 |
| Venezuela | 19.5 | 60.1 | 76.8 | 211.2 |
| Nigeria | 16.7 | 17.1 | 34.3 | 37.2 |
| Middle East | 362.4 | 659.6 | 696.7 | 752.5 |
| World | 667.5 | 1003.2 | 1104.9 | 1383.2 |

Source: BP Statistical Review of World Energy, London, 2011

region's reserves in context. It is worth noting that, despite ever increasing levels of oil production, reserves worldwide have actually increased over the last four decades. Although the reserves of the United States are diminishing due to high levels of production, scientific advances and exploration in new areas have resulted in increasing reserves in most other countries. Saudi Arabia has by far the highest reserve levels, but most of its reserves are known, as is also the case in Kuwait. Other countries in the Middle East have upwardly revised their oil reserves during the last decade, notably Libya and Iran, while outside the region Venezuela, Russia and Kazakhstan seem to be of increasing significance.

Considerations about how much oil to extract are of course influenced by revenue needs. The Arabian Peninsula countries with their relatively small populations and modern infrastructures have much more limited government spending and import needs than countries such as Iran and Iraq, with much larger populations, and run-down infrastructure facilities that have been partly destroyed through wars. From their point of view the ideal scenario in OPEC would be for Saudi Arabia and the small Arab Gulf states to hold down production, both to boost prices and to allow them to export more to maximise immediate revenue. From the Saudi Arabian point of view this is unacceptable, as it would mean possible short-term revenue losses and long-term revenue reductions. The tension between Iraq and Kuwait over the amount of oil each country should produce and OPEC quotas was a contributory factor to the Gulf War.

The major producers of oil in the Middle East are cited in Table 7.2, which shows that Saudi Arabia has by far the highest output level, followed by Iran. Back in 1980 Iraq produced more than Iran but the disruption of the Saddam Hussein era and the subsequent invasion of the country adversely affected the

*Table 7.2* Middle Eastern oil production in a global context (thousand barrels daily)

| Country | 1980 | 1990 | 2000 | 2010 |
|---------|------|------|------|------|
| Algeria | 1139 | 1347 | 1578 | 1809 |
| Libya | 1972 | 1862 | 1475 | 1659 |
| Iran | 1479 | 3270 | 3855 | 4245 |
| Iraq | 2658 | 2149 | 2614 | 2460 |
| Kuwait | 1757 | 964 | 2206 | 2508 |
| Saudi Arabia | 10270 | 7105 | 9491 | 10007 |
| UAE | 1745 | 2283 | 2620 | 2849 |
| Kazakhstan | N/A | 1716 | 744 | 1757 |
| Russia | N/A | 10405 | 6536 | 10270 |
| United States | 10170 | 8914 | 7733 | 7513 |
| Mexico | 2129 | 2977 | 3450 | 2958 |
| Venezuela | 2228 | 2244 | 3239 | 2471 |
| Nigeria | 2059 | 1870 | 2155 | 2402 |
| Middle East | 18882 | 17540 | 23547 | 25188 |
| World | 62948 | 65460 | 74893 | 82095 |

Source: BP Statistical Review of World Energy, London, 2011

oil industry. By 2010 Kuwait produced more than Iraq. Saudi Arabia acts as swing producer in OPEC, sacrificing production to protect prices, and therefore its overall production is little changed over the last three decades. It retains the capacity to produce 11 or even 12 million barrels per day, but as already indicated it will only use this excess if a shock to oil markets, such as a curtailment to Iranian production because of conflict, caused oil prices to soar. Although Saudi Arabia's export earnings would benefit from the higher prices, a worldwide recession resulting from an oil price spike would result in its income from overseas financial assets suffering. Hence Saudi Arabia is a moderating influence in world oil markets. Although the Kingdom's population has grown, its domestic revenue needs are less pressing than those of countries such as Iran, which aim to produce as much oil as possible. Russia, which is not an OPEC member, has taken advantage of Saudi Arabia's restraint to boost its own oil production. Although the economic disruption caused by the collapse of the Soviet Union adversely affected production levels, by 2010 it had again emerged as the world's leading producer of oil, a position Russia intends to retain and defend.

## Oil pricing

Optimum depletion theory suggests that user costs should be added to marginal cost when calculating oil prices.[19] The concept of user cost was first defined by Harold Hotelling as the cost of using a resource today and forgoing tomorrow's profit. In other words, future profits may have to be discounted to calculate user cost, and then this built in to any current oil price calculation. The concept is that of a temporal opportunity cost, the sacrifice of the future for the sake of the present. How great the sacrifice is will clearly depend on the size of a country's reserves. In Saudi Arabia's case with plentiful reserves, oil depleted now will mean little sacrifice of future income.[20] For Algeria or Iran the future sacrifice may be much greater as their reserves are less.

It is the user cost that matters, however, and this depends not only on the relative size of the future income foregone, but the rate at which this is discounted. This in turn will reflect time preferences for current versus future income. Saudi Arabia may put a higher value on future oil income and a lower value on current income than Iraq or Iran. This suggests the rate of discount may be lower for Saudi Arabia than for Algeria or Iran. Hence the higher future sacrifice for the latter countries may not be worth much when discounted at a high rate into present user costs. For Saudi Arabia the lower future sacrifice may be partly offset by the lower discount rate. In other words the calculation of user cost is far from being unambiguous if differences in time preferences are also involved. Pricing to provide for optimal depletion is a much more complex matter than Hotelling suggested, as far as the Middle East is concerned.

## Predicted and actual oil prices

Past predictions of future oil prices have often proved remarkable inaccurate and this has made oil revenue projections virtually impossible in the Middle East. The oil price rises of 1973–74 and 1979 were not predicted, and are usually described as exogenous shocks to the economic system. However, the oil price falls since the mid 1980s were widely predicted, perhaps giving some hope to the forecasters.[21] The Iraq invasion of Kuwait was thought of as a possible catalyst for a third oil price shock, but perhaps thanks to Operation Desert Storm this proved not to be the case as far as the West was concerned.

Exhaustible resource models have now been abandoned by many energy economists, and the pricing of oil is increasingly treated just like any other commodity. The basic problem is that the predictions of exhaustible resource theory concerning steadily rising prices for scarce resources appears to be at variance with the realities of the last 50 years. As oil becomes depleted its price might be expected to rise, reflecting increasing scarcity, but as indicated oil reserves have actually risen worldwide over the last four decades and it appears that demand factors are more important in determining prices than oil supply.

Two factors explain the failure of resource exhaustion theory to explain oil price trends. First is the simple fact that oil is not becoming exhausted. In 1973 there were thirty years of proven reserves worldwide. By 1992 there were over forty years of reserves and this has subsequently increased further to over fifty years. The increase in reserves partly reflected pricing developments, as the oil price rises of the 1970s encouraged oil exploration. It also reflected technical change, particularly in the exploitation of oil in inhospitable environments and the efficient utilisation of oil from small offshore fields. Second, there was the levelling out in the demand for oil in the mature industrial

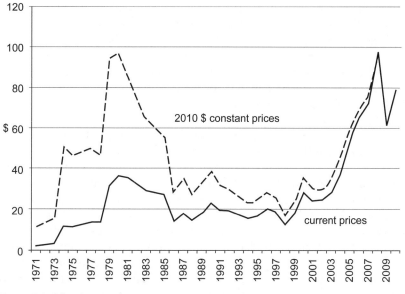

*Figure 7.1* Oil price trends
Source: BP Statistical Review of World Energy, London, 2011

economies already discussed. Increasing efficiency of energy use and the development of substitutes for oil raise questions about its long-term future as a fuel.

Figure 7.1 illustrates oil price trends since 1970. Allowing for inflation, by the 1990s the oil-exporting countries of the Middle East were more or less back to where they were before the oil price shocks of 1973–74. The dollar, in which oil prices were denominated, had itself depreciated against European currencies and the Japanese yen, the currencies in which a substantial part of the civilian imports into the Middle East are denominated. In terms of purchasing power, or the cost of obtaining manufactured goods, the economies of the Middle East that are oil dependent appear to have experienced a continuous deterioration with the two brief exceptions of the oil price shocks. However, since 2002 oil prices have taken off again in both constant and current prices, largely reflecting increased demand from China and India, both of which are at an energy intensive stage of their economic development.[22] How long this is sustained remains to be seen, as in the longer term demand may flatten, either because industrial development slows due to recession, or these Asian economies become restructured towards more knowledge-intensive activities rather than physical manufacturing.

## Spot, future and options oil pricing

Oil is increasingly viewed as just another commodity whose price should be treated accordingly. The fact that it does not seem to be an especially scarce or precious resource means it has lost something of its mystique. Any notion of oil as "liquid gold" seems to have disappeared. Oil substitutes may be slow to develop, especially in the field of transportation, but western consuming nations take an increasingly relaxed view of supplies. One consequence is that there is less concern over long-term contracts and security of supplies.[23] There has been a steady growth in the so-called Rotterdam spot market for oil, which is not physically sited in that Dutch city, but is simply the term used for oil and product deals covering North West Europe.

Long-term contracts, which were much favoured by the major refinery operators in the turbulent 1970s, were much less necessary in the 1990s given the greater oil price stability, and even though oil prices have subsequently risen fixed contracts are less used than in the past. There has in any case been a growth in other hedging instruments, notably futures and options, which means that risk can be reduced without having to resort to the inflexibility of fixed contracts. As London is the major centre for trade in financial derivatives in Europe it is not surprising that dealings in such futures and options contracts were largely concentrated on the city's International Petroleum Exchange, which was acquired by the Intercontinental Exchange in 2001. Following the conversion to electronic trading in 2005 the market was redesignated ICE Futures and the range of energy contracts traded was expanded.[24] There is similar trading on NYMEX Clearpoint in North America, but this is of less interest from the point of view of Middle East producers, as much of the American trading relates to gas and heating oil, with crude oil contracts relating to non-OPEC production from Alaska and Russia.[25]

An oil future is simply an agreement to purchase or sell oil at a predetermined date in the future, often one or three months hence, at a price agreed now. It differs from an oil contract, which usually provides for regular deliveries over a period of time, rather than a once only future transaction. With either type of deal, the parties are tied into a fixed price or prices, which may be advantageous to the buyer in the case of a rise in prices for immediate delivery, referred to as spot prices, as mentioned above. If the spot price is falling, the oil purchaser may regret entering the contract deal or purchasing forward, as it is obligatory to pay the initial price agreed, even where this results in a loss. The loss can be regarded as an opportunity cost rather than an actual cost, as it refers to what might have been, or in other words the value of what was given up in order to secure certainty. Both oil contracts and oil futures can be regarded as hedges against risk.

One way of maintaining greater flexibility in oil dealing is by using the options market. Options are a financial derivative that confer the right to buy or sell, but unlike contracts or futures, it is not obligatory to carry out the transaction. Of course oil contracts and futures can be sold on to third parties, and this releases the original purchaser or seller from the obligation, though in the end someone will have to take delivery or supply the oil. To a large extent, of course, contract and futures prices will reflect expectations about how spot prices will change. If spot prices decline when they were expected to rise, or decline by more than anticipated, then expectations will be revised. This may have a considerable impact on the value of futures.

Suppose, for example, a future for a 1 December delivery was bought for $100 per barrel in October when the oil spot price was $110. By November the spot price has declined to $90 per barrel and it is expected to remain at this level until the end of the year. In these circumstances the holder of the $100 future will face the choice of either using it to purchase oil at an expected $10 per dollars above the December spot price, or of attempting to sell the future and use the cheaper spot market. The latter course of action is likely to be especially unattractive, as given expectations in the market, buyers for the future may be only willing to pay $85.

Oil options represent an attractive means of avoiding being trapped in such loss-making situations. Rather than being a potential victim of adverse market developments, the buyer or seller has a choice of whether to proceed or not to the final transaction. The essential difference with an option is that it does not have to be exercised, unlike a future which implies a predetermined commitment. A right to buy at a fixed price is referred to as a "call" option, and a right to sell a "put" option.

To see how options work, it is best to cite an actual example. Suppose it is 1 July and a refinery owner wants to purchase 400,000 barrels of crude oil for delivery on 1 October. The oil can either be purchased through a future contract, at a guaranteed price of $100 per barrel, or the refinery owner can wait until October and purchase in the spot market at an unknown price. The future brings certainty, but for an initial commitment of $40,000,000 ($100 x 400,000).

Using the spot market is clearly risky and therefore the buyer may seek to hedge instead by the use of options. This involves a much smaller initial outlay than a future contract as the cost of a call option is only $5 per barrel. If the buyer decides to purchase "put" options on 400,000 barrels of oil futures for delivery on 1 October at a price of $110 per barrel the initial cost is therefore only $2,000,000. Suppose by 1 October the spot price was $120 per barrel, the buyer could exercise his option and buy at $110 per barrel. This would be a saving of $10 on the spot price, saving $4,000,000, more than offsetting the initial option cost of $2,000,000. On the other hand, if the spot price was only $100 on 1 October, the buyer would not exercise the option, but would forfeit the $2,000,000 deposit.

The increase in dealing through futures and options has major implications for the market in Middle Eastern oil. Oil contracts have declined in relative significance, and attention has become increasingly focused on spot oil prices. With more use of financial derivatives such as futures and options as hedges, the insurance premium that contracts once enjoyed has been competed away. As a result, bilateral bargaining between individual OPEC suppliers and oil purchasers has become less important. The power of price determination is becoming more remote from Middle Eastern producers, with spot prices of Arabian and Dubai light determined by demand and supply in the Rotterdam market rather than the Gulf. The volume of spot transactions exceeds that of future transactions and options, but these are catching up quickly. Spot oil prices still determine future and option prices, but the situation may well be reversed eventually given the enormous potential for dealings in these derivatives.

## Oil products and refining

The growth of financial derivatives in oil such as futures and options has tended to have a stabilising effect on oil prices, even though the markets are used for speculation as well as hedging. This increased certainty is welcome to OPEC members, but it was to some extent the oil price shocks that gave OPEC its power. Oil prices reacted much less to the Iraqi invasion of Kuwait than they did to the Iranian revolution or the Arab–Israeli War of 1973. These developments, together with the poor outlook which crude oil has in common with other primary commodities, are encouraging Middle Eastern producers to move away from exporting crude oil into refined petroleum and further downstream products. This increases local value added for the oil producing country, brings technology transfer, creates some employment and raises export earnings. It can be viewed as part of an economic diversification strategy, designed to reduce reliance on primary production, and introduce manufacturing, even if it is still closely oil related.

These potential benefits must be qualified, however, and there are several offsetting factors. One major difficulty for Middle Eastern suppliers is the increased logistical problems in the transportation of refined products, which adds to costs and potentially reduces profitability. Oil refineries were historically situated near the markets for petroleum products rather than at the source of crude oil supply on grounds of cost. It is cheaper and easier to ship crude oil than a variety of refined products all of which have to be handled separately. Crude oil can be pumped through pipelines over thousands of miles, but although this is technically feasible for refined products, it is not economically viable. Many refined products are more volatile and flammable than crude oil, and the safety measures involved in their transportation are both complex and costly.

The employment generated by investment in refineries is very limited given the capital intensive nature of the technology. With even further automation in the control systems in recent years, it is now possible for fewer than 100 workers to run a refinery with a throughput of 250,000 barrels a day. In the Gulf the refineries are amongst the most modern and high-technology facilities in the world, requiring largely skilled staff.[26] Most day-to-day running is increasingly handled by local nationals, although migrant workers from the Indian subcontinent and other Arab countries still constitute a majority of the workforce in the Saudi Arabian refineries, but not in Kuwait or Bahrain. When major problems arise, or servicing of complicated equipment is required, expatriates are called in on a short-term basis. Most of these are employed in the companies that supply the equipment, and are not a permanent part of the host country workforce.

Investment in complex refinery operations brings with it technology transfers, and there has been much skill acquisition by local nationals in the Gulf in the field of petroleum technology. Although technicians from the United States, Europe and Japan are still best at handling certain specialised operations, it is possible to foresee a time when a future oil trouble-shooter such as "Red Adair" will be a Kuwaiti, Saudi Arabian or Iranian national. Personnel in the Kuwait Oil Company learnt much from the experience of putting out fires after the Iraqi retreat from their country. All this is positive, especially as it appears that even disastrous conflicts can have some favourable spin-offs.

On the negative side is the isolation of industries such as refining from the rest of the economies in Middle Eastern states. Virtually all equipment is imported, and even the consumables used in the production processes are supplied from abroad. Local multipliers are therefore minimal, and in foreign exchange terms the cost of imported supplies has to be offset against any gains in terms of import savings with refined products or export earnings. Most refineries were geared largely to the local refined products market until the 1970s, and it is only since the 1980s that export refineries have been established in the region.

Saudi Arabia has the largest capacity in the Middle East of 1.8 million barrels a day, followed by Kuwait with a refined throughput of 820,000 per day. With the merger of the Arabian American Oil Company (ARAMCO), and the Saudi Arabian refining company (SAMAREC), ARAMCO has become a major international oil company, in the same league as Exxon and Shell.[27] The company is the world's number three refiner, and can increasingly out-compete the major western oil companies. Iran would like to pursue a similar strategy, but its refining capacity is only 720,000 barrels a day, much of which serves the domestic market.

## Downstream diversification into petrochemicals

The move by the Gulf states into petrochemical production, which was started in the 1970s, was a much bolder step than mere refining. Products such as ethylene and methanol are building blocks, on which whole downstream industries can be based, including all types of plastics from low-grade bags to high-quality materials for vehicle bumpers and similar consumer durable items. Plastics have increasingly been substituted for traditional metal and wooden products, and the petrochemical and plastics industry has become of greater international significance than the steel industry in terms of the value of output. The other major petrochemical product in the Gulf States is urea, which is used for fertiliser production. The South and South East Asian market can be easily served from the Gulf, and this is where the exports are mostly sent.

The region's comparative advantage in petrochemicals derives from the readily available oil feed stock, which minimises transportation costs, and the presence of cheap energy, both in the form of electricity produced by oil and gas fired stations and gas itself. As gas is produced as a by-product of oil production, it makes sound economic sense to harness as an energy source the associated gas that would otherwise be wastefully flared off.

As petrochemical technology is highly complex the states in the Gulf decided to develop the industry through joint venture arrangements with western and East Asian companies that had the necessary expertise, rather than attempting to go it alone.[28] This policy had many advantages, not least as it meant the foreign joint venture partners had an interest in securing value for money from the stage when contracts for the construction of the facilities were being awarded. Their participation also ensured that the output was up to international standards in terms of quality, especially as the foreign joint venture partners were to be purchasers of the output themselves, and had further responsibilities for marketing to third parties.

The Saudi Arabian Basic Industries Corporation has responsibility for petrochemical development in the Kingdom, with most of its facilities located at Jubail on the Gulf. It has separate joint ventures with Shell, Mobil and Exxon for ethane production, and ventures with Mitsubishi, Celanese and Texas Eastern for methane. Its urea venture is with the Taiwan Fertiliser Company. The Jubail site has become the largest single petrochemical complex in the world, and Saudi Arabia already accounts for 10 per cent of world petrochemical exports. In the 1990s a $6 billion expansion scheme was undertaken to double capacity from 10 million tonnes a year and there have subsequently been further increases.[29] Investment has gone into a plant to manufacture acrylonitrile, the nylon intermediate. This may result in further downstream diversification into artificial fibres for textiles.[30] Nevertheless, the petrochemical industry faces supply and pricing challenges that influence future investment and growth.[31]

As a result of all these schemes, it is envisaged that the Gulf will move from being a major supplier of crude oil into high-value added petrochemicals, and eventually further downstream into consumer goods inputs, if not the final products themselves. Although the strategy was not well thought out in the early years, and costly mistakes were made, after more than two decades of effort it has started to take on a momentum of its own. In the 1970s there was little market research undertaken, but this has since become a priority for SABIC when considering any new venture. Other states are diversifying as well as Saudi Arabia, including Bahrain, which has a urea fertiliser plant, and Oman, which has a methanol plant. In the United Arab Emirates there is a small fertiliser plant outside Abu Dhabi. In the longer term Saudi Arabia's main rival in Gulf petrochemicals will be Iran. Though the war with Iraq and US sanctions severely disrupted its programme, production of methane and ethylene plants has recommenced, with an estimated annual output of 4.3 million tons, and a further 1.2 million tons of chemical fertiliser.

## Gas reserves and production

The Middle East has not only oil resources but also considerable reserves of natural gas, both associated with oil fields and independent of oil production. Much of the gas that was hitherto flared is now harnessed, causing less environmental damage and at the same time being put to good use. Gas is a very efficient and clean fuel in comparison to alternatives such as oil and coal, and is increasingly favoured by consuming nations as a source of energy. As Table 7.3 shows, over 40 per cent of the world's natural gas is found in the Middle East, with Iran and Qatar having the largest reserves.

Table 7.4 shows gas production levels, with Iran and Qatar the largest producers in the Middle East followed by Algeria and Iran. For Qatar gas is especially significant as it has vast resources in relation to its small population and the gas income has resulted in the country having the highest per capita GDP in the world. Much of the gas is liquefied before being transported by ship from Qatar, with the country owning the liquefaction facilities, the ships and the terminal plants where the gas is fed into the grids of consuming countries.[32] As a result of this substantial investment Qatar receives over four times the revenue per billion cubic metres than Iran, which is dependent on pipelines and has to pay transit fees.

*Table 7.3* Middle Eastern gas reserves in a global context (trillion cubic metres)

| Country | 1980 | 1990 | 2000 | 2010 |
|---|---|---|---|---|
| Algeria | 3.7 | 3.3 | 4.5 | 4.5 |
| Iran | 14.1 | 17.0 | 26.0 | 29.6 |
| Qatar | 2.8 | 4.6 | 14.4 | 25.3 |
| Saudi Arabia | 3.2 | 5.2 | 6.3 | 8.0 |
| UAE | 2.4 | 5.8 | 6.0 | 6.0 |
| Russia | N/A | N/A | 42.3 | 44.8 |
| United States | 5.6 | 4.8 | 5.0 | 7.7 |
| Venezuela | 1.3 | 3.6 | 4.2 | 5.5 |
| Nigeria | 1.2 | 2.8 | 3.5 | 5.3 |
| Middle East | 24.7 | 38.0 | 59.1 | 75.8 |
| World | 81.0 | 125.7 | 154.3 | 187.1 |

Source: BP Statistical Review of World Energy, London, 2011

*Table 7.4* Middle Eastern gas production in a global context (billion cubic metres)

| Country | 1980 | 1990 | 2000 | 2010 |
|---|---|---|---|---|
| Algeria | 14.2 | 49.3 | 84.4 | 80.4 |
| Iran | 7.1 | 23.2 | 60.2 | 138.5 |
| Qatar | 4.7 | 6.3 | 29.5 | 116.7 |
| Saudi Arabia | 9.7 | 33.5 | 49.8 | 83.9 |
| UAE | 7.5 | 20.4 | 38.4 | 51.0 |
| Russia | N/A | 590.0 | 528.5 | 588.9 |
| United States | 549.4 | 504.3 | 543.2 | 611.0 |
| Venezuela | 14.8 | 22.0 | 27.9 | 28.5 |
| United Kingdom | 34.8 | 36.9 | 108.4 | 57.1 |
| Netherlands | 76.4 | 61.0 | 58.1 | 70.5 |
| Middle East | 37.5 | 101.3 | 208.1 | 460.7 |
| World | 1434.3 | 1980.4 | 2413.4 | 3193.3 |

Source: BP Statistical Review of World Energy, London, 2011

## Oil and development

The role of oil in the economies of the Middle East has changed over time and it is possible to identify stages in its development. Initially the main benefit was financial as, although revenues were modest from the 1930s to the 1960s, these met most of the expenditure needs of the royal households in the Gulf and funded the major proportion of government current spending. As oil production expanded in the 1960s revenues grew, and the quadrupling of oil prices in 1973–74 resulted in a huge windfall. This could be interpreted as the second stage. Oil revenue was viewed primarily as a means of funding investment rather than merely current expenditures, though for some of the Gulf states the revenue was so great that it was possible to put some aside into "funds for future generations". As Middle East production stagnated and declined for many countries, the link between oil prices and development became of crucial importance. This was clear from the infrastructure boom resulting from the 1979 oil price rises, and the virtual halt to major investment projects following the price falls of the 1980s.

A third phase has now started where the volume of exports and price of crude oil is becoming of less significance for the economies of the region. Oil is less important as an output, but more crucial as an input. It is the marketing of refined products and petrochemicals that increasingly matters, not the sales of crude oil. In these circumstances pricing issues become more complex. Low domestic pricing of oil inputs can help the international competitiveness of the Middle Eastern refining and petrochemicals industry, especially during the entry, start up and infant industry phases. In the longer term Middle Eastern crude oil may not be internationally traded; instead it will be oil products exports that will matter. In this situation OPEC's declining significance as a cartel is less damaging to the economies of the Middle East than might otherwise have been the case. Diversification into downstream production means that it matters much less that oil prices are behaving like those of other primary commodities, with cyclical volatility and a long-term tendency to decline. The economies of the Middle East may still be oil dependent, but the nature of this dependence is changing from output to input dependence. This has the merit of being more controllable.

Some of the issues that were prominent in the literature on the oil and development link are arguably now less relevant in a period of lower oil prices. There was a long debate in the 1970s and 1980s about whether oil windfalls were a blessing or curse. One argument for the latter view was the notion that oil dependent economies tended to suffer from "Dutch disease", so called because of the effect of gas exports from the Netherlands in driving up the guilder, making manufacturing exports uncompetitive and imports cheaper, with resultant adverse consequences for unemployment. Although this argument is at first sight persuasive, and there was evidence in its support in the Netherlands, and arguably in Britain, its relevance to the Middle East is open to question.

The countries of the Gulf had little local manufacturing capacity in the 1970s that could have been threatened, and the shortage of labour was more of an issue than unemployment. Oil exports were in any case denominated in dollars, as were most imports, so the level of the exchange rate was of relatively minor importance for trade. A strong exchange rate checked inflationary pressures, and any depreciation would only have resulted in imported inflation which would have added to that generated domestically through supply bottlenecks.

For countries such as Egypt, with manufacturing capacity and non-oil exports such as cotton and textiles, Dutch disease was more likely, especially as oil became increasingly the dominant export after the return of the Suez fields by Israel, and there was also the indirect effect of Gulf oil exports on the exchange rate through remittances. Investigation by economists, notably Bent Hansen, revealed little empirical support for Dutch disease in Egypt. Cotton and textiles were mostly exported to Eastern Europe under bilateral trade deals that had administered prices. Imports were subject to tariffs, quotas, foreign exchange controls and other restrictions. The official exchange rate was itself controlled, although admittedly at a high and possibly over-valued level in the 1970s. It is doubtful, however, if a lower rate would have done much to boost exports given the supply constraints in the Egyptian economy.

Oil revenues were arguably of more consequence at the political economy level, as they reinforced the role of the state by increasing both its power of patronage, and its ability to control economic activity. There was less need to collect other forms of tax revenues because of the significance of oil revenues, and also perhaps less government accountability. Countries in the Gulf all adopted some form of development planning, simply in order to determine their expenditure priorities, and ascertain how spending plans interacted. The consultation when planning the expenditure of oil revenues only extended to the government ministries, however, not the general public. Furthermore, governments frequently ignored their own development plans if circumstances changed, either through new defence and security concerns, or because of the changing price of oil.

These issues will be considered further in the final chapter on the role of the state. The other developmental problem, that of export earnings stability resulting from excessive oil dependence, will be considered in the next chapter on the region's international trade.

# 8   International and intra-regional trade

The Middle East has always been a crossroads for international commerce due to its geographical position between the more populated regions of Europe, South Asia and East Asia. Rather than being a barrier to trade, the deserts of the region have been like oceans, crossed by important trade routes such as that across the Sahara to Nigeria, over the arid lands of central Asia to China or through the Persian Empire to the cities of the Indian subcontinent. The spread of Islam and the Arab conquests served to develop intra-regional trade, as did the spread of the Ottoman Empire in the sixteenth century.[1] Initially the great European powers were to view the region as strategically important for transit trade with the East, a process that was to result in the construction of the Suez Canal and its opening in 1869. By the twentieth century with the discovery of oil, the European countries saw the region as an important trading entity in its own right, whose resources were vital for modern industry and commerce.

It is possible to classify the trading history of the region into three distinct phases, which could well be repeated, as history often is, with demographic and economic change. First, during periods when the region was economically insignificant, the emphasis was on transit trade through re-exporting. Second, there were periods of strong intra-regional trade, which were associated not only with conquest, but also the rise of sufficient economic power to serve the needs of the peoples of the region. Some view such phases as times of economic harmony and contentment, as in the early centuries of Islam and during the heyday of the Ottoman Empire. Third, there were periods of external colonisation, both direct and indirect, when the resources of the Middle East were seen as the property of the international community rather than belonging to those who inhabited the region itself. These resources could be exploited either by peaceful trading relationships or if necessary through force, if regional resistance arose or if obstructions arose.

The era of direct colonialism came to an end in the 1950s and early 1960s with the withdrawal of Britain and France from the region. Many argue, including Islamists as well as secularist socialists and Marxists, that the era of neo-colonialism has been prolonged by the region's significance as a source of global oil reserves. This era is arguably now also coming to a close, partly due to the end of the Cold War and the reduction in the global commitment of the United States, but also because there is less dependence by the West on Middle East oil supplies. It remains to be seen, however, whether strong intra-regional trading links will again emerge to propel the economies of the Middle East forward, or if the region will simply be bypassed by world trade between more dynamic neighbouring areas, a forgotten and neglected backwater, apart from some centres for transit trade.

## Trade and development

The relationship between the extent of international trade and economic advance has been discussed by western economists since the time of Adam Smith, and Muslim historians and philosophers such as Ibn Khaldun were also well aware of the issues involved.[2] The notion that specialisation within nations and exchange between nations can bring economic gains is the essence of the theory of absolute advantage, which is the starting point of most of the modern literature on international trade. David Ricardo's theory of comparative advantage is arguably more relevant to the Middle East than Smith's theory of absolute advantage. The former shows how countries with an absolute disadvantage in all lines of production in relation to other countries can still gain from specialising in producing and selling those items in which they themselves are most efficient. In other words, even if Middle East production is less efficient generally than that of the Far East, there may be some items such as petrochemicals or even cotton yarn where the region is relatively efficient. Far Eastern exporters of vehicles and electrical goods will not have a market in the Middle East unless they accept some goods in exchange. Oil and gas are the major items offered at present, but other commodities on which trade can be based will have to be identified in the longer term if commercial relations are to continue.

For trade in primary commodities such as oil and gas, the so-called "vent for a surplus" theory may have more relevance than absolute or comparative advantage. The rationale is that countries with surplus natural resources, in excess of present and future conceivable national needs, might as well exploit the resources and export the surplus. In exchange the primary producing countries can obtain useful goods that they do not produce themselves, such as high-technology manufactured items, including possibly even weapons to defend their resources. With "vent for a surplus" theory there is no opportunity cost in exporting the primary commodity, as nothing is given up. In contrast with the theories of absolute and comparative advantage, specialisation in one line of production means sacrificing another line. In the Middle East oil industry the capital and technology are imported, and often even the workforce consists of migrant labour. There are no local factors of production re-deployed from other activities. Indeed the growth of oil production has helped finance non-oil development rather than hindered it, although it would be an exaggeration to say that there have been no sacrifices.

In developing economies trade growth theories have particular relevance, notably the model developed by Harry Johnson that distinguishes between pro-trade biased and anti-trade biased growth.[3] Pro-trade biased growth implies that a country is opening up to the world, exporting to exploit its "vent for a surplus", or specialising according to its absolute or comparative advantage. In such circumstances the growth of trade will exceed the growth of gross domestic product. Such growth occurred throughout the nineteenth century as the economies of the Middle East became increasingly open to trade with Europe involving the exchange of primary commodities for manufactured goods. As oil production and exports rose growth could also be described as pro-trade biased. Anti-trade biased growth occurs when countries pursue import substitution policies, producing manufactured goods themselves, even when they are more expensive than competing imports, as economic diversification and industrialisation are seen as desirable goals, the key to modernisation and economic advance. Such policies were followed in Turkey under Ataturk in the 1920s and 1930s, in Egypt under Nasser in the 1950s and 1960s and in Syria under Assad during the 1970s and for much of the 1980s.

## Commodity and merchandise trade

Most of the exports from the Middle East are oil and oil-related products as well as natural gas. For the last half century dependence on energy and related exports has increased and exports of manufactured goods and agricultural produce have been squeezed out. This could be partly attributed to "Dutch disease", whereby overvalued exchange rates resulting from oil and gas exports undermine the competitiveness of other exports.[4] Exchange rate distortions may ironically be less of an issue for the economies of the Gulf Co-operation Council (GCC) countries as these are offset by the relatively low cost of employing migrant labour to service the economies and provide an industrial workforce. It is in Iran and the Arab countries of North Africa where exchange rate distortions may be more significant as the workforce largely comprises local nationals, and although wages are relatively low, so is productivity. In these circumstances any exchange rate distortions further undermine competitiveness.

Governments in the more populous countries of the region, with the notable exception of Turkey, have failed to provide an environment where exports can flourish. One analyst from the IMF using a trade gravity model concludes that part of the problem has been that, insofar as exports are encouraged, there has been excessive stress on the European Union, and no attempt to export to the more rapidly growing markets of Asia, apart from oil and gas exports from the GCC.[5] Even the United States market, still the second largest in the world, is largely neglected.[6] It has also been suggested that poor transport infrastructure also limits trade, especially for the North African countries, although again the situation in the GCC is better.[7] Whatever the reason for slow growth of non-energy exports, there is clearly a cost in terms of development and economic growth.[8]

*Table 8.1* Leading exporters in the Middle East

| Global rank | Country | Value, $ billion | Share, % |
|---|---|---|---|
| 12 | Saudi Arabia | 250 | 1.6 |
| 13 | UAE | 220 | 1.4 |
| 22 | Turkey | 114 | 0.7 |
| 23 | Iran | 101 | 0.7 |
| 29 | Kuwait | 67 | 0.4 |
| 31 | Qatar | 62 | 0.4 |
| 33 | Israel | 58 | 0.4 |
| 34 | Algeria | 57 | 0.4 |
| 36 | Iraq | 53 | 0.4 |
| 39 | Libya | 47 | 0.4 |
| 41 | Oman | 37 | 0.3 |
| 45 | Egypt | 26 | 0.2 |
| 49 | Morocco | 18 | 0.1 |

Source: World Trade Organization, Geneva, 2011

Table 8.1 ranks the economies of the Middle East according to the value of their exports, with Saudi Arabia, the region's largest oil exporter, not surprisingly ranked number one. Indeed Saudi Arabia, a G20 economy, is the twelfth largest exporter in the world. Crude oil accounts for over 80 per cent of Saudi Arabian exports, the rest being largely petrochemical products that bring greater value added. The gap between Saudi Arabia's exports and those of the United Arab Emirates has steadily narrowed, and it is likely that the latter will become the region's leading exporter by 2020. Most of the exports are accounted for by oil and gas from Abu Dhabi but re-exports from Dubai to Iran are also significant despite United States and European Union sanctions. The UAE also has a small but increasingly significant manufacturing sector which supplies neighbouring GCC countries in addition to its role as a servicing centre.

Turkey has become the leading exporter of manufactured goods in the region, supplying both the European Union market, with which it has free trade access, and neighbouring Middle East countries, and increasingly the GCC. The Turkish manufacturing sector has gone from strength to strength in recent years, and the country has the largest textile businesses in Europe. Other exports include designer leather goods and kitchen equipment, with Beko, a subsidiary of Koç Holding, and its rival Vestel leading suppliers of white goods and consumer electrical products to the European Union market. The growth of Turkey's manufacturing sector has been comparable to that of China, with particular dynamism in subcontracting to small and medium sized businesses.[9] The contrast between Turkey's export success and the dismal performance of Egypt is evident from Table 8.1. Turkey has totally eclipsed Iran despite the latter's oil resources, in contrast to the 1970s when Iran was well ahead of Turkey.

The Middle East is less internationally significant as an import market, but as Table 8.2 shows it is Turkey that is the leading importer in the region. It is

*Table 8.2* Leading import markets in the Middle East

| Global rank | Country | Value, $ billion | Share, % |
|---|---|---|---|
| 15 | Turkey | 186 | 1.2 |
| 19 | UAE | 160 | 1.0 |
| 21 | Saudi Arabia | 97 | 0.6 |
| 25 | Iran | 65 | 0.4 |
| 26 | Israel | 61 | 0.4 |
| 31 | Egypt | 53 | 0.3 |
| 36 | Algeria | 40 | 0.3 |
| 38 | Morocco | 35 | 0.3 |
| 44 | Qatar | 23 | 0.2 |
| 45 | Kuwait | 22 | 0.2 |
| 46 | Tunisia | 22 | 0.2 |
| 50 | Oman | 20 | 0.2 |

Source: World Trade Organization, Geneva, 2011

especially significant as a market for European Union exports, but there is increasing competition in the Turkish market from Asian suppliers. Imports include oil and gas, raw materials and supplies for the growing manufacturing sector. Consumer goods are also important now that most trade restrictions have been removed, but although most of these goods are consumed by local nationals, there are also significant sales to visitors to Istanbul, which benefits the city's economy. Istanbul has become a major shopping hub for visitors from neighbouring Balkan countries, Russians and tourists from the Turkic speaking countries of Central Asia, as well as Arab visitors.

The UAE has become the second largest import market in the Middle East, some of which is accounted for by re-exporting to Iran and neighbouring GCC countries from Jebel Ali, the region's major port and logistics hub. However, many of the imports are luxury consumer goods for retailers in Dubai's shopping malls, with the Dubai Mall the largest in the world. The annual shopping festival in Dubai has become the leading event of its type, with middle-class visitors attracted from Asia, Africa and Europe.

## Trade deficit problems

The balance of trade constitutes only part of the balance of payments of a country, and capital inflows can often compensate for trade deficits. As financial inflows through aid and remittances have largely kept the non-oil economies in the Middle East afloat for over five decades, it is easy to be complacent about large and often mounting trade deficits. This has been the case, for example, with the Mubarak government in Egypt, as there was a widespread belief that the United States would always come to the rescue, as it had in the past. Development assistance and past debt write offs have a political price, however, which would not have to be paid if the trading accounts were in better shape. It seems unlikely in any case that such favourable external circumstances will continue to prevail in the future as the United States and the European Union cut government spending to reduce their own fiscal deficits and as the United States questions the value of military assistance to potentially hostile parties. As a consequence, more effort will have to be made to correct trade deficits, either by curtailing imports, which implies domestic hardship, or by export promotion, which will be a completely new experience for the states of the Middle East, and a far from easy challenge.

Substantial trade deficits are the norm for Egypt, Jordan, Morocco and Tunisia. In the case of Jordan imports are almost three times greater than exports, and for Egypt imports are over twice as great as exports despite protectionist policies. Egypt, however, is quite a small import market, especially in relation to its population size of over 80 million; indeed Israel imports more. The UAE, the largest Arab market, imports over three times the amount of Egypt. Despite sanctions, Iran remains the fourth largest import market in the region, most of its imports coming from Asia.

The trade deficits of the states of the region are recurrent rather than cyclical, and it is clear that fundamental economic restructuring will be needed if they are to be significantly reduced, if not eliminated. There has been dialogue about restructuring and economic reform between the International Monetary Fund and many governments in the region for over four decades, and numerous measures have been undertaken, particularly with respect to exchange rate policy. There has been much tampering, but firm resistance to outsiders setting the agenda with respect to basic economic policy, especially that affecting industry or agriculture. Currency devaluation and depreciation have not served to diminish the import bias of consumption growth, as purchasers of imported goods do not appear to be very price sensitive.

Similarly on the export side, the responsiveness of foreign buyers to exchange rate depreciations has been disappointing. The price elasticity of demand for Middle Eastern non-oil exports would appear to be rather low. Of course most Middle Eastern exports are dollar denominated, so export prices do not fall with domestic currency depreciation. The International Monetary Fund advisors are fully aware of this, but point out that with falling domestic exchange rates, dollar export proceeds are worth more but supply costs remain fixed. This increases the profitability of exporting, which should induce production expansion. Unfortunately in the Middle East exporting price signals often fail to work, either because of the supply inflexibility by public sector industries or short-term profit taking by those in the private sector. The challenge is to have export profits ploughed back into investment to bring about further export growth.

## The terms of trade

The economies of the Middle East, like other regions of the developing world, have experienced considerable terms of trade problems, with export prices falling in relation to import prices. Such deterioration in the terms of trade tends to occur with exports of primary commodities in exchange for imports of manufactured goods.[10] World demand for primary commodities often remains static, at least in the short term. If the supply is increased in such circumstances, the price inevitably falls. This is apparent in the case of Middle Eastern oil exports, as already discussed in the previous chapter, but it also applies to the region's exports of agricultural produce and minerals. The basic problem is the low income elasticity of demand for primary commodities in relation to manufactured goods. This phenomenon was first noted by the Prussian economist Engels in the nineteenth century.[11] Bismarck's Prussia was an efficient producer of grains, but when output rose prices tended to fall in relation to the prices of imported manufactured goods from England where the industrial revolution was well advanced. Bismarck's solution was a policy to promote domestic manufacturing with tariffs and other protectionist measures to safeguard the domestic market for the new infant industries.

Similar policies were tried in Egypt in the nineteenth century by Mohammed Ali, who established a mechanised textile industry.[12] Britain, however, did not permit Mohammed Ali to apply tariffs to textile imports from England. It was felt a rival spinning and weaving industry in Egypt could be a long-term threat to the Lancashire cotton textile industry which used imported Egyptian raw cotton. It may have been impossible to thwart Bismarck, but Mohammed Ali was in a much weaker position as he relied on British support to preserve Egypt's semi-independence from the Ottoman Empire. Egypt was therefore forced to abandon its efforts to industrialise and had to rely instead on raw cotton exports for its earnings. It was not until much later in the twentieth century that Egypt could start again, long after all the European countries had emerged as successful industrial powers.

The major evidence of long-term declining primary commodity prices for developing countries was compiled by an Argentinean economist, Raul Prebisch, largely on the basis of prices for Bolivian tin, Brazilian coffee and Central American rubber.[13] Long-run price data for the Middle East is more sketchy, but Roger Owen compiled a long-run price series for Egypt's raw cotton exports which shows falling prices over most of the 1880–1900 period, and again from 1910 onwards.[14] Egypt's cotton production was expanded with British help following the American civil war and the abolition of slavery in the Confederate States. With cotton from the southern states becoming more expensive given the labour intensive nature of the harvesting, Egypt was regarded as a cheap and reliable substitute supply source for the mills of Lancashire. The port of Alexandria was developed, and the railway to Aswan constructed. This was seen as the first stage of a major project to connect all the possessions of the British Empire in Africa from the Cape of Good Hope to Cairo. This project was never completed, but the Aswan railway was of major commercial significance for cotton exports.

Raw cotton is still an important Egyptian export, but the development of mechanised cotton picking in the United States in the 1960s undermined Egypt's labour cost advantage. The introduction of man-made fibres also hurt producers, although the 1980s saw a swing in fashion back to natural fibres which brought some benefit to Egypt. This story of competition from other countries and substitute materials also applied to other Middle Eastern primary commodities. The silk production developed by the French around Mount Lebanon in the nineteenth century supplied the industry in Lyon with fine raw material. The Lebanese Christians in particular benefited from this development, but competition from cheaper Far Eastern silk, mostly from China, made production in the Middle East uneconomic. The same problems arose for Turkish tobacco, which catered for a niche market, while the major growing regions of the United States and Southern Africa achieved commercial dominance in global supplies. A similar picture emerged for Yemeni coffee, which lost out to Latin America producers, who developed large commercial estates. As a result, Yemeni coffee became a novel rarity, whose taste is known to few outside the Arabian Peninsula.

Even more dramatic was the fate of the Gulf pearling industry. During the first two decades of the twentieth century the pearling industry in the Gulf expanded rapidly, with divers obtaining rich natural pearls from the oyster beds off the island of Bahrain and the peninsula of Qatar[15] as well as further down the Gulf in Dubai.[16] The pearls were shipped by *dhow,* the traditional sailing vessels of the Gulf, to Bombay, where they were sorted and graded. They were then re-exported to Europe and North American, to be sold as jewellery. During the 1920s when long strings of pearls were regarded as highly fashionable, output and sales boomed. The Gulf enjoyed a measure of prosperity, at least the *dhow* owners did, if not the divers themselves.[17] In the 1930s the Japanese developed the cultured pearl, which was a much cheaper substitute, being more consistent in quality than natural pearls. Oyster farming was not feasible in the Gulf, as conditions did not compare with Japan's inland sea. With the great slump, buyers, in so far as they purchased pearls, bought the cheaper Japanese variety. The Gulf industry was virtually wiped out by 1935, a precedent that many of the older generation see as a warning for oil.

Those Middle East economies that are still dependent on primary product exports continue to experience terms of trade difficulties. Oil is the dominant primary commodity, and its price has affected the terms of trade of both OPEC states such as Saudi Arabia and lesser non-OPEC oil exporters such as Egypt. There was a significant deterioration in the terms of trade of both these countries in the 1980s and 1990s with similar adverse developments affecting Iran and Algeria. In contrast, those states with a more diversified range of exports such as Turkey and Israel have experienced more favourable terms of trade trends in recent years. Both these countries have also enjoyed more terms of trade stability from year to year. This means a more certain economic environment which facilitates investment and helps ensure smoother economic growth. The two major Middle Eastern producers and exporters of phosphates, Jordan and Morocco, have experienced similar difficulties to the oil dependent states, with the price sometimes doubling from one year to the next, only to half again the following year.

## Export diversification

\*A reduction in dependence on primary product exports is the best way to avoid immiserising growth and the uncertainties of terms of trade instability. Governments throughout the Middle East have export diversification as a policy objective, and often the goals are set out in each country's development plan. Planning for diversification is much more difficult, however, than actually accomplishing the goal. Import substitution is an easier policy to follow, as governments can protect domestic producers through tariffs and quotas. Governments enjoy economic sovereignty over their own national markets, but small and even medium sized countries have little influence over international markets. In the case of the Middle East only Saudi Arabia has some influence over the world oil market, but no other state in the region has any real policy influence over world markets in any primary commodity or manufactured good.

Subsidies can of course be paid to exporters, but governments cannot prevent other states adopting similar policies. Competitive devaluation between countries can also thwart export diversification plans. Only multilateral action can avoid trade wars, never unilateral action, unless a country is in a strong negotiating position because of the sheer size of its domestic market in relation to the world market. The United States and the European Union enjoy considerable bargaining strength that they can exercise in negotiating forums such as the World Trade Organization, which sets the framework for each round of multilateral trade talks. None of the countries of the Middle East acting on its own enjoys such muscle in trade negotiations, and even if they were able to act collectively, which seems an unlikely prospect, their global influence would be limited.

The economies of the Middle East remain more dependent on exports of primary products than most other regions of the Third World, apart from sub-Saharan Africa. There has not been a rapid diversification into exports of manufactured goods as in the major economies of South Asia, South East Asia and Latin America. Nevertheless Turkey, and to a lesser extent Israel, have become diversified exporting states, where the share of exports accounted for by primary products corresponds to levels found in many developed industrial countries. In the cases of Turkey the move away from primary product exports has been dramatic over the period since 1970, with a mere one-third of the total being primary products by the 1990s and less than 20 per cent in 2012. It is only in Syria that primary products still account for over two-thirds of total export proceeds, reflecting the failure of its state-run manufacturing sector. Even Egypt, which remains dependent on oil exports, has seen a significant fall, while in Jordan and Morocco dependence on phosphates and other primary product exports has been much reduced.

## Euro–Arab trading relations

The European Union's interest in the Middle East has always been primarily motivated by economic concerns. There are both positive and negative forces conditioning the relationship. On the positive side in trading terms, the region is of much greater significance for Europe than it is for the United States, because of its importance for Europe's oil imports. The Middle Eastern economies, especially the Gulf states, are also significant export markets for Europe. On the negative side, trans-Mediterranean commerce has declined partly because of the European Union, which has resulted in France, Spain, Italy and Greece being more oriented to the north than the south. The ending of the Cold War and the lifting of the iron curtain resulted in the countries of the European Union becoming more closely connected to their eastern neighbours, many of which have become full members of the Union. Hence since the 1990s it has been the former communist countries that were the major focus of commercial and diplomatic efforts, to some extent at the expense of the Middle East.

European Union exports to the Middle East are shown in Table 8.3, with Turkey by far the most important market followed by the UAE. The value of exports to Egypt was less than one-quarter of those to Turkey. Since 2011 the adverse effects of the Arab Spring have further reduced the significance of exports to Egypt, and the United States and European Union sanctions on Iran have resulted in it being further marginalised, with negative implications for its imports.

To some extent the history of European trade with the Middle East is repeating itself. After the Suez crisis in 1956 Britain and France, the main European powers with continuing interests in the Middle East, tended to turn away from the region. In the case of France this was reinforced by the civil war in Algeria and the legacy of hostility this produced. Nevertheless there was a desire to keep open trade links with the region, not least so that Europe could have export earnings to offset against its payments for oil imports. There was, however, a certain complacency about the Middle East, a tendency to disregard the region and its problems as Europe looked inward to common market integration. The 1967 Arab–Israeli War, which demonstrated the weakness of the Arab countries, tended to reinforce European complacency.

*Table 8.3* EU exports to the Middle East

| Market | Value, $ million | Share, 2010, % | Share, 2005, % |
|---|---|---|---|
| Turkey | 81,121 | 1.6 | 1.4 |
| UAE | 36,734 | 0.7 | 0.8 |
| Saudi Arabia | 30,500 | 0.6 | 0.5 |
| Algeria | 20,598 | 0.4 | 0.3 |
| Egypt | 19,624 | 0.4 | 0.3 |
| Israel | 19,184 | 0.4 | 0.4 |
| Morocco | 18,064 | 0.4 | 0.4 |
| Iran | 15,025 | 0.3 | 0.4 |
| Tunisia | 14,677 | 0.3 | 0.2 |
| Libya | 8,954 | 0.2 | 0.1 |
| Total | 264,481 | 5.3 | 4.8 |

Source: World Trade Organization, Geneva, 2011

It was in this context that the oil price rises as a result of the October 1973 Arab–Israeli War came as a severe shock to Europe. There was the issue of the security of oil imports, and the severe trade deficit problems that the quadrupling of oil prices brought. There was a feeling that Europe should no longer ignore the region. The European Union (or European Economic Community as it then was) decided to pursue two initiatives – the cooperation treaties which represented an extension of the Mediterranean policy to the Arab countries, and the Euro–Arab dialogue. In both cases the European countries were primarily interested in economic objectives, especially promoting exports to pay for their oil imports. For their part the Arabs were more interested in political dialogue, the aim being to separate Europe from American policy over Israel, and ultimately to weaken that policy.

The cooperation agreements were a rather cynical attempt to get the Arab Mediterranean states and Israel to extend trade preferences to the European Union in return for limited concessions on import tariffs and quotas. The arrangements were designed to regulate trade, and were arguably against at least the spirit, if not the letter of GATT, which supports the principle of non-discrimination in trade. As the Arab states were not GATT signatories this did not present a problem. In the agreements the Arab countries are treated individually, rather than as a bloc, yet the European Union itself deals as a bloc. This puts Brussels trade negotiators in a powerful position given the huge size of the European Union market compared to that of each Arab country.[18] Egypt, the largest Arab country in terms of population size, has a market for imports less than half the size of Portugal's, one of the poorest periphery countries in the European Union.

The cooperation agreements provide for an annual cycle of meetings between European Union and Arab trade officials from each of the countries in turn. Trade ministers are present at some meetings, but details of quotas and tariffs for particular items are usually dealt with at the civil servant level. The annual rounds have become almost a ritual since the late 1970s, with little of substance achieved; indeed they have been unable to safeguard existing trade. It was clear, for example, that the enlargement of the European Union in 1986 to include Spain and Portugal would create problems for citrus exports from Morocco and Tunisia. Yet no action was taken, and once Spanish and Portuguese production rose in response to the favourable prices under the Common Agricultural Policy, imports from Morocco and Tunisia were duly curtailed. Similarly the Common Market agreement between the European Union and the Republic of Cyprus had adverse implications for Egyptian exports of early potatoes which compete with those from Cyprus, yet the Co-operation Agreement with Cairo did nothing to safeguard its position.[19]

Egypt also lost out to Turkey over textiles, although exports from both countries to the European Union were restricted under the multifibre arrangements. Turkey, however, as an aspiring member of the European Union, has a Free Trade Agreement. This provides for more favourable treatment than a Co-operation Agreement. The only Arab country to express

*Table 8.4* EU imports from the Middle East

| Source | Value, $ million | Share, 2010, % | Share, 2005, % |
|---|---|---|---|
| Turkey | 55,796 | 1.0 | 1.1 |
| Libya | 38,092 | 0.7 | 0.6 |
| Algeria | 27,690 | 0.5 | 0.6 |
| Saudi Arabia | 21,117 | 0.4 | 0.7 |
| Iran | 18,995 | 0.4 | 0.3 |
| Israel | 14,732 | 0.3 | 0.3 |
| Tunisia | 12,608 | 0.2 | 0.2 |
| Qatar | 10,316 | 0.2 | 0.0 |
| Morocco | 10,244 | 0.2 | 0.3 |
| Egypt | 9,551 | 0.2 | 0.2 |
| Iraq | 9,470 | 0.2 | 0.1 |
| Total | 228,611 | 4.3 | 4.4 |

Source: World Trade Organization, Geneva, 2011

interest in joining the European Union is Morocco, but by definition the Union is European, which Morocco is certainly not, and Turkey is arguably not, despite the fact that the area to the west of the Bosporus is in Europe. Greece is of course hostile to Turkish membership, at least until the Cyprus issue is resolved, but there is also resistance from Germany and other member states because of the provision for free mobility of labour within the European Union. There is, however, a desire not to offend the Ankara government, as Turkey is a key military ally that is highly valued by the United States, and the country also represents for Europe the moderate and acceptable face of Islam.

Turkey is also by far the largest supplier of imports to the European Union as Table 8.4 shows. Most of these imports are manufactured goods. Libya is significant as a source of oil imports given its geographical proximity to the European Union, and Italy in particular. The instability and destruction during the final months of the Gaddafi regime disrupted production and imports in 2011, but these have since recovered and the goodwill generated by the Anglo-French intervention in providing an air shield for the rebel forces has positive implications for trade and wider economic relations.

## Europe and Arab–Israeli differences

For the Arab states the main achievement of the Euro–Arab dialogue of the 1970s was seen as the Venice Declaration of 1980 by European leaders. This referred to the recognition of the legitimate rights of the Palestinian people. It went well beyond United Nations resolutions 242 and 338 in stating that:

> A just solution must finally be found to the Palestinian problem, which is not simply one of refugees. The Palestinian people, which are conscious of existing as such, must be placed in a position, by an appropriate process

defined within the framework of the comprehensive peace settlement, to exercise fully its right to self determination.[20]

This declaration was music to the ears of all those Arab states that rejected the Camp David peace process, and the United States' attempts to encourage bilateral talks between individual Arab states and Israel at that time. It appeared that the Europeans were prepared to go much further in their recognition of Palestinian grievances than either the Carter administration or the incoming Reagan leadership. It could, of course, be dismissed as empty rhetoric by those with little power to move events, but to Arab leaders at the time, apart from the Egyptians, it was warmly welcomed.

It was the Co-operation Agreement with Israel in 1974 that led to the later bilateral agreements with the Arab countries in 1975 and 1976. The agreement with Israel was partly a result of Britain's entry into the European Union in 1973, as the United Kingdom had been a significant market for Israeli citrus produce following on from the days of the Palestine mandate, and the Jerusalem trade officials wanted to protect this trade as far as possible. After the Co-operation Agreement was concluded it immediately became apparent that it would be very one-sided to include Israel in such arrangements, but exclude the Arab Mediterranean states. The issue arose in the course of deliberations in Brussels concerning the aftermath of the 1973 Arab–Israeli War and the resultant Arab boycott of oil sales to the Netherlands, which in Rotterdam had the largest refining capacity in the European Union. Although the boycott was unrelated to the Co-operation Agreement issue, and was more a consequence of Dutch national policy, it became clear that some initiative should be undertaken with respect to the Arab Mediterranean states.

In fact trade relations with the European Union were to prove difficult for Israel, not least because Europe had the agriculture of its own Mediterranean states to protect, and there was the constant concern of not wanting to offend the Arab states. With Israel obtaining most of its military hardware from the United States, there were not even the interests of the French and British armaments industries to consider, which, had circumstances been different, might have been lobbying for offset trade agreements to enable Israel to pay for its arms imports. The European countries were largely restricted to supplying inputs to the Israeli consumer goods industries, automobiles and commercial vehicles.

One particularly contentious issue for Israel and the European Union has been the question of how to handle the trade of the Occupied Territories. Israel did not favour Gaza and the West Bank being given separate quotas for their exports to the European Union as this might imply some sort of de facto recognition for a separate Palestinian entity. On the other hand there was a reluctance to include citrus exports from the Arab run packaging stations in Gaza under the Israeli quota, as this would reduce sales and revenues for Israeli producers. For the European Union the amounts were modest, but the Israelis were pressed into a position by their own exporters to allow a separate quota for the Occupied Territories as an escape valve. For once in the Middle East, economic pragmatism won out over issues of principle.

## Oil and petrochemical trade

The Middle East is of most importance to the European Union as a source of oil imports. Only the United Kingdom had significant oil supplies of its own, and even for it, North Sea production has gradually declined as reserves became depleted. In contrast Saudi Arabia has sufficient reserves for over 80 years of production at current levels, and Iran sufficient reserves for 50 years of production. The European Union accounts for almost 18 per cent of total world oil consumption, but less than 1 per cent of world production. In contrast the countries of the Middle East account for over one-third of world oil production, and over two-thirds of reserves, but a mere 10 per cent of global consumption. Middle Eastern gas supplies are also of importance to Europe, especially those from Iran and Algeria, which have the second and fourth highest reserves in the world respectively, Russia and Qatar being the other major suppliers. There is more gas than oil in the North Sea, but reserves within the European Union's continental shelf only account for 3 per cent of the world total compared to one-third of the total for the Middle East.

These figures show how dependent the European Union is on Middle East energy supplies, and how vulnerable to any supply disruption. The events of 1973–74, and the further oil price rises in 1979 following the Iranian revolution highlighted this dependence and taught the countries of the European Union a lesson. Nevertheless there was no coherent energy policy at the European level, apart from restrictions on national energy subsidies, and the policies inherited from the European Coal and Steel Community which has been phased out. It is at the national level that policy shifts have occurred. Rather than shield consumers from the effects of rising oil prices in the 1970s and early 1980s, European governments raised their own taxes on oil and petroleum products. This encouraged the development of efficient engines, and replacement purchase of more modern vehicles by private motorists and road haulage companies. At the same time other fuels were substituted for oil for heating purposes, although gas, the preferred alternative, may increase long-term vulnerability to Russian and Middle Eastern suppliers as North Sea reserves become exhausted. The French embarked on an ambitious nuclear energy programme, and by the mid 1990s obtained over four-fifths of their electricity from nuclear stations.

As a consequence, oil consumption in the major countries of the European Union steadied or actually fell for most of the 1980s and 1990s, and imports from the Middle East declined significantly in volume terms. China and Japan are much larger purchasers of Middle East oil than the European Union, and the newly industrialising countries of South and South East Asia have also become more important purchasers. With the fall in nominal oil prices from the peak of over $36 per barrel in 1980 to under $13 in 1986, and their subsequent fluctuation in the $16 to $20 range until the 1990s, the European Union has enjoyed massive savings on its oil import bill. These were of course eliminated during the last decade as oil prices rose to more than $100 per barrel, but allowing for inflation and the reduced value of the US dollar, oil prices were no higher in 2012 than they had been in the immediate aftermath of the Iranian revolution. As a result the European Union still enjoys a healthy trade surplus with Saudi Arabia of over $9 billion, while the United States has a deficit with the Kingdom. Libya is the only major oil producing nation that still maintains a surplus in its trade with the European Union, amounting to almost $18 billion annually.

There are of course no European tariffs or quotas on oil or gas imports, but tariffs are levied on petrochemical products. This has caused considerable controversy in the Gulf, especially as Saudi Arabia has aimed at becoming a major exporter of petrochemicals in an attempt to increase local value added.[21] The major concern for the Gulf States was the 13.5 per cent tariff which the European Union levied on Saudi Arabian petrochemicals to protect the industry in Europe and allow time for adjustment. Many rounds of talks between European Community and Gulf Co-operation Council officials have failed to resolve the issues, but there has been some movement with around 10 per cent of the exports supplied by the Saudi Basic Industries Corporation allowed in without tariff protection. On the Gulf side there is the recognition that tariffs are preferable to outright quotas, as at least there is no maximum placed on sales of petrochemicals. On the European side the allegation is still made that Saudi Arabia subsidises its methanol and ethylene production by pricing the gas inputs at below local market levels, and below the world market prices paid by European oil and chemical companies.[22]

## Foreign receipts and payments for commercial services

As economies develop, commercial services become more significant, notably earnings from banking and other financial activity, transportation services, tourism, health, education and professional activities, including information technology and consulting. Although services make up 60 per cent of world production, they only account for 20 per cent of world trade.[23] In the case of the Middle East the share of services is even less, at below 10 per cent.

Turkey is the major supplier of commercial services in the region, as Table 8.5 shows, with tourist earnings, oil pipeline revenues and transport services accounting for much of the total. Israel, despite the relatively small size of its economy, is a major provider of commercial services, tourism, information technology and scientific consultancy. In the case of Egypt the major source of services revenues are Suez Canal transit fees, earnings from the Suez–Mediterranean pipeline and tourist earnings. There is much potential for media earnings from television programmes and films, as well as Arabic software applications, given the significance of the country in the Arab world. Arabic media earnings are also significant in the case of Lebanon, but financial services have never regained their pre-civil war status, as discussed in Chapter 5.

*Table 8.5* Leading Middle East earnings from commercial services

| Global rank | Country | Value, $ billion | Share, % |
| --- | --- | --- | --- |
| 16 | Turkey | 33 | 1.2 |
| 20 | Israel | 25 | 0.9 |
| 21 | Egypt | 25 | 0.8 |
| 25 | Lebanon | 15 | 0.5 |
| 29 | Morocco | 12 | 0.4 |
| 31 | UAE | 11 | 0.4 |
| 33 | Saudi Arabia | 10 | 0.4 |
| 36 | Iran | 8 | 0.3 |
| 38 | Kuwait | 7 | 0.2 |
| 40 | Syria | 5 | 0.2 |

Source: World Trade Organization, Geneva, 2011

*Table 8.6* Leading Middle East payments for commercial services

| Global rank | Country | Value, $ billion | Share, % |
| --- | --- | --- | --- |
| 11 | Saudi Arabia | 51 | 1.9 |
| 16 | UAE | 41 | 1.5 |
| 23 | Iran | 19 | 0.7 |
| 24 | Turkey | 18 | 0.7 |
| 18 | Israel | 18 | 0.7 |
| 29 | Egypt | 13 | 0.5 |
| 30 | Lebanon | 13 | 0.5 |
| 32 | Kuwait | 12 | 0.4 |
| 34 | Algeria | 11 | 0.4 |

Source: World Trade Organization, Geneva, 2011

The UAE is a services hub, but much of the activity is recorded as re-exports rather than as commercial services.

Most countries in the Middle East have deficits for commercial services, with payments greatly exceeding receipts, as shown in Table 8.6. The exceptions are Israel and Egypt, which maintain surpluses, largely reflecting the nature of their services earnings, as already discussed. The largest spending on commercial services is Saudi Arabia, reflecting the size of its economy. Its commercial services deficit exceeds $40 billion annually, largely reflecting the relative underdevelopment of its commercial services sector. The UAE is also a major spender on commercial services, although its earnings are slightly higher than those of Saudi Arabia, largely a result of Dubai's significance as a hub for commercial services.

## Arab economic integration

Much of the Middle East was part of the Ottoman Empire, but long before the collapse of the Empire, penetration by the European powers had undermined local economic linkages. Trade as a consequence was oriented towards

Europe from the nineteenth century onward, and it was only after the retreat of Britain and France from the region that there was a renewed interest in regional links. These were pan-Arab, however, rather than encompassing Turkey or even Iran, though Iran has its own links with the Arab oil-exporting countries through OPEC, and both it and Turkey are represented in the Organisation of Islamic Cooperation COI, which created the Islamic Development Bank as an instrument to promote Muslim economic cooperation. Only Israel is excluded from regional forums, as an artificial state created by outside powers.

Attempts at Arab economic cooperation date from as early as 1950 when the Arab Joint Defence and Economic Co-operation Agreement was signed under the auspicious of the Arab League.[24] Multilateral agreement was reached on the regulation of transit trade in 1953, but in practice this failed to amount to much, as overland links from the most populous Arab state, Egypt, would have to transit through the state of Israel. It was subject to a trade boycott by the Arab states, but this hurt all parties, and not only Israel.

The most ambitious attempt at Arab economic cooperation was instigated by Nasser in 1958 with the founding of the United Arab Republic. With the two major participants, Syria and Egypt, separated geographically by Israel, it never stood much chance of success.[25] Then there was the Arab Common Market agreement of 1964 between Jordan, Iraq, Syria and Egypt.[26] The agreement was politically motivated by the desire for pan-Arab cooperation, but the model adopted was inspired by the early success of the economic integration efforts of the original six members of the European Economic Community. This was ambitious on paper, but never really took off, and again it was the Israeli factor that damaged the agreement, as Egypt was virtually suspended after the Camp David accords. Jordan did, however, benefit considerably from the arrangement, as Arab trade was significant for its economy, especially the small business sector, which served the Iraqi market as well as Jordan. There can be little doubt that Jordan, because of its small size, has much to gain from regional efforts for economic cooperation, although trade volumes with Iraq have proved disappointing since the overthrow of Saddam Hussein.

It is at the sub-regional level that economic links have been developed most fully, notably through the Gulf Co-operation Council (GCC). Although this failed as a defensive body to prevent the Gulf War, and there is little prospect of it acting as a coherent military counterweight to Iran, as an economic alliance it has achieved some success. Like the European Union, the GCC states allow free labour mobility of their own nationals between member states, which facilitated the exodus of Kuwaitis after the Iraqi invasion. Capital movements are unregulated, and Bahrain is allowed to function as an offshore financial centre for the Arabian Peninsula states, which encourages its orientation to Saudi Arabia rather than Iran. Dubai, with its highly successful duty free zone at Jebel Ali, serves as a transit and warehouse centre for GCC trade, which has helped its re-exports to the Arab side of the Gulf rather than Iran. In the recent past, including the period after the Iranian revolution, Dubai served as a centre for illegal imports into the Islamic Republic. There has also been some more solidly based trade within the GCC, notably the export of oil pipes from Kuwait to neighbouring states, and construction materials from the factories on Saudi Arabia's Dammam industrial estate in Eastern Province.

The impact of such trade is limited, however, compared to that between European Union countries, and is hardly likely to cement regional bonds or even build significant bridges. Nevertheless, attempts at regional economic cooperation continue and even the World Bank has identified this as a promising area for investigation in its initiative to encourage economic research in the Middle East and North Africa. The fact that its forum, the body set up in June 1993 in Cairo to encourage such research, had to be renamed the "Forum for Economic Research in the Arab Countries, Iran and Turkey" says much about the aspirations for economic cooperation. The term "Middle East" was dropped, as this included Israel, which was not wanted as a participant. Many cooperation endeavours appear ill fated. The Arab Common Market effort was revived in 1989 with the Arab Co-operation Council encompassing Egypt, Iraq, Jordan and Yemen. This has a more limited agenda than Nasser's original project, as it only provided for joint industrial fairs in each of the capitals, a gradual reduction of some tariffs, and preferences for labour from the signatory states when work permits were issues.[27] The Gulf States refused to participate because of this, but the whole scheme was to fall apart in any case with the Iraqi invasion of Kuwait. Similarly the Arab Maghreb Union between Morocco, Algeria and Tunisia set up the same period appears to have become moribund following the Algerian election fiasco and the virtual undeclared war between the Algerian security forces and Islamist opposition.

## The extent of regional trade

The value of regional trade increased substantially during the 1970s and early 1980s from a mere $3.1 billion in 1973 to $27.5 billion by 1981, but subsequently declined even in nominal current price terms, the low of $12.6 billion being reached in 1986. Although there was some revival in the late 1980s to $20.5 billion, this was less than half the 1981 figure if real values are taken, allowing for inflation. The figures showed that there was, and to some extent remains, a close relationship between oil revenues and the value of regional trade. It was the oil price rises of 1973–74 and 1979 that resulted in at least a doubling of the value of trade between the Arab countries, and a similar pattern was repeated after 2002 when oil prices increased substantially with increased exports to China and India.

Only a small portion of intra-regional trade was accounted for by the increased payments by the Arab oil-importing states, as countries such as Jordan obtained their oil at concessional rates well below the international market price. Saudi Arabia and Kuwait became unwilling to supply oil to Jordan on such favourable terms in 1977 when evidence emerged that Jordanian petroleum dealers were reselling concessional oil imports at near the full world market price to third parties. It was this that prompted Jordan to turn to Iraq for its main oil supplies, largely through counter trade deals under which oil was swapped for Jordanian consumer non-durables such as detergents, soaps and medical supplies. Services were also included in the arrangements, notably road haulage and the use of the port of Aqaba. These "invisible earnings" were not included in the trade statistics, but they were to become an especially important lifeline for Iraq during its war with Iran.

A major factor promoting Arab trade was the financial transfers from the oil-exporting states to the poorer states. Remittances fuelled part of this, as did bilateral inter-governmental assistance. Palestinian and Jordanian migrant workers in the Gulf would continue to purchase some Jordanian goods even when they were resident in Saudi Arabia or Kuwait. The same applied to a lesser extent in the case of Egyptian and Lebanese migrants. There were also barter deals between Arab governments, such as those between Egypt, Iraq and Libya, under which Egyptian assembled cars were swapped for oil for Egypt's refineries. Of course such deals were relatively small in scale by international standards, and it is important to see Arab trade in context. The proportion of Arab trade in relation to the region's total international trade has fluctuated between 5.6 and 10.3 per cent over the 1973–2011 period, the more encouraging figures of over 8 per cent occurring during the most recent five years.[28] This proportion of intra-Arab trade is small, however, compared with the European Union, whose internal trade accounts for more than 55 per cent of the total.

The proportion of intra-Arab trade increased in the late 1980s partly as a result of the decline in the value of the oil trade of the region with the rest of the world. As well as this somewhat negative factor, there are more positive forces at work. A major factor in the past restraining Arab trade has been the severe foreign exchange restrictions and currency inconvertibility of the northern Arab states. No amount of institution building could compensate for this basic fact of life. There was little point in paying lip service to the concept of an Arab Common Market while at the same time not permitting the necessary payments for traded goods to be made. The GCC was arguably more successful as a trading entity because all the currencies of the Gulf oil-exporting countries are freely convertible.

The moves towards payments liberalisation in Egypt, Syria and Jordan, and the new emphasis on the market determining the exchange rates has arguably done more to promote Arab trade than all the over-ambitious institution building by governments in the past. It is through liberalisation that the climate is created for Arab merchants to get on with their trading. Ultimately it is the businessmen who have to do the dealing; government's role is to provide an environment where transactions costs are reduced as far as possible with the minimum of bureaucratic impediments to the movement of goods.

As in the European Union the proportion of regional trade is highest for the smaller countries with more restricted industrial bases and only limited possibilities for import substitution because of domestic market size.[29] Bahrain,

Jordan and Lebanon have the most highly integrated regional trading links. The figure for Lebanon is probably a substantial underestimate as official figures do not include illicit smuggling into Syria, which is extensive.

Egypt, Saudi Arabia and Libya appear to be the least regionally integrated countries.[30] In the case of the latter two states, regional trade is insignificant in comparison with oil trade with the outside world. Libya also suffers from its geographical position, as it is neither in the Maghreb or Mashreq. It could of course serve as a bridge between the western and eastern Arab world, but is regarded by most other Arab governments as being on the fringes in every sense of the word rather than being a core state, although with the ending of the Gaddafi regime perceptions are changing. Egypt's trade with other Arab states is also hindered by it being cut off from its eastern neighbours by Israel, as already indicated, and the poor communications infrastructure linking it with Jordan and Saudi Arabia.[31] Its protected industries overlap with those of other Arab countries rather than being complementary.[32] Competition from other producers within the region would be unwelcome to the Egyptian government if it resulted in state sector industries losing domestic market share, and perhaps collapsing with unfortunate consequences for employment. The Arab Spring has not changed domestic economic preoccupations or protectionist tendencies.

## Conclusions

Although commercial relations with Europe have declined in significance, there is little sign of any promising regional economic cohesion in the Middle East. Regional trade links remain weak, labour mobility is limited and governmental financial transfers have virtually ceased. Despite so called open door policies such as Egypt's *infitah*, it is by no means clear that the economies of the region are really opening up either internationally or even to their neighbours. The oil-exporting states of the Gulf are of course highly dependent on and integrated with the outside world, but they had become more isolated economically from their northern Arab neighbours and the Arab Spring has not helped. These northern Arab countries may well turn in on themselves in the coming years, as Iran did following its Islamic revolution. Such an orientation may bring greater economic hardship, but some at least within the region may feel this is a price worth paying in order to be able to exercise domestic fiscal, investment and trade policy choices. Those smaller countries such as Jordan, which can never be even partially self-sufficient, are likely to be in an especially difficult position. It is these countries that have most to gain from regional integration, and in its absence their economies will at best mark time.

# 9   The role of the state

In the Middle East the state is often portrayed as playing an all-powerful role, with most of the discussion on the economy focusing on government policy rather than businesses or entrepreneurs.[1] Theories on the role of the state were discussed in Chapter 2, drawing on the economic development and political economy literature. The aim in this chapter is to focus on the Middle Eastern experience, examining both those issues that are especially important in the region, such as the economic impact of military spending by the state, and issues where the region's experience parallels that of other developing countries, as in relation to the structural adjustment policies advocated by the International Monetary Fund, including economic liberalisation and privatisation. Issues of governance are also discussed, as good or poor practices in economic and financial management by the state also influence corporate governance.

## Governments and economic decision taking

Until the Arab Spring the notion of a strong, autocratic, centralised leadership prevailed in the economic as well as the political sphere. It is too early to say if this has changed. There is a "top man syndrome", with the emphasis on the personal ambitions of the ruler for the state. Economic policies were, and in many cases still are, enacted through ministerial decrees rather than a consultative process involving parliamentarians. The spending budgets of government departments are largely determined through bilateral bargaining between the minister responsible and the president's or prime minister's office. Cabinet discussions are a formalised ritual where opposing views are seldom expressed, and parliamentary approval a mere rubber stamping exercise. Decision making is always at the level of the boss, rather than as part of a team exercise, and the views of individual economic agents, the ordinary citizens, are seldom, if ever, actively sought.

Even prior to the Arab Spring it would have been misleading, however, to regard all regimes in the Middle East as dictatorial on economic matters and totally unresponsive to public opinion. Turkey is a parliamentary democracy where voters' opinions matter as much as in the West, and the Iranian and Egyptian parliaments do at least question government economic policy, even if they do not necessarily affect its outcome. For Israelis elections really matter, as indeed they do for the Palestinians in the occupied territories, even though they have had no opportunity to yield real economic power as yet. In Saudi Arabia there is a right to audiences with the ruler and ministers, although frank feelings are seldom expressed at these formalised gatherings. The basic difference between the Middle East and the West is not in the economic and political institutions, but in the social attitudes of the rulers and the ruled. It is not the legal detail and administrative framework which matters, but popular perceptions of government and what it can achieve in the spheres of economic policy and development.

One issue is why political power is sought in the first place, whether it is because of personal mission, an ambition to lead and direct, or simply as a way of ensuring that the ruling group obtains maximum economic benefit from the expropriation of the nation's resources.[2] Economic patronage is an important means of reinforcing political power; indeed, those who did not exercise such patronage would be regarded by many in the Middle East as too inept to rule. Where particular groups occupy powerful positions, such as the *Alawi* sect in Syria, which included President Assad, or the *al-Takriti* clan in Iraq, which included President Saddam Hussein, they expect a financial as well as a political pay-off. Governing parties worldwide represent particular interest groups, but in the Middle East those close to power are often small minorities, whose membership is closed. Membership of the *Baathist* political party may have been open to anyone in Syria and Iraq, but in the inner ruling circles it was family background and religious affiliation that really mattered, even with regimes that were nominally socialist and secular.

Labels can be deceptive in the Middle East and the actual workings of particular regimes often do not correspond to supposed allegiances. There is a considerable amount of misinterpretation, especially in the West, regarding the economic policy orientation of Middle Eastern states. Iran is depicted as a backward, theocratic state, with economic policies that belong in the medieval ages rather than in the modern world. Yet Ayatollah Khomeini was in many respects a reformer, propounding a reinterpretation of *Shi'ite* religious ideas, which helped make religion more popular than ever amongst the ordinary people. Listening to or playing music had been regarded as sinful by many in the religious establishment, but Khomeini removed this prohibition. Literature and the arts generally had become fossilised under the old religious establishment associated with Ayatollah Shari'it Madari, which had collaborated with the Shah's regime. As a result western secular cultural influences had grown. What Khomeni recognised was the need for Islam to modernise, to ensure its successful revival, and challenge secularist tendencies.

In the economic sphere Khomeni gave his blessing to a young, largely unknown economist, Abu'l Hasan Bani Sadr, who had spent many years working on a doctoral dissertation at the Sorbonne in Paris in the field of Islamic economics. Bani Sadr was elected President of the Islamic Republic in January 1980, and immediately started to remodel the economy along Islamic lines, instigating in particular the measures that were to cumulate in the Islamic banking legislation of 1983.[3] Bani Sadr championed the rights of poor Muslims and set a radical economic agenda for income and wealth redistribution. As a politically inexperienced academic he was to be out-manoeuvred by Beheshti, Khamenei and Rafsanjani, especially because of his inept handling of the American hostage crisis, when the embassy staffs in Tehran were imprisoned for 444 days. It was Rafsanjani, the protector of the *bazzari* interests, and a former merchant himself, who was to accede to power, despite Khomeni's initial support for Bani Sadr's more radical economic programme.

## Economic power and appropriation

In the Middle East, as in many other regions of the world, those who exercise the levers of economic power invariably use it to the advantage of themselves and the interest groups they represent. Under the Ottomans, landowners throughout the Empire paid taxes to the state and in return were given military protection.[4] Most paid willingly as the payment guaranteed their security of tenure and ensured that the landholders could benefit from the investment they made in the land. Tenants and agricultural labourers did not pay taxes, which meant that the Ottoman administration was not accountable to them for its actions. At least there was an economic link between a large number of Ottoman citizens, the landlords and the rulers of the Empire. The agricultural surplus was appropriated, but the government provided some service in return, and had a reasonably wide constituency to serve.

Oil has served to weaken the links between ruler and ruled in the Middle East, to an extent not found elsewhere. The revenue accrues to governments, who have the power to disburse it as they see fit. Until the 1950s no distinction was made between the personal finances of the ruling families and government finance. Oil revenues simply accrued to the ruling families and there were no formal structures to govern its disbursement, and indeed no systems of accountability or even the reporting of financial balances. Formal government structures were gradually introduced, and the ministries expanded considerably in terms of numbers of civil servants, but the ministers themselves remained members of the ruling families or closely associated with the royals. This situation still prevails, with some notable exceptions such as the Saudi Arabian oil ministers from the time of Sheikh Yamani onward. Such a crucial position required a person with considerable ability, not merely the right connections; a fact that was recognised at an early stage by the Saudi Arabian King.

In the Arabian Peninsula the main constituency outside the ruling families is the merchants. There are, of course, merchant princes within the ruling families.[5] Most of the richer merchants have acquired their fortunes by having agencies or franchises to act as exclusive distributors of imports from Asia and Europe. This makes them opposed to all but minimum import duties and against constraints on trade such as quotas, unless they are running import-substitution ventures themselves. The merchants favour a high level of government spending financed from oil revenue, as this keeps the wheels of domestic trade and commerce turning to their financial advantage. There is also a willingness to see government employment expand because this boosts demand. The merchants even favour a relatively liberal policy on work permits as immigrant workers are also customers and their entry eases wage pressures in an otherwise tight labour market. This keeps the merchant's own business costs down, but deters local citizens from seeking private sector employment, especially as government employment means shorter hours and often much higher remuneration. However, all too often the local merchants have little interest in employing their fellow citizens.

Governments that are forced to rely on their own citizens for tax revenues are inevitably more accountable to them than those that do not. In the United States in the eighteenth century a political slogan was "No taxation without representation". Although such views have long been out of fashion in the West, especially amongst the thinkers of the left, they may explain the lack of political accountability by many governments in the Middle East. In the oil-exporting states of the Gulf there is no income tax because oil provides most of the fiscal revenue, and in these circumstances it is more difficult to make a case for representative government and public expenditure accountability. Oil has not only weakened the link between governments and peoples in the OPEC states of the Middle East, but also freed governments from account-ability to their own people in some of the other states of the region. Syria, Jordan and Egypt all received substantial bilateral aid from Saudi Arabia and the other Gulf states, which reduced domestic fiscal pressures. In the case of Egypt the Camp David Accords and the peace treaty with Israel resulted in the curtailment of such assistance, but then the United States stepped in with substantial help, arguably making the Sadat and Mubarak governments more accountable to Washington than to ordinary Egyptians.

Not only were states "corrupted", but arguably so were groups such as the Palestinian leadership who could rely on backing from the Gulf states rather than contributions from their own people. Once these contributions stopped following the Gulf War the leaders of the Palestinian Liberation Organisation started to look around for alternative backing, and Hamas turned to Iran. The same applied to the various warring parties in Lebanon, whose reliance on different external financial backers tended to keep them in a state of mutual hostility, arguably prolonging the Civil War and making reconciliation more difficult. The collapse of the Lebanese currency following the conclusion of the war demonstrated just how significant these financial flows had become, as the war itself had kept the financing going and sustained the economy.

## The fiscal position

A major economic responsibility of any government is to manage its own finances, including the raising of funds to cover expenditure through taxation and borrowing. Clearly, spending cannot be fixed without reference to taxation and the borrowing capacity of governments, but in the Middle East, as with so much else, oil revenues and official inward flows have blurred the position. There has been more scope for government discretion over how much public spending to permit, and not merely the composition of the expenditure. For the oil exporting states the issue in the 1970s and early 1980s was to determine how much to spend in any one year and how much to set aside for future years or even future generations. Later in the 1980s and 1990s the position deteriorated significantly as oil revenues were considerably lower, but financial discipline was still not a virtue associated with Middle Eastern governments, even though there were moves to determine expenditure priorities in a more coherent fashion. Increasing oil revenues after 2001 reduced the need for financial discipline, and the reaction in the oil exporting countries to the Arab Spring was to increase substantially the salaries of local nationals working in the public sector, hardly a sustainable position in the long term.

Expenditure management remains a rather crude affair in the major oil-exporting states of the region, with the implementation of projects being slowed down or even halted in response to budgetary pressures. In some cases there has been simply delay and deferment of payments to foreign contractors for work already completed. As those tendering for contracts in the Middle East often build uncertainty premiums into their offers, it is ultimately the governments of the region themselves who have to pay the price for such discretion and ability to manoeuvre.

Government revenues and expenditure as a proportion of gross domestic product for the GCC countries is shown in Table 9.1. These figures illustrate the size of government and the extent of its involvement in the economy. It is appropriate to consider the countries of the GCC as a group, as four of the six have significant revenues from oil and gas, and the other two, Bahrain and Oman, have benefited from fiscal transfers from their more resource-rich

*Table 9.1* Government revenue and expenditure as a proportion of GDP in the GCC (per cent)

| Country | | 2005 | 2010 | 2012 | 2014 |
|---|---|---|---|---|---|
| Bahrain | Revenue | 32.4 | 24.3 | 25.9 | 23.6 |
| | Expenditure | 30.4 | 32.1 | 33.0 | 32.8 |
| Kuwait | Revenue | 59.6 | 60.7 | 60.0 | 57.8 |
| | Expenditure | 40.0 | 38.0 | 36.3 | 36.8 |
| Oman | Revenue | 46.4 | 40.0 | 45.3 | 41.0 |
| | Expenditure | 29.3 | 33.8 | 35.8 | 37.0 |
| Qatar | Revenue | 35.0 | 30.8 | 29.4 | 28.2 |
| | Expenditure | 24.6 | 28.2 | 25.7 | 26.8 |
| Saudi Arabia | Revenue | 46.4 | 40.0 | 45.3 | 41.0 |
| | Expenditure | 29.3 | 33.8 | 35.8 | 37.0 |
| UAE | Revenue | 38.6 | 28.3 | 32.0 | 30.7 |
| | Expenditure | 17.4 | 24.7 | 22.3 | 21.9 |

Source: IMF, *World Economic Outlook Database*, Washington, January 2012

neighbours, although not as much as they would like, and certainly well below the magnitude of fiscal transfers in the European Union from north to south. The consistency of the revenue and expenditure figures for each country over time is worth noting, indicating that in the GCC as elsewhere, fiscal adjustments take time. Kuwait has the highest relative level of both revenue and expenditure, the latter reflecting the generous welfare provision for all Kuwaiti citizens, which has been sustained over many decades. Qatar and the UAE have even more generous provision, but it costs less as the numbers of local citizens are much smaller. All the countries enjoy budgetary surpluses with the exception of Bahrain, but the surplus is reducing for Oman, which has few oil resources, and for Saudi Arabia, which has a much larger population and major social and economic challenges, with many citizens feeling that the state is not doing enough to support them.

The government revenue and expenditure position is very different for the northern Middle Eastern countries, as Table 9.2 shows. The Iraqi government spends more than the other countries relatively, but much of this has been on security, given the continuing lawlessness in the country. Nevertheless, expenditure is being curtailed as the situation gradually improves and a fiscal surplus is predicted for 2014. The Israeli government also plays a major role in the economy despite years of encouraging the private sector, partly reflecting the continued burden of security expenditure. With its oil revenues Iran might be expected to run a substantial budget surplus but as the figures show this is not the case, reflecting economic mismanagement and distorted spending priorities, not least the nuclear programme. Turkey in contrast is much better managed, with the fiscal position tightly controlled. Egypt, Jordan and Syria face chronic fiscal deficits, which are unlikely to improve.

*Table 9.2* Government revenue and expenditure as a proportion of GDP in the northern Middle East (per cent)

| Country | | 2005 | 2010 | 2012 | 2014 |
|---|---|---|---|---|---|
| Egypt | Revenue | 27.7 | 25.1 | 25.4 | 27.5 |
| | Expenditure | 35.5 | 33.4 | 35.5 | 34.8 |
| Iran | Revenue | 23.5 | 23.4 | 24.2 | 23.5 |
| | Expenditure | 24.5 | 21.7 | 23.2 | 22.8 |
| Iraq | Revenue | 85.7 | 75.6 | 73.0 | 74.3 |
| | Expenditure | 87.1 | 84.7 | 80.9 | 62.2 |
| Israel | Revenue | 41.8 | 40.0 | 41.8 | 42.3 |
| | Expenditure | 44.6 | 44.1 | 44.0 | 43.5 |
| Jordan | Revenue | 30.1. | 24.8 | 24.4 | 24.3 |
| | Expenditure | 34.3 | 30.2 | 30.4 | 29.3 |
| Syria | Revenue | 20.9 | 21.8 | 21.3 | 22.1 |
| | Expenditure | 22.9 | 26.8 | 30.3 | 30.6 |
| Turkey | Revenue | 31.4 | 32.7 | 33.6 | 33.0 |
| | Expenditure | 33.8 | 35.5 | 34.6 | 33.9 |

Source: IMF, *World Economic Outlook Database*, Washington, January 2012

## The military expenditure priority

The Middle East has been a region of conflict throughout the last seventy years. The Arab–Israeli conflict has inflicted heavy economic costs on the region since 1948, as although the 1948, 1956, 1967 and 1973 wars were short-lived, each distorted expenditure decisions for years before and after. The *intifadah* or uprising in the Occupied Territories from 1988 onwards imposed large security costs on Israel, and severely disrupted economic activity in the West Bank and Gaza. The same applied in the case of the civil war in Lebanon from 1974 onwards, and the Israeli occupation of southern Lebanon after 1983. In addition to those conflicts directly involving Israel there have also been the Iraq–Iran War of the 1980s, the Gulf War in 1991, the invasion of Iraq, civil war in Sudan and the eventual division of the country in 2011, and the turmoil associated with and following the Arab Spring, notably in Libya, Syria and Yemen where there was much bloodshed and economic disruption. This list is by no means exhaustive, as there have also been numerous disputes with the potential for conflict, such as the contested sovereignty of three Gulf islands, Abu Musa, Greater Tunb and Lesser Tunb, by the UAE and Iran. The list of conflicts goes on and on, with new sources of differences arising as some of the old conflicts get resolved.

Apart from the human cost of the many conflicts, which are not really measurable, there are also the potentially quantifiable economic costs.[6] Government spending on armaments has an opportunity cost for civilian development expenditure, which as a consequence is curtailed. Investment spending on infrastructure and industrial support suffers, as does recurrent expenditure on education and health that can be so vital for human resource development.[7]

Military spending as a proportion of GDP in the Middle East is shown in Table 9.3. The 1990 figure for Kuwait was distorted by the need to rebuild its own military capability in the aftermath of the invasion by Iraq and the subsequent liberation, and more significantly by the funds paid to the governments of the allied military forces who undertook the liberation. It is Saudi Arabia

*Table 9.3* Military expenditure in the Middle East as a proportion of GDP (per cent)

| Country | 1990 | 2000 | 2009 |
|---|---|---|---|
| Bahrain | 4.8 | 4.0 | 3.7 |
| Egypt | 4.7 | 3.2 | 2.1 |
| Iran | 2.0 | 3.7 | 1.8 |
| Israel | 12.5 | 7.8 | 6.3 |
| Jordan | 7.8 | 6.3 | 6.1 |
| Kuwait | 48.5 | 7.2 | 4.4 |
| Oman | 16.5 | 10.8 | 9.7 |
| Saudi Arabia | 14.0 | 10.6 | 11.2 |
| Syria | 6.4 | 5.5 | 4.0 |
| Turkey | 3.5 | 3.7 | 2.7 |

Source: Stockholm International Peace Research Institute, *Military Spending Database*, 2011

and Oman who are the largest relative military spenders, partly because of expensive purchases of aircraft such as the Typhoon. However, a significant part of the Saudi Arabian military budget covers items such as hospital provision and bloated administrative expenditure. In some respects much of the defence budget can be considered a form of welfare expenditure. This also applies in Egypt, but its defence budget is relatively smaller, although this excludes assistance from the United States exceeding one billion dollars annually. It is notable, however, that defence spending as a proportion of GDP has been falling throughout the region, with the most marked declines in Israel and Egypt, reflecting a peace dividend despite some continued hostile rhetoric.

It is informative to consider the absolute amounts of military spending, as this shows the regional ranking. As Table 9.4 shows, Saudi Arabia has long been the leading spender and its military budget has increased enormously in recent years. Turkey was the second largest spender in 2000 and 2010, followed by Israel. Expenditure by other countries is considerably smaller, but it is interesting to note that in 2010 both Kuwait and Oman spent more than Egypt, a much larger and more populous country, and which under Nasser projected itself as the major military power in the Arab world, even though the reality proved very different in the 1967 war.

If the Middle East moves into a more peaceful period of its history, it will be interesting to see if there is a real "peace dividend" similar to that which has benefited the former belligerents in the Cold War. Given Egyptian defence spending trends since the signing of its peace treaty with Israel, the omens are better than might have been expected, but a more generalised settlement of the Arab–Israeli conflict may bring greater gains.[8] As already indicated, the Israeli figure for defence expenditure in relation to total government spending is falling, but from a very high base. Yet these still high figures are an underestimate of the full resource costs, as the wages bill of a largely conscript army does not take account of the fact that the men involved, and in the case of Israel also the women, could be more productively employed elsewhere in the economy.

*Table 9.4* Military expenditure in the Middle East ($ million)

|              | 1990   | 2000   | 2010   |
|--------------|--------|--------|--------|
| Bahrain      | 271    | 378    | 731    |
| Egypt        | 3,796  | 3,900  | 3,914  |
| Iran         | 2,279  | 7,816  | N/A    |
| Israel       | 10,132 | 12,121 | 12,001 |
| Jordan       | 612    | 761    | 1,363  |
| Kuwait       | 15,422 | 3,906  | 4,411  |
| Oman         | 2,620  | 2,724  | 4,047  |
| Saudi Arabia | 22,256 | 24,714 | 45,245 |
| Syria        | 1,059  | 1,760  | 2,236  |
| Turkey       | 12,384 | 19,420 | 15,634 |

Source: Stockholm International Peace Research Institute, *Military Spending Database*, 2011

Even with low manpower costs in the armed services, most Middle Eastern states spend more on military salaries than on those for teachers or health personnel. In Jordan military expenditure is greater than the combined amounts for education and health. In troubled Iraq the comparable figure is over five times the education and health bill, a legacy of the Anglo-American occupation. In Iraq there are six military and security employees for every teacher and ten for every doctor.

Most military expenditure in the Middle East is on imported arms, as local defence industries, apart from that of Israel, have limited capabilities. Arms imports represent a huge foreign exchange burden and a serious leakage from the economies of the Middle East to defence equipment manufacturers in the West. Saudi Arabia and Iraq were by far the greatest spenders on arms imports over the period since 1990, with expenditure averaging over $2 billion a year. Turkey and Egypt each spend over $1 billion annually on arms imports, even though military supplies from the United States are often acquired at prices that do not reflect the full research and development costs of the equipment. Smaller, so-called frontline states in the conflict with Israel spend substantial amounts on arms imports, an annual average of $689 million for Syria and a surprisingly large $572 million in the case of Jordan.

Government spending on defence has created a local armaments industry in Israel that produces relatively sophisticated equipment, from missiles to fighter aircraft, usually adapted from the original American designs. Israel's defence and airspace industry undertakes some sub-contracting work for American companies, and has been successful in exporting cut price versions of United States equipment to developing countries in Africa and Latin America. Hence, in its case, there are certainly economic benefits from government spending on defence, with export penetration as well as local multiplier effects. Israel with its limited resources can never hope to be at the forefront of military technology, as brains are not a substitute for the money it takes to develop sophisticated defence equipment. However, Israel has benefited significantly from its close defence relationship with the United States, and there is much sharing of military technology.

Elsewhere in the Middle East offset contracts have been negotiated with western arms suppliers, notably in the case of Saudi Arabia. The Typhoon and earlier Tornado aircraft supplied by British Aerospace are maintained and serviced within Saudi Arabia rather than being flown back to the United Kingdom. Similar accords have been reached between Egypt and the United States for tanks, trainer aircraft and helicopters, with the western companies involved providing technical support. These deals are in the nature of import substitution ventures, with a high price being paid to obtain the offset work. Whether this is economically or financially justifiable must be open to serious question.

The other major benefit from the military spending has been skills acquisition, and arguably the dynamic benefits that come from nation building. In the case of a country such as the UAE, the armed services bring conscripts and professionals together from different sheikhdoms that in the past have had divergent loyalties.

Their cohesion into a fighting force to serve the whole country brings about a change of outlook, and supplants the narrow allegiance of the tribal group. The same applies in diverse and heterogeneous countries such as Saudi Arabia and Iran, where being a conscript is an educational experience in itself. Service personnel also learn useful skills, as the army cadet who learns to maintain and repair a tank today may be able to look after heavy goods vehicles tomorrow. Those who can manage computer guided weapons can apply their software applications skills in the civilian sector at a later date. It can of course be argued that such skill acquisition through military service is expensive and often irrelevant, but in a region such as the Middle East where a comparable level of civilian training may simply not be available, it may serve a useful purpose.

## The costs of conflict

Conflicts are far from over in the Middle East but in the years ahead civil strife within countries is likely to be the major security concern rather than wars between countries. Civil strife can be highly economically damaging if it is on the scale of the Lebanese or Syrian civil wars which resulted in a collapse in government control and near anarchy in some parts of the country, but this is unlikely in most Middle Eastern states. More probable are continuing terrorist incidents from groups such as the Kurds in Turkey, and Hamas and Hezbollah in Israel. Such incidents inflict economic costs, especially for soft targets such as the tourist industry, but they are unlikely to be serious impediments to development. Much better organised groups, such as ETA in Spain, the IRA in Britain and various extremist organisations in India, have been only able to inflict marginal economic damage, and have not had any significant impact on either industry or services. There is little reason to think that the experience in the Middle East will be any different, especially given the record to date.

It is clear from the events of the Arab Spring and the outcomes of the subsequent elections that many Muslims in the Middle East were dissatisfied with the secularist governments in the region, but few, and even fewer of the truly devout, saw terrorism against the state as the way forward. Most, being religious people, see provision of help for fellow Muslims as the best course of action, providing welfare systems for the poor who the state failed to look after, religious education, and financial services such as Islamic banks and investment companies. The aim was to win the hearts and minds of the masses through peaceful social and economic actions, and to teach by example. Some armed incidents have only been a reaction to terror by the state, rather than actions instigated by Muslim groups themselves. Democratic societies should welcome such peaceful challenges, which bring infusions of new ideas. It was in those Middle Eastern states where there was a lack of democracy, such as Assad's Syria or Gaddifi's Libya, which saw the Islamists as the greatest danger and pursued oppressive policies.

If peace does prevail between Israel and its neighbours, the economic situation in the Middle East heartland could be transformed. New infrastructure links could give Jordan direct access to the Mediterranean for its trade, Egypt could benefit from overland links with Syria, and Gaza could become a duty-free entrepôt centre. Regional complementaries could be harnessed for the common good, with, for example, Israeli irrigation expertise combined with Gulf capital to introduce different types of crop production with more market appeal. The tourist potential of the Eliat and Aqaba area could be developed jointly, making the region much more attractive for the overseas visitor. Palestinians could develop their financial institutions, such as the Arab Bank, to become significant regional and perhaps even international enterprises.

All this could give a much more balanced development from a sounder base than the oil boom of the 1970s. It may be an exaggeration to speak of the effects of a "peace boom" surpassing those of the oil boom, but there is little doubt that the region has enormous potential. By removing the restraints on trade that have existed ever since the state of Israel was created in the Middle Eastern heartland, and by shifting human energies in a more positive direction, there is much that can be achieved in the coming years and decades. The Arab Spring should not be seen as a threat to Israel, indeed it should be welcomed as an opportunity for renewal even if dialogue is unlikely in the short term.

## Development planning

Governments have asserted their control over Middle Eastern economies as much through development planning as through the annual fiscal rounds. Nevertheless development planning has been as unsuccessful in the Middle East as in other parts of the Third World, and there has been much questioning in recent years of its usefulness, although planning bureaucracies continue to exist. In the case of the Middle East the exclusion of military expenditure from development planning may be one factor explaining the poor results, especially given the scale of defence budgets. Most governments in the region continue to draft five-year development plans, however, although how seriously they are treated by the key decision makers varies considerably from country to country.

The oil exporting countries tended to view development plans as a shopping list. Each was a statement of government intentions for the coming five-year period, and a listing of priorities. In so far as the compiling and publication of this information prompted public discussion of economic policy it served a useful purposes, but unfortunately in the Middle East planning processes were unnecessarily secretive and there was little popular consultation. In the Far East governments listen to industrialists, entrepreneurs and bankers and then draw up economic policies to serve these interests. In the Middle East ministers and bureaucrats have tended to draw up the plans, and then present them to the country as a fait accompli. The planning documents were seen as directives, to be enforced through administrative controls that owed their legitimacy to the plans themselves. Plans tended to be regarded as ends rather than means by those charged with their implementation, which encouraged inflexible attitudes rather than the flexibility that was arguably needed as resources varied with the state of the international oil market.

Most development plans in the Middle East are indicative, which means that they itemise state spending targets in broad categories, and set targets which it is hoped the private sector may attain. With more stress on private investment in recent years the government's ability to meet targets is reduced, but increased reliance on the private sector reflects partly changing ideology, but more importantly, constraints brought about by the relative reduction in oil revenues and financial inflows. The most ambitious comprehensive planning in the past was attempted by Syria and Algeria, both of which constructed elaborate input–output models for their economies, with estimates of inter- and intra-sectorial linkages. These models drew to some extent on Soviet planning methods, but also followed input–output methods pioneered by the development economist, Jan Tinbergen.[9] The reality, however, seldom matched the plans, and in practice the planners became very isolated from what was happening in the real economy. In Iraq there were also some attempts at comprehensive planning, but the requirements of civilian investment were always treated as secondary to the needs of the military by the country's rulers.[10]

The more modern planning techniques such as cost benefit analysis have been largely neglected by governments in the region, although international agencies have applied such techniques to particular projects. It was the World Bank's cost benefit appraisal of the Aswan high dam in Egypt in the 1950s that made it decide not to fund the scheme, which opened the door to the Soviet Union to proceed instead.[11] The concern of the nationalist governments of the 1950s and 1960s in the region was with production rather than prices. Governments controlled prices for social objectives, and tried to restrain market forces rather than harnessing them to promote development. Basic foodstuffs were subsidised to help the urban poor, and energy was subsidised to promote industrial development. Exchange rates were distorted by foreign exchange and import controls in the more populous states and non oil exporting countries, but the calculation of shadow prices was an exercise undertaken by academic economists, not those in government or the planning agencies.

In other words, prices as a means of achieving planning objectives were ignored in favour of the quantitative rationing of resources by the state. This has had the same unfortunate consequences for the Middle East as for the states of Eastern Europe. Planning has become out of fashion and somewhat discredited, although the ministries remain. Unfortunately some of the beneficial features of planning, such as optimisation techniques and social accounting, have never really been tried in the region, and seem likely to remain untested as governments move from one extreme position to another, following international fashion rather than addressing domestic realities.

## Economic liberalisation and structural adjustment

Egypt, Jordan, Morocco and Tunisia have to varying degrees implemented the classic type of economic liberalisation and structural adjustment policy much favoured by the International Monetary Fund.[12] Often governments have been obliged to adopt such policies as a condition of receiving IMF balance of payment funding assistance. Multinational banks and western creditors have frequently stressed that IMF structural adjustment programmes should be in place, so that the countries can more easily meet their payments obligations, and secure access to international commercial credits for trade finance on more favourable terms.

The IMF policies have often proved deeply unpopular, as governments have been obliged to exercise fiscal restraint, curtail subsidies on fuel and foodstuffs, and charge higher, and supposedly more economic prices for basic services such as electricity and domestic water. The rationale behind such policies has been the belief that sound fiscal conditions are a necessary precondition for development, and that they will result in a more favourable economic climate in which the private sector should flourish. The aim is to remove the price distortions that inevitably arise with subsidies, so that markets can function more efficiently, and to reduce government intervention in economic activity in the long run so that the private sector will not be "crowded out" by the state.

There are two major sets of issues that arise from such policies. First, are they an infringement of economic sovereignty, and does it mean that governments such as those in Egypt were mere captives of the IMF, at least in their economic policy marking? Second, does the economic "medicine" actually work, and are the assumptions underlying such policies actually relevant to the economic conditions in the Middle East? One criticism of the IMF and to a lesser extent the World Bank is that they have a standard set of policy prescriptions reflecting the fashion for emphasising the need to overcome supply side rigidities by some western economists. Are supply side rigidities a major problem in the Middle East, and has excessive government intervention actually crippled enterprise and the private sector more generally?

It has been arguably convenient for some Middle Eastern governments to blame the IMF for their economic predicament, as it deflects some of the popular criticism that inevitably arises with economic austerity measures. The IMF has in any case learnt from its early mistakes, and there is a desire not to undermine governments which it believes offers the best hope for reform in the long run, by forcing them to undertake unpopular short run panic measures. The food riots in 1977 in Cairo were something of a turning point not only for the Sadat government, but also for IMF officials, who saw the folly of trying to change too much too quickly. The governments under Mubarak were much more cautious in their approach to reform, but they still kept the support of the IMF until their demise with the Arab Spring of 2011.

In Turkey the major reforms followed the 1980 coup, and it could be argued that the technocrats under Ozal could not have implemented the structural adjustment measures had it not been for the strong backing of the military, and the suppression of any dissent from those on the left. As the 1980s advanced the austerity measures were relaxed, but the substantial improvement in the balance of trade, and the rise in Turkish exports, was seen as proof that the policy worked. It can be argued that it was not a powerful IMF, but rather a strong Turkish government, that brought about these favourable results. Indeed it was only when the discipline was relaxed in the late 1980s that inflationary problems returned, and the balance of trade went back into substantial deficit.

Iran has been attempting to introduce structural adjustment measures of its own during the 1990s, independently of the IMF, but arguably much in line with what it recommends, demonstrating that there is not necessarily a conflict between the position of Islamists and the conventional economic wisdom of international institutions. The currency was allowed to float down in response to market pressures, which has resulted in a rise of non-oil exports from $1 to $5 billion over the 1990–95 period. Imports have been allocated according to ability to pay, rather than by the planners, and the law on foreign investment was changed to allow multinational companies to have a majority share holding in Iranian joint ventures. Although relations with the West were difficult, the country looked for partners elsewhere.[13] Unfortunately the impact of sanctions, and economic mismanagement, especially under President Mahmoud Ahmedinajad, has resulted in the gains from the earlier measures being reversed and a marked economic deterioration.

The major criticism of structural adjustment programmes is that they can worsen income distribution, and increase the difficulties of the very poor as the price of basic commodities rises. In Egypt real earnings fell by 10 per cent over the 1987–90 period, and those of employees in the state sector decreased by a quarter as inflation rose towards 20 per cent. In Turkey real earnings fell by almost 40 per cent over the 1979–86 period, although since then they have risen as economic discipline has been relaxed. Critics of structural adjustment argue that the greater international competitiveness is achieved at enormous social cost. In Egypt and Algeria one-quarter of the population continues to live in what the United Nations development programme defines as absolute poverty. The proportion in Tunisia, which the IMF often regards as an economic success, had risen to 17 per cent before the revolution. The numbers in absolute poverty are also rising in Iran, with the proportion exceeding 30 per cent, to some extent a result of rapid population growth amongst the poor, but also reflecting recent economic policy changes that have taken the inflation rate to 21 per cent.

## Nationalisation and privatisation

The twentieth century has witnessed much debate over state ownership of productive resources, with socialists urging the state to take control of the commanding heights of the economy in order to protect the workers from exploitation by monopoly capitalism, while those on the political right urged governments to restrict their activities, to free business from damaging inter-ference by incompetent, and sometimes even corrupt, bureaucrats. This debate has been echoed in the Middle East, with state ownership of economic resources increasing over the 1920–70 period and then retreating as nationalisation gave way to moves towards privatisation.

Arguments over the control of productive resources have a long history in the Middle East, and it would be a mistake to view governments in the region as merely copying policies being pursued elsewhere. Economists in the region are of course aware of policy changes in Europe and North America, and inter-national bodies such as the IMF and World Bank have in recent years favoured liberalisation and the encouragement of the private sector. Govern-ments in the Middle East have always favoured the control of strategic resources, however, so that internal conflicts between private parties were avoided, and the over ambitious did not harm the interests of their neighbours. Although land ownership has usually been private in the Middle East, water resources, which are arguably more vital, have always been controlled by the state. Historical records indicate that there was government management of water resources in ancient Egypt and Mesopotamia; indeed the Pharaohs derived much of their economic power from their ability to ration water supplies to particular users.

Against this background it is scarcely surprising that Nasser wanted to nationalise the Suez Canal in 1956, taking control from the Anglo-French company that had hitherto collected and disbursed the revenues, mostly to its own shareholders in Europe. Nasser also took control of other foreign interests in the country, notably the banking system, which was also controlled by French and British capital. The textile mills, which were founded by local merchants and landlords in the 1920s and 1930s, were also nationalised under Nasser, as he distrusted the owners, and was concerned that they were sending the profits abroad, rather than reinvesting in Egypt. Some were of course doing this because of their lack of confidence in Nasser, and their desire to have assets abroad as a safeguard in case they had to leave if their situation became difficult.

In Turkey and Iran from the 1920s, and in the Gulf from the 1970s, the state took the lead in heavy industrialisation largely because the private sector was both unable and unwilling to invest in such ventures. It was not a ques-tion of taking over existing assets by the state, but rather the finance of new investment where domestic private capital markets were small or non-existent. The industries involved included steel production, oil refining, petrochemicals, vehicle assembly and the servicing of military supplies.

There is little doubt that most of the heavy industries in the Middle East would not have been developed without state intervention, although just how beneficial these industries have been is open to debate. Where industries continue to need subsidised inputs for their survival they are arguably more of an economic burden than an asset. Much of the steel industry in the Middle East uses old technology, which causes considerable pollution. In many respects it is in an even worse state than the plants in Eastern Europe which in many cases have been closed, yet there would be considerable political opposition if there were similar closures in the Middle East, as these plants are still regarded by many as symbols of the region's industrial progress. It is only in the Gulf, where steel mills using modern gas reduction techniques have been built, that the industry is really viable.

Commercial viability has become more of an issue in recent years with the moves towards economic liberalism and the privatisation of state owned assets. Privatisation is proceeding very slowly in the Middle East, but liberalisation policies are much more advanced. The latter includes the phasing out of state subsidies on foodstuffs, energy and industrial inputs, and the reduction and abolition of foreign exchange controls, including multiple exchange rate arrangements. Egypt moved in this direction in 1989, and in 1993 Iran abolished its three tiered exchange rate system that discriminated in favour of imports of capital equipment and industrial inputs with a single floating rate determined by market forces.[14] Turkey had already followed this course a decade earlier. Despite payments liberalisation for traded goods, some controls still remain on capital transfers in all Middle Eastern states, apart from those in the Gulf. Foreign investment is actively encouraged, however, with free repatriation of profits. Even the former Marxist state, South Yemen, now unified with the North, was trying to encourage foreign direct investment in a new duty free zone established at the port of Aden. It appears that the new economic liberalism was appearing in some of the most unlikely places, although this may have been the last ploy of a dying regime.

Western multinational companies remain cautious over Middle Eastern investment, and continue to be wary of political risk. As most regimes in the Middle East lasted considerably longer than those in the democratic West, it is by no means clear that such fears were justified. The concern, however, was that change would be violent, and that there could be abrupt policy reversals that could threaten and undermine businesses, especially those under foreign control. The Arab Spring has shown that many of these concerns were indeed justified. There has been less direct investment by multinationals in the Middle East than in any other region of the Third World apart from sub-Saharan Africa. The Japanese multinationals are especially notable by their absence, as although these firms are leading suppliers of exports to the region, they appear reluctant to commit themselves to any long-term manufacturing ventures. Their only significant investments in recent years have been with the Saudi Arabian Basic Industries Corporation (SABIC), which has built petrochemical and fertiliser plants. Even in this case the foreign companies tried to keep their joint venture stakes to the minimum required to stay in the projects.

If privatisation measures were broadly adopted and implemented, this would undoubtedly encourage foreign direct investment, but this still seems a distant prospect. Saudi Arabia has sold one-quarter of the state share in SABIC to private local investors but there is a reluctance to sell the remainder in view of the strategic importance of the company and its contribution to government revenue. Egypt embarked on a very cautious privatisation programme involving medium sized companies in fields such as food processing, textiles and construction supplies as well as a few leading hotels.[15] Major state industries such as steel making are excluded on strategic grounds, as is Egyptair, the Egyptian state airline, and the privatisation of the banks has proceeded very slowly. In the case of the state manufacturing facilities it is doubtful if buyers could be found in any case, unless debts were written off and losses underpinned. The state airline could be a more promising possibility, as the Jordanian experience with selling off Alia, the Royal Jordanian Airline, showed.

None of the imaginative privatisation schemes attempted in Eastern Europe or the former Soviet Union have been tried in the Middle East. Privatisation may only result in industries been sold off to a few already wealthy speculative investors rather than any mass subscription to share ownership. A voucher system whereby purchase certificates are distributed to the entire adult population, as in the Czech Republic, could be one answer. It would not bring any revenue to Middle Eastern governments, but it would ensure that the relative value of different enterprises was established, and it would give the ordinary citizens the means to participate directly in financial markets and the commanding heights of the economy. Popular capitalism could deliver for the region the economic growth that eluded past socialist planners.

## Development and democracy

The link between development and democracy is a much debated issue by political scientists and those concerned with international relations, but perhaps given less attention by economists.[16] Which comes first is far from clear, as, for example, in much of Eastern Europe political reform came before economic development, while in China the reverse seems to be the case. Has the lack of democracy in most of the Middle East and the autocratic style of government been an impediment to development or actually aided the process?[17]

There are of course disadvantages if decision making is concentrated in just a few hands, with all directions from the top down. In Middle East politics, and indeed business, power is concentrated at the top, and there is a lack of delegation of decision making. This may mean that economic policy makers and top businessmen have simply too many minor decisions to make, and progress gets thwarted by delays because those with the power get overwhelmed. The absence of popular participation means that there are fewer economic agents to harness, and the team spirit gets lost. On the other hand there are fewer problems of coordination and delays in trying to reach agreement. Popular consultation can often result in inertia, as the planning processes over environmentally sensitive schemes in Europe illustrate. Such problems are seldom encountered in the Middle East.

In the Middle East governments are often more concerned with power politics and international relations than domestic economic concerns. The ordinary people are very interested in the basic economic developments affecting their own lives, but as politicians come from the wealthier classes they are somewhat removed from such mundane concerns. In Egypt it was the rise in the price of bread in 1977 that brought anti-government rioting to the streets of every major city in the country, but there were no popular demonstrations against Sadat's peace treaty with Israel, a source of deep concern to many in the political class. Despite such events government complacency over economic issues remains. The economy was regarded as safe, almost non-controversial, while the real heat of political debate was reserved over issues such as relations with the western powers, inter-Arab disputes, and differences with Iran and how to deal with the Israelis.

There is little real economic democracy in the Middle East that would imply widespread participation in and consultation on economic policy matters. Riots, such as those of the Arab Spring, represent the ultimate public veto, but expressing a negative view is less satisfactory than people indicating what they actually want. Much economic power in the Middle East is vested in the finance ministers and their senior civil servants, with planning ministers and those involved in planning departments being usually less important. Central banks have no independence, and are seldom consulted on economic policy matters, although the governor of the central bank may attend formal meetings to listen. As government expenditure policy is the main means of controlling the economy, and monetary policy plays at best a minor role, this tends to reduce the influence of the central bank in any case.

Many economic policy changes are simply introduced by ministerial decree, which implies little or no parliamentary accountability. Indeed it often seems that finance ministers are more accountable internationally to bodies such as the IMF than they are domestically to their own parliaments. Increasingly the ministers are technocrats, many of whom are trained economists, which means that at least they have a good grasp of the economic issues if not always the political constraints. Economists are often poor communicators, however, and as a result finance ministers often fail to get their message across to others in government, and usually carry little political weight. Many feel most comfortable when dealing with their own civil servants, rather than answering questions in parliament or even the queries of other ministers.

## Perceptions of corruption and the Arab Spring

There were many political and economic causes of the Arab Spring, but perceptions that the regimes in Tunisia, Egypt, Syria and Yemen were totally corrupt were a major factor prompting public discontent and frustration. There is widespread agreement and extensive evidence that corruption impedes economic development,[18] even if in some societies it can be seen as lubricating the wheels of economic activity.[19] Corruption takes many forms, from unofficial commissions and kickbacks for middle men with public procurement to favouritism in recruitment towards relatives or those prepared to pay bribes. All such practices have a direct cost in terms of reducing economic growth and ensuring the benefits of growth are skewed towards a minority.[20]

*Table 9.5* Corruption perception index for the Middle East

| Rank | Country | Score | Rank | Country | Score |
|---|---|---|---|---|---|
| 22 | Qatar | 7.2 | 80 | Morocco | 3.4 |
| 28 | UAE | 6.8 | 112 | Algeria | 2.9 |
| 36 | Israel | 5.8 | 112 | Egypt | 2.9 |
| 46 | Bahrain | 5.1 | 120 | Iran | 2.7 |
| 50 | Oman | 4.8 | 129 | Syria | 2.6 |
| 54 | Kuwait | 4.6 | 134 | Lebanon | 2.5 |
| 56 | Jordan | 4.5 | 164 | Yemen | 2.1 |
| 57 | Saudi Arabia | 4.4 | 168 | Libya | 2.0 |
| 61 | Turkey | 4.2 | 175 | Iraq | 1.8 |
| 73 | Tunisia | 3.8 | 177 | Sudan | 1.6 |

Source: Transparency International, London, 2011

In the Middle East corruption is not new, indeed it arguably has deep roots dating back many centuries.[21] However, the data from Transparency International cited in Table 9.5 shows that there is much variation across the region in perceptions of corruption, and care should be taken not to make sweeping generalisations. Sudan, Iraq, Libya under Gaddafi and Yemen were seen as amongst the most corrupt countries in the world, closely followed by Lebanon and Syria under Assad, while Iran and Egypt also had poor scores. In contrast the GCC countries, and Qatar and the UAE in particular, scored well, indeed their corruption scores were well below those in many European countries. Even Bahrain, despite the inter-communal discontent, scored well. The corruption perception index reflects the opinions of the public sector practices by external agencies and observers as well as expatriates living in each country included. These are of course value judgements, but they carry much credibility internationally. In the Middle East many regard the indicators as understating the degree of corrupt practice, especially in the most corrupt countries. What Table 9.5 shows is that there is much that these countries could learn in terms of tacking corruption from the better performers in the region and that the dissemination of good practice would be highly desirable.

Corruption in the public sector is often related to poor corporate governance in the private sector. The position in the Middle East has received much more international attention during the last decade partly because of the agenda of the Organisation for Economic Co-operation and Development (OECD) in promoting good corporate governance worldwide. This is viewed as essential for a more thriving private sector that can become the driver for greater prosperity in increasingly market driven economies. If the government cannot regulate itself, there is little hope of transparency and sound business practice in the private sector. In order to promote better corporate governance in the Middle East, Hawkamah was established in Dubai in February 2006 with support from the OECD and the International Finance Corporation (IFC), the affiliate of the World Bank that aims to encourage and enhance private sector activity. Previously there had been two Middle East corporate governance conferences, and it was these that resulted in the founding of the new institution.[22]

One of the activities of Hawkamah is to rank stock market listed companies in the Middle East in terms of the soundness and integrity of their governance practices. As Table 9.6 shows, companies from the GCC dominate the top 10 rankings; indeed over three-quarters of the top 50 listed companies are accounted for by Saudi Arabia, Qatar and the UAE. These are also the countries that have good governance rankings for their public sectors. There are nevertheless exceptions, notably MobiNile and Orascom Construction of Egypt, multinational companies based in Cairo and listed on the Egyptian Stock Market, that exhibit high integrity and good financial reporting practice in spite of operating in many jurisdictions where the rule of law, including commercial law, is less than adequate.

State corruption inhibits business development and there is, not surprisingly, a relationship between the corruption perception rankings and those for the ease of doing business calculated by the IFC. As Table 9.7 shows, the GCC states are favourably ranked for ease of doing business, Saudi Arabia,

*Table 9.6* Top 10 listed companies in the Middle East for corporate governance

| Rank | Country | Company | Sector |
|------|---------|---------|--------|
| 1 | UAE | Etisalat | Telecoms |
| 2 | UAE | DP World | Logistics |
| 3 | Saudi Arabia | SAVOLA | Wholesaling |
| 4 | Jordan | Arab Bank | Financials |
| 5 | Egypt | MobiNil | Telecoms |
| 6 | UAE | National Bank of Abu Dhabi | Financials |
| 7 | Egypt | Orascom Construction | Real Estate and Infrastructure |
| 8 | Qatar | Qtel | Telecoms |
| 9 | Morocco | Maroc Telecom | Telecoms |
| 10 | Qatar | Al Khaliji Commercial Bank | Financials |

Source: S&P Hawkamah, *Environmental, Social and Governance Metrics*, Dubai, 2012

*Table 9.7* Ease of doing business in the GCC

| Economy | Rank for ease of business | Construction permits, days | Cost of registering property, % value | Enforcing contracts, days |
|---------|---------|---------|---------|---------|
| Bahrain | 38 | 43 | 2.7 | 635 |
| Kuwait | 67 | 130 | 0.5 | 566 |
| Oman | 49 | 174 | 3.0 | 598 |
| Qatar | 36 | 70 | 0.3 | 570 |
| Saudi Arabia | 12 | 75 | 0.0 | 635 |
| UAE | 33 | 46 | 2.0 | 537 |

Source: International Finance Corporation, *Doing Business Rankings*, Washington, 2012

perhaps surprisingly, being the leader. As indicated earlier the Kingdom attracts by far the largest share of inward investment in the region, and although foreign companies are motivated by the opportunities in playing a significant role in resource development, the climate for business undoubtly helps. The zero cost of registering property is seen as helpful, as is the short times for obtaining construction permits and for contract enforcement. The Saudi Arabian legal system for commercial contracts is regarded as functioning comparatively well.

In contrast, in the non-GCC states of the Middle East the climate for business is much less favourable, as Table 9.8 shows. In Egypt it takes almost three years on average to enforce commercial contracts where there are payments defaults or subcontractors failing to meet the terms of their engagement either through inferior work or delays in meeting agreed schedules. In Iran registration costs over 10 per cent of the value of the property and in Syria almost 28 per cent, figures possibly indicative of corruption in the registration process. It takes almost one year to obtain construction permits in Iran, hardly an encouraging situation for foreign companies already taking risks because of United States and European Union sanctions.

If the Arab Spring is to bear fruit and bring political and economic advance, it is not only parliamentary democracy and accountable government that can help economic development. Much will depend on the integrity of those elected and holding positions of power. There has been much support for the Islamist parties as they are perceived as more honest and less corrupt than the former government parties which were mere instruments of the regimes. However these parties will not succeed, or indeed remain in power long, unless there is economic advancement.

An important prerequisite for such advancement is sound corporate governance as successful business are built and sustained through good reporting

*Table 9.8* Ease of doing business in the Middle East excluding the GCC

| Economy | Rank for ease of business | Construction permits, days | Cost of registering property, % value | Enforcing contracts, days |
|---------|---------------------------|----------------------------|----------------------------------------|---------------------------|
| Algeria | 148 | 281 | 7.1 | 630 |
| Egypt | 110 | 218 | 0.8 | 1,010 |
| Iran | 144 | 320 | 10.5 | 505 |
| Iraq | 164 | 187 | 6.9 | 520 |
| Jordan | 96 | 70 | 7.5 | 689 |
| Lebanon | 104 | 219 | 5.8 | 721 |
| Morocco | 94 | 97 | 4.9 | 510 |
| Syria | 134 | 104 | 27.9 | 872 |
| Tunisia | 46 | 88 | 6.1 | 565 |
| Turkey | 71 | 189 | 3.3 | 420 |
| Yemen | 99 | 116 | 3.8 | 520 |

Source: International Finance Corporation, *Doing Business Rankings*, Washington, 2012

practices. The new governments need to look at the legal provision for the private sector and investors, and create a political climate where just and honest business practice is the norm. Islamic teaching stresses these attributes and the importance of good morals and the highest ethical standards in economic and financial management.[23] There have been some achievements in these areas, mainly in the GCC. There is an opportunity to create a distinctive Islamic form of capitalism, but it will take time.[24] This could be the unique contribution of the Middle East to the global economy. The region already has two G20 members, Saudi Arabia and Turkey, who can influence decision making at the highest level. Too often in the past the Middle East has merely imported economic ideas and development concepts instigated outside the region. There may be a chance to reverse this process.

# Notes

## 1 Introduction

1 Samir Amin, *Maldevelopment: Anatomy of a Global Failure*, Zed Books, London, 1990.
2 Michael P. Todaro and Stephen C. Smith, *Economic Development,* Pearson, Harlow, 2009.
3 Frederick Nixson, *Development Economics*, Heinemann, London, 2001.
4 Peter Cramp, *Economic Development*, Anforme, London, 2007.
5 W. Arthur Lewis, *The Theory of Economic Growth*, Irwin, Homewood, Illinois, 1995.
6 Charles K. Wilber and Kenneth P. Jameson, *The Political Economy of Development and Underdevelopment*, McGraw Hill, New York, 6th edition, 1995.
7 Amartya Sen, *Development as Freedom*, Anchor Books, New York, 1999.
8 Paul Rivlin, *Arab Economies in the Twenty-First Century*, Cambridge University Press, Cambridge, 2009, pp. 61–94.
9 Bent Hansen, *Egypt and Turkey: Political Economy of Poverty, Equity and Growth*, Oxford University Press, Oxford, 1991.
10 Many identify 1950 as the starting point for the contemporary Middle East; see Tarik Yousef, "Development, growth and policy reform in the Middle East and North Africa since 1950", *Journal of Economic Perspectives*, Volume 18, Number 3, Summer 2004, pp. 91–115.
11 Roger Owen, *The Middle East in the World Economy, 1800–1914*, Methuen, London, 1981.
12 Charles Issawi, *An Economic History of the Middle East*, Methuen, London, 1982.
13 George Sabagh (ed.) *The Modern Economic and Social History of the Middle East in its World Context,* Cambridge University Press, Cambridge, 1989.
14 Elie Kedourie (ed.), *The Middle Eastern Economies: Studies in Economics and Economic History,* Frank Cass, London, 1977.
15 Rajeev K. Goel and Michael A. Nelson, "Corruption in MENA countries: an empirical investigation", in Serdar Sayan (ed.), *Economic Performance in the Middle East and North Africa: Institutions, Corruption and Reform*, Routledge, London and New York, 2009, pp. 13–24.
16 Clement Henry and Robert Springborg, *Globalisation and the Politics of Development in the Middle East*, Cambridge University Press, Cambridge, 2001, pp. 134–67.
17 Peter Bauer, *The Development Frontier: Essays in Applied Economics*, Harvester Wheatsheaf, Hemel Hempstead, Herts, 1991.
18 This is especially true of the Gulf. See Gill Crystal, *Oil and Politics in the Gulf, Rulers and Merchants in Kuwait and Qatar*, Cambridge University Press, Cambridge, 1990.
19 Abdullah Yusuf Ali, *The Meaning of the Holy Qur'an*, Islamic Book Trust, Kuala Lumpur, 2007, Sura 9:111.

20 Ibid., Sura 83:1–4.
21 Maxime Rodinson, *Islam and Capitalism*, Penguin Books, Harmondsworth, Middlesex, 1966.
22 M. Umer Chapra, *Islam and the Economic Challenge*, Islamic Foundation, Leicester, 1992.
23 Said El-Naggar (ed.), *Privatisation and Structural Adjustment in the Arab Countries*, International Monetary Fund, Washington DC, 1989.
24 Tim Niblock and Emma Murphy (eds), *Economic Liberalisation in the Middle East*, I.B. Tauris, London, 1992.
25 Farid A. Muna, *The Arab Executive*, St Martin's Press, New York, 1980.
26 Alan Gelb, *Oil Windfalls, Blessing or Curse*, Oxford University Press, for the World Bank, Oxford, 1988.
27 Rodney Wilson with Abdullah Al-Salamah, Monica Malik and Ahmed Al-Rajhi, *Economic Development in Saudi Arabia*, Routledge Curzon, London, 2004, pp. 94–125.
28 Hazwm Beblawi and Giacomo Luciani (eds), *The Rentier State*, Croom Helm, London, 1987.
29 Jahangir Amuzegar, *Iran's Economy under the Islamic Republic*, I.B. Tauris, London, 1997.
30 Massoud Karshenas, *Oil, State and Industrialisation in Iran*, Cambridge University Press, Cambridge, 1991.
31 Kazem Alamdari, *Why the Middle East Lagged Behind: The Case of Iran*, University Press of America, Lanham, 2005.
32 Abdelali Jbili, Vitali Kramarenko and José Bailén, *Islamic Republic of Iran: Managing the Transition to a Market Economy*, International Monetary Fund, Washington, 2007.
33 Z.Y. Hershlag, *The Contemporary Turkish Economy*, Routledge, London, 1988.
34 Tevfik F. Nas and Mehmet Odekon (eds), *Economics and Politics of Turkish Liberalization*, Associated University Presses, New Jersey, 1992.
35 Ziya Öniş and Fikret Şenses, *Turkey and the Global Economy: Neo-liberal Restructuring and Integration in the Post Crisis Era*, Routledge, London, 2009.
36 Zülküf Aydın, *The Political Economy of Turkey*, Pluto Press, London, 2005.
37 Roberto Aliboni, Ali Hillal Dessouki, Saad Eddin Ibrahim, Giacomo Luciani and Piercarlo Padoan (eds), *Egypt's Economic Potential*, Croom Helm, London, 1984.
38 Gouda Abdel-Khalek, *Stabilisation and Adjustment in Egypt: Reform or De-Industrialisation?* Edward Elgar, Cheltenham, 2001.
39 Khalid Ikram, *The Egyptian Economy*, 1952–2000, Routledge, London, 2006.
40 Robert Bowker, *Egypt and the Politics of Change in the Arab Middle East*, Edward Elgar, Cheltenham, 2010.
41 Frederic P. Miller, Agnes F. Vandome, and John McBrewster, *The Economy of Egypt*, VDM Publishing House, Saarbrücken, Germany, 2009.
42 Assaf Razin and Efraim Sadka, *The Economy of Modern Israel: Malaise and Promise*, University of Chicago Press, Chicago 1993.
43 Avi Ben-Bassat. *The Israeli Economy, 1985–1998*, Massachusetts Institute of Technology Press, Cambridge, Massachusetts, 2002.
44 Jonathan Nitzan and Shimshon Bichler, *The Global Political Economy of Israel*, Pluto Press, London, 2002.
45 Jacob Metzer, *The Divided Economy of Mandatory Palestine*, Cambridge University Press, Cambridge, 1998.
46 Raja Khalidi, *The Arab Economy in Israel*, Croom Helm, London, 1988.
47 Shir Hever, *The Political Economy of Israel's Occupation*, Pluto Press, London, 2010.
48 Ali D. Johany, Michel Berne and J. Wilson Mixon, *The Saudi Arabia Economy*, Croom Helm, London, 1986.
49 M.W. Khouja and P.G. Sadler, *The Economy of Kuwait*, Macmillan, London, 1979.

50 Bichara Khader and Bashir El-Wifati (eds), *The Economic Development of Libya*, Croom Helm, London, 1987.
51 Paul Aarts and Gerd Nonneman, *Saudi Arabia in the Balance: Political Economy, Society and Foreign Affairs*, New York University Press, New York, 2006.
52 Tim Niblock, *The Political Economy of Saudi Arabia*, Routledge, London 2007.
53 Steffen Hertog, *Princes, Brokers and Bureaucrats: Oil and the State in Saudi Arabia*, Cornell University Press, Ithaca, 2010.
54 Christopher Davidson, *Dubai: The Vulnerability of Success*, Hurst and Company, London, 2008.
55 Christopher Davidson, *Abu Dhabi: Oil and Beyond*, Columbia University Press, Ithaca, 2009.
56 Rodney Wilson, *The Economies of the Middle East*, Macmillan, London, 1979.
57 Alan Richards and John Waterbury, *A Political Economy of the Middle East: State, Class and Economic Development*, Westview Press, Boulder, 3rd edition, 2007.

## 2 Modelling Middle East economic development

1 Robert Dorfman, "Economic development from the beginning to Rostow", *Journal of Economic Literature*, Volume 29, Number 2, 1991, pp. 573–91.
2 Joseph Schumpeter, *The Theory of Economic Development*, Harvard University Press, Cambridge, Massachusettes,1934.
3 Charles Issawi, "The economic and social foundations of democracy in the Middle East", *International Affairs*, January 1956, reprinted in Charles Issawi, *The Arab World's Legacy*, Darwin Press, Princeton, 1981. Although originally written over half a century ago, much of the analysis remains relevant.
4 Alan Richards and John Waterbury, *A Political Economy of the Middle East*, Westview Press, Boulder, Colarado, 1990, pp. 146–55.
5 Rony Gabbay, *Communism and Agrarian Reform in Iraq*, Croom Helm, London, 1978, pp. 108–22.
6 Alexander Gerschenkron, *Economic Backwardness in Historical Perspective*, Harvard University Press, Cambridge, Massachusettes, 1962.
7 John Page and Lawrence MacDonald, *The East Asian Miracle: Economic Growth and Public Policy*, Oxford University Press for the World Bank, Oxford, 1993.
8 Yair Aharini, *The Israeli Economy: Dreams and Realities*, Routledge, London, 1991, pp. 275–314.
9 Ziya Önis, "Organisation of export-oriented industrialisation: the Turkish foreign trade companies in a comparative perspective", in Tevfik F. Nas and Mehmet Odekon (eds), *Economics and Politics of Turkish Liberalisation*, Lehigh University Press and Associated University Press, London, 1992, pp. 73–100.
10 W.W. Rostow, *The Stages of Economic Growth: A Non-Communist Manifesto*, Cambridge University Press, Cambridge, 1961.
11 Essam Montasser, "The Arab economy and its development strategy: a new Arab economic order", in Malcolm H. Kerr and El Sayed Yassin, *Rich and Poor States in the Middle East*, Westview Press, Boulder, Colorado, 1982, pp. 99–128.
12 Arne Jon Isachsen, Carl B. Hamilton and Thorvaldur Gylfason, *Understanding the Market Economy*, Oxford University Press, Oxford, pp. 77–98.
13 Clifford Geettz, "The Bazaar economy: information and search in peasant marketing", *American Economic Review*, Volume 68, Number 2, 1978, pp. 28–32.
14 Jean Philippe Platteau, "Behind the market stage where real societies exist: the role of public and private order institutions", *Journal of Development Studies*, Volume 30, Number 3, 1994, pp. 533–77.
15 Rodney Wilson, "Japan's exports to the Middle East: directional and commodity trends and price behaviour", *Middle East Journal*, Volume 38, Number 3, 1984, pp. 454–73.

16 Rodney Wilson, *Banking and Finance in the Arab Middle East*, Macmillan, London, 1983, pp. 9–11.

17 Iliya Harik and Denis J. Sullivan, *Privatisation and Liberalisation in the Middle East*, Indiana University Press, Bloomington, 1992, pp. 1–23.

18 Barry W. Poulson, *Economic Development: Private and Public Choice*, West Publishing, Minneapolis, 1994, p. 98.

19 Delwin Roy, "The hidden economy of Egypt", *Middle Eastern Studies*, Volume 28, Number 4, 1992, pp. 689–711. Casual empiricism and press reports would indicate that Roy's analysis is even more relevant for Syria and Iraq.

20 Roger Owen, *The Middle East in the World Economy, 1800–1914*, Methuen, London, 1981, pp. 2–23.

21 Giacomo Luciani, "Allocative versus production states: a theoretical framework", in Hazem Beblawi and Giacomo Luciani (eds), *The Rentier State*, Croom Helm, London, 1987, pp. 63–82.

22 Gerald M. Meier, *Politics and Policy Making in Developing Countries: Perspectives in the New Political Economy*, ICS Press, San Francisco, 1991.

23 Mark N. Cooper, *The Transformation of Egypt*, Croom Helm, London, 1982, pp. 91–125.

24 Philip J. Robbins, "Politics and the 1986 electoral law in Jordan", in Rodney Wilson (ed.), *Politics and the Economy in Jordan*, Routledge, London, 1991, pp. 184–207.

25 Patrick Conway, "Algeria: windfalls in a socialist economy", in Alan Gelb (ed.), *Oil Windfalls: Blessing or Curse?*, Oxford University Press for the World Bank, Oxford, 1988, pp. 147–69.

## 3 Growth and structural change

1 P. Jackson and C. Lockhart (eds), *The Cambridge History of Iran: The Timurid and Safavid Periods*, Volume 6, Cambridge University Press, Cambridge, 1986.

2 Charles Issawi, *An Economic History of the Middle East and North Africa*, Methuen, London, 1982, pp. 48–49.

3 World Bank estimates.

4 Richard Pomfret, *Diverse Paths of Economic Development*, Harvester Wheatsheaf, New York, 1992, p. 3.

5 Yair Aharoni, *The Israeli Economy: Dreams and Realities*, Routledge, London, 1991.

6 For a discussion of longer-term inflationary trends in Turkey, see Z.Y. Hershlag, *The Contemporary Turkish Economy*, Routledge, London, 1988, pp. 98–109.

7 Malcolm Gillis, Dwight Perkins, Michael Roemer and Donald Snodgrass, *Economic Development*, 3rd edition, W.W. Norton, New York, 1992, pp. 551–52.

8 Rodney Wilson, "Development of transport infrastructure for inter-state trade throughout the eastern Arab world", in Gerd Nonneman (ed.), *The Middle East and Europe: An Integrated Communities Approach*, Federal Trust for Education and Research, London, 1992, pp. 175–78.

9 Ali Johany, Michel Berne and Wilson Mixon, *The Saudi Arabian Economy*, Croom Helm, London, 1986, pp. 115–16.

10 David Coleman and Frederick Nixon, *Economics of Change in Less Developed Countries*, 2nd edition, Philip Allan, Oxford, 1986, pp. 206–8.

11 Walter Elkan, *An Introduction to Development Economics*, Penguin Books, Harmondsworth, Middlesex, 1978, pp. 17–18.

12 David Hallam, "International investment in developing country agriculture: issues and challenges", *Food Security*, Volume 3, Number 1, 2011, pp. 91–98.

13 Roger Owen, *The Middle East in the World Economy, 1800–1914*, Methuen, London, 1981, pp. 69–71.

14 Peter Bauer, *The Development Frontier: Essays in Applied Economics*, Harvester Wheatsheaf, Hemel Hempstead, Herts., 1991, pp. 122–40.

15 Z.Y. Hershlag, *The Contemporary Turkish Economy*, Routledge, London, 1988, pp. 4–5.

16 Roberto Aliboni, Ali Hillal Dessouki, Saad Eddin Ibrahim, Giacomo Luciani and Piercarlo Padoan, *Egypt's Economic Potential*, Croom Helm, London, 1984, p. 136.

17 In recent years Egypt has actually imported low-grade cotton for its textile industry. It makes more economic sense to export locally grown high-grade cotton, which commands a better price in international markets.

18 Ian Seccombe and Rodney Wilson, *Trade and Finance in Jordan*, Durham University, Centre for Middle East and Islamic Studies, Occasional Paper No. 33, 1987, pp. 19–21.

19 Rodney Wilson, *Banking and Finance in the Arab Middle East*, Macmillan, London, 1983, pp. 56–63.

20 W.W. Rostow, *Stages of Economic Growth*, Cambridge University Press, Cambridge, 1960, pp. 1–25.

21 Cevat Tosun, Dallen Timothy and Yüksel Öztürk, "Tourism growth, national development and regional inequality in Turkey", *Journal of Sustainable Tourism*, Volume 11, Numbers 2–3, 2003, pp. 133–61.

22 Adel S. Al-Dosary and Syed Masur Rahman, "The role of the private sector towards Saudisation (localisation)", *International Journal of Arab Culture, Management and Sustainable Development*, Volume 1, Number 2, 2009, pp. 131–43.

23 Ragnar Nurkse, *Problems of Capital Formation in Underdeveloped Countries*, Oxford University Press, Oxford, 1953, pp. 10–27.

24 Paul N. Rosenstein-Rodan, "Problems of industrialisation of Eastern and South-eastern Europe", *Economic Journal*, Volume 53, Number 210–11, June–September 1943, pp. 210–11.

25 Albert O. Hirschman, *The Strategy of Economic Development*, Yale University Press, New Haven, Conn., 1958, pp. 10–22.

26 Tim Niblock and Emma Murphy (eds), *Economic Liberalisation in the Middle East*, I.B. Tauris, London, 1992, pp. 3–14.

27 William Cuddihy, "Agricultural prices, farm mechanization and the demand for labour", in Alan Richards and Philip Martin (eds), *Migration, Mechanization and Agricultural Labour Markets in Egypt*, Westview Press, Boulder, Col., 1983, pp. 225–34.

28 Louis Turner and James Bedore, *Middle East Industrialisation: A Study of Saudi and Iranian Downstream Investments*, Royal Institute for International Affairs, London, 1979, pp. 7–24.

29 Galal Amin, *The Modernisation of Poverty*, Brill, Leiden, 1974, pp. 8–24.

30 Rodney Wilson, *The Economies of the Middle East*, Macmillan, London, 1979, pp. 8–12.

31 Jahangir Amuzegar, *Iran's Economy under the Islamic Republic*, I.B. Tauris, London, 1992, pp. 3–25.

32 Abbas Ali, "Middle East competitiveness in the 21st century's global market", *The Academy of Management Executives*, Volume 13, Number 1, 1999, pp. 102–8.

## 4 Population growth and employment

1 Thomas Frejka, "Long term prospects for world population growth", *Population and Development Review*, Volume 7, Number 3, 1981, pp. 489–511; Dudley Kirk, "Demographic transition theory", *Population Studies*, Volume 50, Issue 3, 1996, pp. 361–87.

2 Richard Easterlin, "Modernisation and fertility: a critical essay", in R. Bulatao and R. Lee (eds), *Determinants of Fertility in Developing Countries*, Academic Press, New York, Volume 2, pp. 562–86; John C. Caldwell, "Towards a restatement

of demographic transition theory", *Population and Development Review*, Volume 2, Numbers 3–4, 1976, pp. 321–66.

3 Michael Teitelbaum, "Relevance of demographic transition theory for developing countries", *Science*, Number 188, 1977, pp. 420–25.

4 World Bank Database estimates.

5 Unni Wikan, *Life Among the Poor in Cairo*, Tavistock Publications, London, 1980, pp. 157–59.

6 Ziauddin Sardar, *Islamic Futures: The Shape of Ideas to Come*, Mansell, London, 1985, pp. 121–22.

7 Edward William Lane, *The Manners and Customs of Modern Egyptians*, Everyman Library, London, 1908, pp. 60–64.

8 Rodney Wilson, "Education priorities for a service dominated economy: the case of Kuwait", *Teaching Public Administration*, Volume 9, Number 1, Spring 1989, pp. 52–59.

9 The supply of low-cost teachers in countries such as Egypt has made class size less of a problem. See Alan Richards and John Waterbury, *A Political Economy of the Middle East*, Westview Press, Boulder, Col., 1990, pp. 121–22.

10 Frederick Harbison, "Human resources development planning in modernising economies", *International Labour Review*, Volume 85, Number 5, 1962, pp. 1–23.

11 Rodney Wilson, "Western, Soviet and Egyptian influences on Iraq's development planning", in Tim Niblock (ed.), *Iraq: The Contemporary State*, Croom Helm, London, 1982, pp. 238–39.

12 W. Arthur Lewis, *The Theory of Economic Growth*, Irwin, Homewood, Illinois, 1955, pp. 25–45.

13 Robert Mabro, "Industrial growth, agricultural underemployment and the Lewis model: the Egyptian case, 1937–75", *Journal of Development Studies*, Volume 3, Number 4, July 1967, pp. 330–45.

14 John Harris and Michael Todaro, "Migration, unemployment and development: a two-sector analysis", *American Economic Review*, Volume 60, Number 1, March 1970, pp. 126–52.

15 Georges Sabagh, "Migration and social mobility in Egypt", in Malcolm Kerr and El Sayed Yassin (eds), *Rich and Poor States in the Middle East: Egypt and the New Arab Order*, Westview Press, Boulder, Col., 1982, pp. 71–95.

16 Alan Richards, Philip Martin and Rifaat Nagaar, "Labour shortages in Egyptian agriculture", in Alan Richards and Philip Martin (eds), *Migration, Mechanisation and Agricultural Labour Markets in Egypt*, Westview Press, Boulder, Col., 1983, pp. 21–44.

17 Mark Cooper, *The Transformation of Egypt*, Croom Helm, London, 1982, pp. 51–52.

18 World Bank Database.

19 Malcolm Gillis, Dwight Perkins, Michael Roemer and Douglas Snodgrass, *Economics of Development*, 3rd edition, W.W. Norton, New York, 1992, pp. 561–64.

20 J.S. Birks, I.J. Seccombe and C.A. Sinclair, "Migrant workers in the Arab Gulf: the impact of declining oil revenues", *International Labour Review*, Volume 20, Number 4, Winter 1986, pp. 799–814.

21 Susan Paine, *Exporting Workers: The Turkish Case*, Cambridge University Press, Cambridge, 1974.

22 Stace Birks, "The demographic challenge in the Arab Gulf", in Brian Pridham (ed.), *The Arab World*, Croom Helm, London, 1988, pp. 131–52.

23 An alternative model is provided by Naiem Sherbiny and Ishmail Serageldin, "Expatriate labour and economic growth: Saudi demand for Egyptian labour", in Malcolm Kerr and El Sayed Yassin (eds), *Rich and Poor States in the Middle East*, Westview Press, Boulder, Col., 1982, pp. 225–57.

24 Monther Share, "The use of Jordanian workers' remittances", in Bichara Khader and Adnan Badran (eds), *The Economic Development of Jordan*, Croom Helm, London, 1987, pp. 32–44.

25 Saad Eddin Ibrahim, *The New Arab Social Order*, Westview Press, Boulder, Col., 1982, pp. 63–94.
26 Fatima-Zohra Oufriha, "Aspects of the brain drain in Algeria", in A.B. Zahlan (ed.), *The Arab Brain Drain*, Ithaca Press, London, 1981, pp. 100–14.
27 Stace Birks and Clive Sinclair, *Arab Manpower*, Croom Helm, London, 1980, pp. 114–15.
28 Larbi Talha, Le *Salariat immigré dans la crise*, Éditions du Centre National de la Recherche Scientifique, Paris, 1989, pp. 165–237.

## 5 Capital markets, savings and investment

1 Authors such as Richard Pomfret stress the central role of capital formation in development but this is discussed in terms of macro monetary and fiscal policy, with the microeconomics of capital markets and private savings largely ignored. See *Diverse Paths of Economic Development*, Harvester Wheatsheaf, New York, 1992, pp. 16–18 and 129–42.
2 *The New Palgrave* on economic development concentrates on taxation and foreign aid, but also ignores the efficiency of capital markets. Éprime Eshag, "Fiscal and monetary policies in developing countries", and Hollis Chenery, "Foreign aid", are the only two contributions in this field in John Eatwell, Murray Milgate and Peter Newman (eds), *The New Palgrave: Economic Development*, Macmillan, London, 1989, pp. 130–44.
3 Charles C. Okeahalam, "Institutions and financial market development in the MENA region", *Progress in Development Studies*, Volume 5, Number 4, 2005, pp. 310–28.
4 J.G. Gurley and E.S. Shaw, "Financial structure and economic development", *Economic Development and Cultural Change*, Volume 15, Number 1, 1967, 257–68.
5 Rodney Wilson, "The role of commercial banking in the Jordanian economy", in Bichara Khader and Aidnan Badran (eds), *The Economic Development of Jordan*, Croom Helm, London, 1987, pp. 45–61.
6 Maxwell Fry, "Money and capital: financial deepening in economic development", *Journal of Money, Credit and Banking*, Volume 10, Number 4, 1979, pp. 464–75.
7 Geoffrey Jones, *The Imperial Bank of Persia, Banking and Empire in Iran: The History of the British Bank of the Middle East*, Cambridge University Press, Cambridge, 1986, Volume 1, pp. 40–54.
8 Roger Owen, *The Middle East and the World Economy*, Methuen, London, 1981, pp. 100–10.
9 Geoffrey Jones, *The Imperial Bank of Persia, Banking and Empire in Iran: The History of the British Bank of the Middle East*, Cambridge University Press, Cambridge, 1986, Volume 1, pp. 207–8 and 217–18.
10 Marius Deeb, "Bank Misr and the emergence of the local bourgeoisie in Egypt", in Elie Kedourie (ed.), *The Middle Eastern Economy: Studies in Economics and Economic History*, Frank Cass, London, 1976, pp. 69–86.
11 Rodney Wilson, "The evolution of the Saudi banking system and its relationship with Bahrain", in Tim Niblock (ed.), *State, Society and Economy in Saudi Arabia*, Croom Helm, London, 1982, pp. 278–300.
12 Geoffrey Jones, *Banking and Oil: The History of the British Bank of the Middle East*, Cambridge University Press, Cambridge, 1987, Volume 2, pp. 214–41.
13 Charles Issawi, *An Economic History of the Middle East and North Africa*, Methuen, London, 1982, pp. 185–86.
14 Information on exchange rate policy and currency regulations for all Arab countries is published annually in the *Arab Banking and Finance Directory*, Tele-Gulf Publications, Bahrain.

15 Arthur Young, *Saudi Arabia: The Making of a Financial Giant*, Longmans for New York University Press, New York, 1983, pp. 91–97.

16 For an historical profile of Egypt's debt, see Bent Hansen, *The Political Economy of Poverty, Equity and Growth: Egypt and Turkey*, Oxford University Press for the World Bank, Oxford, 1991, pp. 216–18.

17 A.P. Thirlwall, *Financing Economic Development*, Macmillan, London, 1976, pp. 13–17.

18 Henry T. Azzam, "Bahrain's offshore banking centre", *Arab Gulf Journal*, Volume 4, Number 1, 1984, pp. 23–35.

19 Rodney Wilson, *Cyprus and the International Economy*, Macmillan, London, 1992, pp. 89–91.

20 Central Bank of Egypt, *Annual Report, 1990–91*, Cairo, 1992, p. 134.

21 Ayman Shafiq Fayyad Abdul-Hadi, *Stock Markets of the Arab World: Trends, Problems and Prospects for Integration*, Routledge, London, 1988, pp. 19–47.

22 Susan Creane, Rishi Goyal, A. Mushfiq and Randa Sab, *Financial Development in the Middle East and North Africa*, International Monetary Fund, Washington, 2003, pp. 1–16.

23 www.sagia.gov.sa.

24 www.invest.gov.tr.

## 6  An Islamic model for economic development

1 Wolfgang Sacks, "Progress and development", in Paul Ekins and Manfred Max-Neef, *Real Life Economics: Understanding Wealth Creation*, Routledge, London, 1992, pp. 156–61.

2 M. Umer Chapra, *Islam and the Economic Challenge*, Islamic Foundation, Leicester, 1992, pp. 28–36.

3 W. Montgomery Watt, *Islamic Fundamentalism and Modernity*, Routledge, London, 1989, pp. 3–8.

4 Akbar S. Ahmed, *Postmodernism and Islam: Predicament and Promise*, Routledge, London, 1992, pp. 33–37.

5 Muhammad Nejatullah Siddiqi, *Muslim Economic Thinking: A Survey of Contemporary Literature*, Islamic Foundation, Leicester, 1981, pp. 2–3 and 10–15.

6 Ingrid Hahne Rima, *Development of Economic Analysis*, 5th edn, Irwin, Homewood, Ill., 1991, pp. 13–20.

7 M.A. Mannan, *Islamic Economics: Theory and Practice*, Hodder & Stoughton, London, 1986, pp. 22–24.

8 Masudul Alam Choudhury, *The Principles of Islamic Political Economy*, Macmillan, London, 1992, pp. 9–40.

9 Abdullah Yusuf Ali, *The Holy Koran: Text, Translation and Commentary*, That es-Salasil, Kuwait, 1988, Sura iv, verse 12, p. 182.

10 Ibid., Sura 39:10, p. 1240.

11 Ibid., Sura 4:29, pp. 188–89.

12 Ibid., Sura 35:29, p. 1161.

13 Ibid., Sura 102:1, p. 1180.

14 Ibid., Sura 4:32, p. 189.

15 Ibid., Sura 17:35, p. 704.

16 Ibid., Sura 17:36, p. 704.

17 Ibid., Sura 30:40, p. 1062.

18 Ibid., Sura 24:38, p. 909.

19 Ibid., Sura 64:15–17, pp. 1559–60.

20 Ibid., Sura 17:18, p. 699.

21 Ibid., Sura 16:71, p. 675.

22 Ibid., Sura 8:41, p. 425.
23 Ibid., Sura 2:275, pp. 111–12.
24 Ibid., Sura 2:280, p. 113.
25 Ibid., Sura 9:34, pp. 449–50.
26 Ibid., Sura 2:254, p. 102.
27 Ibid., Sura 2:267, p. 108.
28 Ibid., Sura 2:271, p. 110.
29 Ibid., Sura 2:261, p. 106.
30 Ibid., Sura 2:265, p. 107.
31 Rodney Wilson, *Islamic Business: Theory and Practice*, Economist Intelligence Unit Special Report, no. 221, London, 1985, p. 24.
32 M. Umer Chapra, *Towards a Just Monetary System*, Islamic Foundation, Leicester, 1985, pp. 71–77.
33 Waqar Masood Khan, *Towards an Interest Free Islamic Economic System*, Islamic Foundation, Leicester, 1985, pp. 28–33 and 73–79.
34 John R. Presley, *Directory of Islamic Financial Institutions*, Macmillan, London, 1988, p. 22.
35 Saad Al Harran, *Islamic Finance: Partnership Financing*, Pelanduk Publishing, Selangor, Malaysia, 1993, pp. 95–97.
36 Ann Elizabeth Mayer, "Islamic banking and credit policies in the Sadat era: the social origins of Islamic banking in Egypt", *Arab Law Quarterly*, Volume 1, Part 1, 1985, pp. 32–50.
37 Rodney Wilson, *Banking and Finance in the Arab Middle East*, Macmillan, London, 1983, pp. 80–86.
38 Ahmed El Ashker, *The Islamic Business Enterprise*, Croom Helm, London, 1987, pp. 115–40.
39 Hossein Aryan, "Iran: the impact of Islamisation on the financial system", in Rodney Wilson (ed.), *Islamic Financial Markets*, Routledge, London, 1990, pp. 155–70.
40 Monzer Kahf, "Zakat: unresolved issues in contemporary *Fiqh*", in Abdul Hasan Sadeq, Ataul Huq Pramanik and Nik Hassan (eds), *Development and Finance in Islam*, International Islamic University Press, Selangor, Malaysia, 1991, pp. 173–90.
41 Muhammad Nejatullah Siddiqi, *Insurance in an Islamic Economy*, Islamic Foundation, Leicester, 1985, pp. 27–46.
42 Afzalur Rahman, *Economic Doctrines of Islam: Banking and Insurance*, Muslim Schools Trust, London, 1979, pp. 217–42.

## 7  Oil and development

1 British Petroleum, *Statistical Review of World Energy*, London, June 2011, pp. 6 and 20.
2 British Petroleum, *Energy Outlook 2030*, London, January 2012, p. 30.
3 Alessandro Roncaglia, *The International Oil Market*, Macmillan, London, 1985, pp. 24ff.
4 Albert Danielsen, *The Evolution of OPEC*, Harcourt Brace Jovanovich, New York, 1982, pp. 56–60.
5 John Chesshire, "The energy demand impact of conservation technology", in David Hawdon (ed.), *Oil Prices in the 1990s*, Macmillan, London, 1989, pp. 39–53.
6 Stephen Hemsley Longrigg, *Oil in the Middle East: Its Discovery and Development*, Oxford University Press, Oxford, 1954, pp. 17–24.
7 Mostafa Elm, *Oil, Power and Principle: Iran's Oil Nationalisation and its Aftermath*, Syracuse University Press, New York, 1992, pp. 23–43.
8 Ali D. Johany, Michel Berne and J. Wilson Mixon, *The Saudi Arabian Economy*, Croom Helm, London, 1986, pp. 30–31.

9 Louis Turner, *Oil Companies in the International System*, George Allen & Unwin, London, 1983, pp. 44–47.

10 Mana Saeed Ai-Otaiba, *OPEC and the Petroleum Industry*, Croom Helm, London, 1975, pp. 77–107.

11 Ian Seymour, *OPEC: Instrument of Change*, Macmillan, London, 1980, pp. 18–54.

12 Benjamin Shwadran, *Middle East Oil: Issues and Problems*, Schenkman, Cambridge, Mass., 1977, pp. 7–16.

13 Maurice Adelman, *The World Petroleum Market*, Johns Hopkins University Press, Baltimore, Md, 1972, pp. 250–64.

14 Sheikh R. Ali, *Oil and Power: Political Dynamics in the Middle East*, Frances Pinter Publishers, London, 1987, pp. 53–65.

15 Roy Licklider, *Political Power and the Arab Oil Weapon*, University of California Press, Berkeley, 1988, pp. 28–62.

16 Abdelkader Maachou, *OAPEC and Arab Petroleum*, Berger-Levrault, Paris, 1982, pp. 40–44.

17 Ali D. Johany, *The Myth of the OPEC Cartel*, John Wiley, Chichester, 1980, pp. 17–32.

18 Robert Belgrave, *Energy: Two Decades of Crises*, Gower, London, 1983, pp. 314–19.

19 Anthony C. Fisher, *Resources and Environmental Economics*, Cambridge University Press, Cambridge, 1981, pp. 10–36.

20 Georg Koopmann, Klaus Matthies and Beate Reszat, *Oil and the International Economy: Lessons from Two Price Shocks*, Transaction, Hamburg, pp. 46–47.

21 Edward Morse, "An overview: gains, costs and dilemmas", in Joan Pearce (ed.), *The Third Oil Price Shock: The Effects of Lower Prices*, Routledge and Kegan Paul, London, 1983, pp. 1–31.

22 Flynt Leverett and Jeffrey Bader, "Managing China–US energy competition in the Middle East", *The Washington Quarterly*, Volume 29, Number 1, 2005, pp. 187–201.

23 Maurice A. Adelman, "The ecnomics of the international oil industry", in Judith Rees and Peter Odell (eds), *The International Oil Industry*, Macmillan, London, 1987, p. 51.

24 www.theice.com/futures_europe.jhtml

25 http://www.cmegroup.com/trading/energy/

26 Focus on Saudi Arabia, "Chemicals, refining and greener fuel the targets", *The Times*, London, 23 September 1992, p. 26.

27 Deborah Hargreaves and Mark Nicholson, "Merger unleashes new powerhouse", *The Financial Times*, London, 17 June 1993, p. 23.

28 Louis Turner and James Bedore, *Middle East Industrialisation: A Study of Saudi and Iranian Downstream Investments*, Saxon House, London, 1979, pp. 17–21.

29 Mark Nicholson, "Gargantuan ambition", *The Financial Times Report on Saudi Arabia*, London, 30 January 1992, p. 3.

30 Robert Bailey and John Whelan, *The Gulf*, Committee for Middle East Trade, London, 1990, pp. 31–34.

31 Prema Viswanathan and John Richardson, *Saudi Arabia's Petrochemical Industry Faces New Challenges*, International Chemical Information Services (ICIS), Singapore, 5 May 2010, pp. 1–4.

32 R. Chedid, M. Kobrosly and R. Ghajar, "The potential of gas-to-liquid technology in the energy market: the case of Qatar", *Energy Policy*, Volume 35, Issue 10, October 2007, pp. 4799–4811.

## 8 International and intra-regional trade

1 Hamid Hosseini, "Understanding the market mechanism before Adam Smith: economic thought in Medieval Islam", *History of Political Economy*, Volume 27, Number 3, 1995, pp. 539–61.

2 Jean David C. Boulakia, "Ibn Khaldun: a fourteenth century economist", *Journal of Political Economy*, Volume 79, Number 5, 1971, pp. 1105–18; Deiter Weiss, "Ibn Khaldun on economic transformation", *International Journal of Middle Eastern Studies*, Volume 27, Issue 1, 1995, pp. 29–37.

3 Harry Johnson, "Economic development and international trade", in Harry Johnson (ed.), *Money, Trade and Economic Growth*, Harvard University Press, Cambridge, Mass., 1962, pp. 21–40.

4 Jean-Marie Boland and Francoise Patrick, "Rent seeking and resource booms", *Journal of Development Economics*, Volume 61, Number 3, 2000, pp. 527–42.

5 Ludvig Soderling, *Is the Middle East and North Africa Region Achieving its Trade Potential?*, IMF Working Paper, Number 05/90, Washington, May 2005, pp. 1–24.

6 Nicolas Péridy, "Towards a new trade policy between the USA and the Middle Eastern countries: eliminating trade resistance and export potential", *The World Economy*, Volume 28, Issue 4, 2005, pp. 491–518.

7 Julia Devlin and Peter Yee, "Trade logistics in developing countries: the case of the Middle East", *The World Economy*, Volume 28, Issue 3, 2005, pp. 435–56.

8 Patrick Messerlin and Bernard M. Hoekman, *Harnessing Trade for Development and Growth in the Middle East*, Council on Foreign Relations, New York, 2002, pp. 1–20.

9 Ozden Bayazit and Birsen Karpak, "An analytical network process based framework for successful total quality management: an assessment of Turkish manufacturing readiness", *International Journal of Production Economics*, Volume 105, Issue 1, 2007, pp. 79–96.

10 Enrique G. Mendoza, "The terms of trade, the real exchange rate and economic fluctuations", *International Economic Review*, Volume 36, Number 1, 1995, pp. 101–37.

11 Josef Zweimüller, "Schumpeterian entrepreneurs meet Engel's law: the impact of inequality on innovation driven growth", *Journal of Economic Growth*, Volume 5, Number 2, 2000, pp. 185–206.

12 Roger Owen, *The Middle East in the World Economy, 1800–1914*, Methuen, London, 1981, pp. 69–73.

13 Raul Prebisch, "Commercial policy in the underdeveloped countries", *American Economic Review*, Volume 74, Number 2, 1964, pp. 305–26.

14 Roger Owen, *Cotton and the Egyptian Economy*, Oxford University Press, Oxford, 1969, pp. 196–97.

15 Rodney Wilson, *The Economies of the Middle East*, Macmillan, London, 1979, pp. 74–75.

16 Fatma Al-Sayegh, "Merchants role in a changing society: the case of Dubai", *Middle Eastern Studies*, Volume 34, Issue 1, 1998, pp. 87–102.

17 Richard Le Baron Bowen, "The pearl fisheries of the Persian Gulf", *Middle East Journal*, Volume 5, Number 2, 1951, pp. 161–80.

18 Rodney Wilson, *Euro–Arab Trade: Prospects to the 1990s*, Economist Intelligence Unit Special Report, no. 1105, London, 1988, pp. 25–29.

19 Rodney Wilson, *Cyprus and the International Economy*, Macmillan, London and St Martin's Press, New York, 1992, pp. 60–77.

20 Saleh Al Mani and Salah Al Shaikhly, *The Euro–Arab Dialogue*, Frances Pinter, London, 1983, p. 142.

21 Ali Johany, Michel Berne and Wilson Mixon, *The Saudi Arabian Economy*, Croom Helm, London, 1986, pp. 119–30.

22 Robert Bailey and John Whelan, *The Gulf: British Business at Risk*, Committee for Middle East Trade, London, 1995, pp. 31–34.

23 Caroline Freund and Diana Weinhold, "The internet and international trade in services", *American Economic Review*, Volume 92, Number 2, 2002, pp. 236–40.

24 Elias Ghantus, *Arab Industrial Integration*, Croom Helm, London, 1982, pp. 59–60.

25 B. Momani, "A Middle East free trade area: economic interdependence and peace considered", *The World Economy*, Volume 30, Issue 11, pp. 1683–1700.

26 Jamal Eddine Zarrouk, "Intra-Arab trade: determinants and prospects for expansion", in Said El Naggar (ed.), *Foreign and Intratrade Policies of the Arab Countries*, International Monetary Fund, Washington, D.C., 1992, pp. 152–53.

27 Fayçal Lakhoua, *Past and Present of Arab Economic Integration: Analysis and Evaluation of the Institutions, the Achievements and the Shortcomings*, Initiative to Encourage Economic Research in the Middle East and North Africa, Cairo, 1993, pp. 24–25.

28 Arab Trade Financing Program, *Annual Report 2010*, Arab Trade Financing Program, Abu Dhabi, p. 11.

29 Abdessatar Grissa, *Arab Economic Integration: Current Reality and Future Prospects*, Initiative to Encourage Economic Research in the Middle East and North Africa, Cairo, 1993, pp. 1–2.

30 Hassan Al-Atrash and Tarik Yousef, *Intra-Arab Trade: Is it Too Little?* International Monetary Fund Working Paper WP/00/10, January 2000, pp. 1–19.

31 Rodney Wilson, "Development of transport infrastructure for inter-state trade throughout the Eastern Arab world", in Gerd Nonneman (ed.), *The Middle East and Europe: An Integrated Communities Approach*, Federal Trust, London, 1992, pp. 175–78.

32 Allen Dennis, *The Impact of Regional Trade Agreements and Trade Facilitation in the Middle East and North Africa*, World Bank Policy Research Working Paper, Number 3837, Washington, 2006, pp. 3–6.

# 9 The role of the state

1 Alan Richards and John Waterbury, *A Political Economy of the Middle East: State, Class and Economic Development*, Westview Press, Boulder, Col., 1990, pp. 20–33.

2 "Globalisation, governance and leadership development in the Middle East", in Beverly Dawn Metcalfe and Fouad Mimouni (eds), *Leadership Development in the Middle East*, Edward Elgar, Cheltenham, 2011, pp. 61–85.

3 Zubair Iqbal and Abbas Mirakhor, *Islamic Banking*, International Monetary Fund Occasional Paper Number 49, Washington, D.C., pp. 9–31.

4 Roger Owen, *The Middle East in the World Economy, 1800–1914*, Methuen, London, 1981, pp. 12–35.

5 Jill Crystal, *Oil and Politics: Rulers and Merchants in Kuwait and Qatar*, Cambridge University Press, Cambridge, 1990, pp. 5–15.

6 James H. Lebovic and Ashfaq Ishaq, "Military burden, security needs and economic growth in the Middle East", *Journal of Conflict Resolution*, Volume 31, Number 1, 1987, pp. 106–38.

7 Suleiman Abu-Bader and Aamer S. Abu-Qarn, "Government expenditure, military spending and economic growth: causality evidence from Egypt, Israel and Syria", *Journal of Policy Modelling*, Volume 25, Issues 6–7, 2003, pp. 567–83.

8 Malcolm Knight, Norman Loayza and Delano Villanueva, *The Peace Dividend: Military Spending Cuts and Economic Growth*, World Bank Policy Research Working Paper Number 1577, Washington, February 1996, pp. 1–60.

9 Jan Tinbergen, *Central Planning*, Yale University Press, Cambridge, Mass., 1976, pp. 1–15.

10 Rodney Wilson, "Western, Soviet and Egyptian influences on Iraq's development planning", in Tim Niblock (ed.), *Iraq: The Contemporary State*, Croom Helm, London, 1982. pp. 219–40.

11 Robert Mabro, *The Egyptian Economy, 1952–1972*, Oxford University Press, Oxford, 1974, pp. 83–106.

12 Karen Pfeifer, "How Tunisia, Morocco, Jordan and even Egypt became IMF 'Success Stories' in the 1990s", in Middle East Research and Information Project (MERIP), *Reform or Reaction? Dilemmas of Economic Development in the Middle East*, Middle East Report, Number 210, Spring, 1999, pp. 23–27.

13 Afshin Molavi, "Buying time in Tehran: Iran and the China Model", *Foreign Affairs*, Volume 83, Number 6, 2004, pp. 9–16.

14 Lucio Sarno, "Real exchange rate behavior in the Middle East: a re-examination", *Economic Letters*, Volume 66, Issue 2, 2000, pp. 127–36.

15 Tony Walker, "Public sector liability for Egypt", *The Financial Times*, 18 March 1993, p. 6.

16 Bruce Bueno de Mesquita and George W. Downs, "Development and democracy", *Foreign Affairs*, Volume 84, Number 5, 2005, pp. 77–86.

17 Rodney Wilson, "Economic democracy: state direction and popular participation", in *Proceedings of the British Society for Middle Eastern Studies Conference*, St Andrews University, St Andrews, 1992, pp. 521–31.

18 Stephen J. H. Dearden, *Corruption and Economic Development*, Manchester Metropolitan University, Economic Development and Policy Study Group Discussion Paper Number 18, 2000, pp. 1–14.

19 Shang-Jin Wei, *Corruption in Economic Development: Beneficial Grease, Minor Annoyance or Major Obstacle?*, Staff Paper, Kennedy School of Government, Harvard University, 1999, pp. 1–28.

20 Pak Hung Mo, "Corruption and economic growth", *Journal of Comparative Economics*, Volume 29, Issue 1, 2001, pp. 66–79.

21 Timur Kuran, "Why the Middle East is economically underdeveloped: historical mechanisms of institutional stagnation", *Journal of Economic Perspectives*, Volume 18, Number 1, 2004, pp. 71–90.

22 Nasser Saidi, *Corporate Governance in MENA Countries: Improving Transparency and Disclosure*, Lebanese Transparency Association, Beirut, 2004, pp. 16–26.

23 Rodney Wilson, "Islam and Business", *Thunderbird International Business Review*, Volume 48, Number 1, 2006, pp. 109–23.

24 Rodney Wilson, "Islam et Capitalisme Reconsidérés", *Maghreb-Machrek*, No. 187, 2006, pp. 29–44.

# Bibliography

Aarts, Paul and Nonneman, Gerd, *Saudi Arabia in the Balance: Political Economy, Society and Foreign Affairs*, New York University Press, New York, 2006.

Abbas, Ali, "Middle East competitiveness in the 21st century's global market", *The Academy of Management Executives*, Volume 13, Number 1, 1999, pp. 102–8.

Abdel-Khalek, Gouda, *Stabilisation and Adjustment in Egypt: Reform or De-Industrialisation?* Edward Elgar, Cheltenham, United Kingdom, 2001.

Abdul-Hadi and Ayman Shafiq Fayyad, *Stock Markets of the Arab World: Trends, Problems and Prospects for Integration*, Routledge, London, 1988.

Abu-Bader, Suleiman and Abu-Qarn, Aamer S., "Government expenditure, military spending and economic growth: causality evidence from Egypt, Israel and Syria", *Journal of Policy Modelling*, Volume 25, Issues 6–7, 2003, pp. 567–83.

Adelman, Maurice A., "The economics of the international oil industry", in Rees, Judith and Odell, Peter (eds), *The International Oil Industry*, Macmillan, London, 1987.

Adelman, Maurice, *The World Petroleum Market*, Johns Hopkins University Press, Baltimore, Md, 1972.

Aharini, Yair, *The Israeli Economy: Dreams and Realities*, Routledge, London, 1991.

Ahmed, Akbar S., *Postmodernism and Islam: Predicament and Promise*, Routledge, London, 1992.

Al Harran, Saad, *Islamic Finance: Partnership Financing*, Pelanduk Publishing, Selangor, Malaysia, 1993.

Al Mani, Saleh and Al Shaikhly, Salah, *The Euro-Arab Dialogue,* Frances Pinter, London, 1983.

Alamdari, Kazem, *Why the Middle East Lagged Behind: The Case of Iran*, University Press of America, Lanham, 2005.

Al-Atrash, Hassan and Yousef, Tarik, *Intra-Arab Trade: Is it too Little?* International Monetary Fund Working Paper WP/00/10, Washington, January 2000.

Al-Dosary, Adel S. and Rahman, Syed Masur, "The role of the private sector towards Saudisation (localisation)", *International Journal of Arab Culture, Management and Sustainable Development*, Volume 1, Number 2, 2009, pp. 131–43.

Ali, Abdullah Yusuf, *The Holy Koran: Text, Translation and Commentary*, That es-Salasil, Kuwait, 1988.

Ali, Abdullah Yusuf, *The Meaning of the Holy Qur'an*, Islamic Book Trust, Kuala Lumpur, 2007.

Ali, Sheikh R., *Oil and Power: Political Dynamics in the Middle East*, Frances Pinter Publishers, London, 1987.

Aliboni, Roberto, Dessouki, Ali Hillal, Ibrahim, Saad Eddin, Luciani, Giacomo and Padoan, Piercarlo (eds), *Egypt's Economic Potential*, Croom Helm, London, 1984.

Al-Otaiba, Mana Saeed, *OPEC and the Petroleum Industry*, Croom Helm, London, 1975.

Al-Sayegh, Fatma, "Merchants' role in a changing society: the case of Dubai", *Middle Eastern Studies*, Volume 34, Issue 1, 1998, pp. 87–102.

Amin, Galal, *The Modernisation of Poverty*, Brill, Leiden, 1974.

Amin, Samir, *Maldevelopment: Anatomy of a Global Failure*, Zed Books, London, 1990.

Amuzegar, Jahangir, *Iran's Economy under the Islamic Republic*, I.B. Tauris, London, 1997.

Aryan, Hossein, "Iran: the impact of Islamisation on the financial system", in Wilson, Rodney (ed.), *Islamic Financial Markets,* Routledge, London, 1990, pp. 155–70.

Aydın, Zülküf, *The Political Economy of Turkey*, Pluto Press, London, 2005.

Azzam, Henry T., "Bahrain's offshore banking centre", *Arab Gulf Journal*, Volume 4, Number 1, 1984, pp. 23–35.

Bailey, Robert and Whelan, John, *The Gulf*, Committee for Middle East Trade, London, 1990.

Bailey, Robert and Whelan, John, *The Gulf: British Business at Risk*, Committee for Middle East Trade, London, 1995.

Bauer, Peter, *The Development Frontier: Essays in Applied Economics*, Harvester Wheatsheaf, Hemel Hempstead, Herts., 1991.

Bayazit, Ozden and Karpak, Birsen, "An analytical network process based framework for successful total quality management: an assessment of Turkish manufacturing readiness", *International Journal of Production Economics*, Volume 105, Issue 1, 2007, pp. 79–96.

Beblawi, Hassan and Luciani, Giacomo (eds), *The Rentier State*, Croom Helm, London, 1987.

Belgrave, Robert, *Energy: Two Decades of Crises*, Gower, London, 1983.

Ben-Bassat, Avi, *The Israeli Economy, 1985–1998*, Massachusetts Institute of Technology Press, Cambridge, Mass., 2002.

Birks, J.S., Seccombe, I.J. and Sinclair, C.A., "Migrant workers in the Arab Gulf: the impact of declining oil revenues", *International Labour Review*, Volume 20, Number 4, Winter 1986, pp. 799–814.

Birks, Stace and Sinclair, Clive, *Arab Manpower*, Croom Helm, London, 1980.

Birks, Stace, "The demographic challenge in the Arab Gulf", in Pridham, Brian (ed.), *The Arab World*, Croom Helm, London, 1988, pp. 131–52.

Boland, Jean-Marie and Patrick, Francoise, "Rent seeking and resource booms", *Journal of Development Economics*, Volume 61, Number 3, 2000, pp. 527–42.

Boulakia, Jean David C., "Ibn Khaldun: a fourteenth century economist", *Journal of Political Economy*, Volume 79, Number 5, 1971, pp. 1105–18.

Bowen, Richard Le Baron, "The pearl fisheries of the Persian Gulf", *Middle East Journal*, Volume 5, Number 2, 1951, pp. 161–80.

Bowker, Robert, *Egypt and the Politics of Change in the Arab Middle East*, Edward Elgar, Cheltenham, United Kingdom, 2010.

British Petroleum, *Energy Outlook 2030*, London, January 2012.

British Petroleum, *Statistical Review of World Energy*, London, June 2011.

Caldwell, John C., "Towards a restatement of demographic transition theory", *Population and Development Review*, Volume 2, Numbers 3–4, 1976, pp. 321–66.

Chapra, M. Umer, *Islam and the Economic Challenge*, Islamic Foundation, Leicester, 1992.

Chapra, M. Umer, *Towards a Just Monetary System*, Islamic Foundation, Leicester, 1985.

Chedid, R., Kobrosly, M. and Ghajar, R., "The potential of gas to-liquid technology in the energy market: the case of Qatar", *Energy Policy*, Volume 35, Issue 10, October 2007, pp. 4799–4811.

Chenery, Hollis, "Foreign aid", in Eatwell, John, Milgate, Murray and Newman, Peter (eds), *The New Palgrave: Economic Development*, Macmillan, London, 1989, pp. 130–44.

Cheshire, John, "The energy demand impact of conservation technology", in Hawdon, David (ed.), *Oil Prices in the 1990s*, Macmillan, London, 1989.

Choudhury, Masudul Alam, *The Principles of Islamic Political Economy*, Macmillan, London, 1992.

Coleman, David and Nixon, Frederick, *Economics of Change in Less Developed Countries*, 2nd edition, Philip Allan, Oxford, 1986.

Conway, Patrick, "Algeria: windfalls in a socialist economy," in Alan Gelb (ed.), *Oil Windfalls: Blessing or Curse?*, Oxford University Press for the World Bank, Oxford, 1988, pp. 147–69.

Cooper, Mark N., *The Transformation of Egypt*, Croom Helm, London, 1982.

Cramp, Peter, *Economic Development*, Anforme, London, 2007.

Creane, Susan, Goyal, Rishi, Mushfiq, A. and Sab, Randa, *Financial Development in the Middle East and North Africa*, International Monetary Fund, Washington, 2003.

Crystal, Gill, *Oil and Politics in the Gulf, Rulers and Merchants in Kuwait and Qatar*, Cambridge University Press, Cambridge, 1990.

Cuddihy, William, "Agricultural prices, farm mechanization and the demand for labour", in Alan Richards and Philip Martin (eds), *Migration, Mechanization and Agricultural Labour Markets in Egypt*, Westview Press, Boulder, Col., 1983, pp. 225–34.

Danielsen, Albert, *The Evolution of OPEC*, Harcourt Brace Jovanovich, New York, 1982.

Davidson, Christopher, *Abu Dhabi: Oil and Beyond*, Columbia University Press, Ithaca, 2009.

Davidson, Christopher, *Dubai: The Vulnerability of Success*, Hurst and Company, London, 2008.

de Mesquita, Bruce Bueno and Downs, George W., "Development and democracy", *Foreign Affairs*, Volume 84, Number 5, 2005, pp. 77–86.

Dearden, Stephen J. H., *Corruption and Economic Development*, Manchester Metropolitan University, Economic Development and Policy Study Group Discussion Paper Number 18, 2000, pp. 1–14.

Deeb, Marius, "Bank Misr and the emergence of the local bourgeoisie in Egypt", in Kedourie, Elie (ed.), *The Middle Eastern Economy: Studies in Economics and Economic History*, Frank Cass, London, 1976, pp. 69–86.

Dennis, Allen, *The Impact of Regional Trade Agreements and Trade Facilitation in the Middle East and North Africa*, World Bank Policy Research Working Paper, Number 3837, Washington, 2006.

Devlin, Julia and Yee, Peter, "Trade logistics in developing countries: the case of the Middle East", *The World Economy*, Volume 28, Issue 3, 2005, pp. 435–56.

Dorfman, Robert, "Economic development from the beginning to Rostow", *Journal of Economic Literature*, Volume 29, Number 2, 1991, pp. 573–91.

Easterlin, Richard, "Modernisation and fertility: a critical essay", in R. Bulatao and R. Lee (eds.), *Determinants of Fertility in Developing Countries*, Academic Press, New York, Volume 2, pp. 562–86.

El Ashker, Ahmed, *The Islamic Business Enterprise*, Croom Helm, London, 1987.

Elkan, Walter, *An Introduction to Development Economics*, Penguin Books, Harmondsworth, Middlesex, 1978.

Elm, Mostafa, *Oil, Power and Principle: Iran's Oil Nationalisation and its Aftermath*, Syracuse University Press, New York, 1992.

El-Naggar, Said (ed.), *Privatisation and Structural Adjustment in the Arab Countries*, International Monetary Fund, Washington DC, 1989.

Fisher, Anthony C., *Resources and Environmental Economics*, Cambridge University Press, Cambridge, 1981.

Frejka, Thomas, "Long term prospects for world population growth", *Population and Development Review*, Volume 7, Number 3, 1981, pp. 489–511.

Freund, Caroline and Weinhold, Diana, "The internet and international trade in services", *American Economic Review*, Volume 92, Number 2, 2002, pp. 236–40.

Fry, Maxwell, "Money and capital: financial deepening in economic development", *Journal of Money, Credit and Banking*, Volume 10, Number 4, 1979, pp. 464–75.

Gabbay, Rony, *Communism and Agrarian Reform in Iraq*, Croom Helm, London, 1978.

Geertz, Clifford, "The Bazaar economy: information and search in peasant marketing", *American Economic Review*, Volume 68, Number 2, 1978, pp. 28–32.

Gelb, Alan, *Oil Windfalls, Blessing or Curse*, Oxford University Press, for the World Bank, Oxford, 1988.

Gerschenkron, Alexander, *Economic Backwardness in Historical Perspective*, Harvard University Press, Cambridge, Mass., 1962.

Ghantus, Elias, *Arab Industrial Integration*, Croom Helm, London, 1982.

Gillis, Malcolm, Perkins, Dwight, Roemer, Michael and Snodgrass, Douglas, *Economics of Development*, 3rd edition, W.W. Norton, New York, 1992.

Goel, Rajeev K. and Nelson, Michael A., "Corruption in MENA countries: an empirical investigation", in Sayan, Serdar (ed.), *Economic Performance in the Middle East and North Africa: Institutions, Corruption and Reform*, Routledge London and New York, 2009, pp. 13–24.

Grissa, Abdessatar, *Arab Economic Integration: Current Reality and Future Prospects*, Initiative to Encourage Economic Research in the Middle East and North Africa, Cairo, 1993.

Gurley, J.G. and Shaw, E.S., "Financial structure and economic development", *Economic Development and Cultural Change*, Volume 15, Number 1, 1967, pp. 257–68.

Hallam, David, "International investment in developing country agriculture: issues and challenges", *Food Security*, Volume 3, Number 1, 2011, pp. 91–98.

Hansen, Bent, *The Political Economy of Poverty, Equity and Growth: Egypt and Turkey*, Oxford University Press for the World Bank, Oxford, 1991.

Harbison, Frederick, "Human resources development planning in modernising economies", *International Labour Review*, Volume 85, Number 5, 1962, pp. 1–23.

Hargreaves, Deborah and Nicholson, Mark, "Merger unleashes new powerhouse", *The Financial Times*, London, 17 June 1993, p. 23.

Harik, Iliya and Sullivan, Denis J., *Privatisation and Liberalisation in the Middle East*, Indiana University Press, Bloomington, 1992.

Harris, John and Todaro, Michael, "Migration, unemployment and development: a two-sector analysis", *American Economic Review*, Volume 60, Number 1, March 1970, pp. 126–52.

Henry, Clement and Springborg, Robert, *Globalisation and the Politics of Development in the Middle East*, Cambridge University Press, Cambridge, 2001, pp. 134–67.

Hershlag, Z.Y., *The Contemporary Turkish Economy*, Routledge, London, 1988.

Hertog, Steffen, *Princes, Brokers and Bureaucrats, Oil and the State in Saudi Arabia*, Cornell University Press, Ithaca, 2010.

Hever, Shir, *The Political Economy of Israel's Occupation*, Pluto Press, London, 2010.

Hirschman, Albert O., *The Strategy of Economic Development*, Yale University Press, New Haven, Conn., 1958.

Hosseini, Hamid, "Understanding the market mechanism before Adam Smith: economic thought in Medieval Islam", *History of Political Economy*, Volume 27, Number 3, 1995, pp. 539–61.

Ibrahim, Saad Eddin, *The New Arab Social Order*, Westview Press, Boulder, Col., 1982.

Ikram, Khalid, *The Egyptian Economy, 1952–2000*, Routledge, London, 2006.

Iqbal, Zubair and Mirakhor, Abbas, *Islamic Banking*, International Monetary Fund Occasional Paper Number 49, Washington, D.C., 1987.

Isachsen, Arne Jon, Hamilton, Carl B. and Gylfason, Thorvaldur, *Understanding the Market Economy*, Oxford University Press, Oxford, 1993.

Issawi, Charles, "The economic and social foundations of democracy in the Middle East," *International Affairs*, January 1956, reprinted in Issawi, Charles, *The Arab World's Legacy*, Darwin Press, Princeton, 1981.

Issawi, Charles, *An Economic History of the Middle East and North Africa*, Methuen, London, 1982.

Jackson, P. and Lockhart, C. (eds), *The Cambridge History of Iran: The Timurid and Safavid Periods*, Volume 6, Cambridge University Press, Cambridge, 1986.

Jbili, Abdelali, Kramarenko, Vitali and Bailén, José, *Islamic Republic of Iran: Managing the Transition to a Market Economy*, International Monetary Fund, Washington D.C., 2007.

Johany, Ali D., *The Myth of the OPEC Cartel*, John Wiley, Chichester, 1980.

Johany, Ali D., Berne, Michel and Mixon, J. Wilson, *The Saudi Arabia Economy*, Croom Helm, London, 1986.

Johnson, Harry, "Economic development and international trade", in Johnson, Harry (ed.), *Money, Trade and Economic Growth*, Harvard University Press, Cambridge, Mass., 1962, pp. 21–40.

Jones, Geoffrey, *Banking and Oil: The History of the British Bank of the Middle East*, Volume 2, Cambridge University Press, Cambridge, 1987.

Jones, Geoffrey, *The Imperial Bank of Persia, Banking and Empire in Iran: The History of the British Bank of the Middle East*, Volume 1, Cambridge University Press, Cambridge, 1986.

Khaf, Monzer, "Zakat: unresolved issues in contemporary Fiqh", in Sadeq, Abdul Hasan, Pramanik, Ataul Huq and Hassan, Nik (eds), *Development and Finance in Islam*, International Islamic University Press, Selangor, Malaysia, 1991, pp. 173–90.

Karshenas, Massoud, *Oil, State and Industrialisation in Iran*, Cambridge University Press, Cambridge, 1991.

Kedourie, Elie (ed.), *The Middle Eastern Economies: Studies in Economics and Economic History*, Frank Cass, London, 1977.

Khader, Bichara and El-Wifati, Bashir (eds), *The Economic Development of Libya*, Croom Helm, London, 1987.

Khalidi, Raja, *The Arab Economy in Israel*, Croom Helm, London, 1988.

Khan, Waqar Masood, *Towards an Interest Free Islamic Economic System*, Islamic Foundation, Leicester, 1985.

Khouja, M.W. and Sadler, P.G., *The Economy of Kuwait*, Macmillan, London, 1979.

Kirk, Dudley, "Demographic transition theory", *Population Studies*, Volume 50, Issue 3, 1996, pp. 361–87.

Knight, Malcolm, Loayza, Norman and Villanueva, Delano, *The Peace Dividend: Military Spending Cuts and Economic Growth*, World Bank Policy Research Working Paper Number 1577, Washington, February 1996, pp. 1–60.

Koopmann, Georg, Matthies, Klaus and Reszat, Beate, *Oil and the International Economy: Lessons from Two Price Shocks*, Transaction Press, Hamburg, 1984.

Kuran, Timur, "Why the Middle East is economically underdeveloped: historical mechanisms of institutional stagnation", *Journal of Economic Perspectives*, Volume 18, Number 1, 2004, pp. 71–90.

Lakhoua, Fayçal, *Past and Present of Arab Economic Integration: Analysis and Evaluation of the Institutions, the Achievements and the Shortcomings*, Initiative to Encourage Economic Research in the Middle East and North Africa, Cairo, 1993.

Lane, Edward William, *The Manners and Customs of Modern Egyptians*, Everyman Library, London, 1908.

Lebovic, James H. and Ishaq, Ashfaq, "Military burden, security needs and economic growth in the Middle East", *Journal of Conflict Resolution*, Volume 31, Number 1, 1987, pp. 106–38.

Leverett, Flynt and Bader, Jeffrey, "Managing China US energy competition in the Middle East", *The Washington Quarterly*, Volume 29, Number 1, 2005, pp. 187–201.

Lewis, W. Arthur, *The Theory of Economic Growth*, Irwin, Homewood, Illinois, 1995.

Licklider, Roy, *Political Power and the Arab Oil Weapon*, University of California Press, Berkeley, 1988.

Longrigg, Stephen Hemsley, *Oil in the Middle East: Its Discovery and Development*, Oxford University Press, Oxford, 1954.

Luciani, Giacomo, "Allocative versus production states: a theoretical framework", in Beblawi, Hazem and Luciani, Giacomo (eds), *The Rentier State*, Croom Helm, London, 1987, pp. 63–82.

Maachou, Abdelkader, *OAPEC and Arab Petroleum*, Berger-Levrault, Paris, 1982.

Mabro, Robert, "Industrial growth, agricultural underemployment and the Lewis model: the Egyptian case, 1937–75", *Journal of Development Studies*, Volume 3, Number 4, July 1967, pp. 330–45.

Mabro, Robert, *The Egyptian Economy, 1952–1972*, Oxford University Press, Oxford, 1974.

Mannan, M.A., *Islamic Economics: Theory and Practice*, Hodder and Stoughton, London, 1986.

Mayer, Ann Elizabeth, "Islamic banking and credit policies in the Sadat era: the social origins of Islamic banking in Egypt", *Arab Law Quarterly*, Volume 1, Part 1, 1985, pp. 32–50.

Meier, Gerald M., *Politics and Policy Making in Developing Countries: Perspectives in the New Political Economy*, ICS Press, San Francisco, 1991.

Mendoza, Enrique G., "The terms of trade, the real exchange rate and economic fluctuations", *International Economic Review*, Volume 36, Number 1, 1995, pp. 101–37.

Messerlin, Patrick and Hoekman, Bernard M., *Harnessing Trade for Development and Growth in the Middle East*, Council on Foreign Relations, New York, 2002, pp. 1–20.

Metzer, Jacob, *The Divided Economy of Mandatory Palestine*, Cambridge University Press, Cambridge, 1998.

Miller, Frederic P, Vandome, Agnes F, and McBrewster, John, *The Economy of Egypt*, VDM Publishing House, Saarbrücken, Germany, 2009.

Mo, Pak Hung, "Corruption and economic growth", *Journal of Comparative Economics*, Volume 29, Issue 1, 2001, pp. 66–79.

Molavi, Afshin, "Buying time in Tehran: Iran and the China Model", *Foreign Affairs*, Volume 83, Number 6, 2004, pp. 9–16.

Momani, B., "A Middle East free trade area: economic interdependence and peace considered", *The World Economy*, Volume 30, Issue 11, pp. 1683–1700.

Montasser, Essam, "The Arab economy and its development strategy: a new Arab economic order", in Kerr, Malcolm H. and Yassin, El Sayed, *Rich and Poor States in the Middle East*, Westview Press, Boulder, Colorado, 1982, pp. 99–128.

Morse, Edward, "An overview: gains, costs and dilemmas", in Pearce, Joan (ed.), *The Third Oil Price Shock: The Effects of Lower Prices*, Routledge and Kegan Paul, London, 1983, pp. 1–31.

Muna, Farid A., *The Arab Executive*, St Martin's Press, New York, 1980.

Nas, Tevfik F. and Odekon, Mehmet (eds), *Economics and Politics of Turkish Liberalization*, Associated University Presses, New Jersey, 1992.

Niblock, Tim, *The Political Economy of Saudi Arabia*, Routledge, London, 2007.

Niblock, Tim and Murphy, Emma (eds), *Economic Liberalisation in the Middle East*, I.B. Tauris, London, 1992.

Nicholson, Mark, "Gargantuan ambition", *The Financial Times Report on Saudi Arabia*, London, 30 January 1992, p. 3.

Nitzan, Jonathan, *The Global Political Economy of Israel*, Pluto Press, London, 2002.

Nixson, Frederick, *Development Economics*, Heinemann, London, 2001.

Nurkse, Ragnar, *Problems of Capital Formation in Underdeveloped Countries*, Oxford University Press, Oxford, 1953.

Okeahalam, Charles C., "Institutions and financial market development in the MENA region", *Progress in Development Studies*, Volume 5, Number 4, 2005, pp. 310–28.

Öniş, Ziya and Şenses, Fikret, *Turkey and the Global Economy: Neo-Liberal Restructuring and Integration in the Post Crisis Era*, Routledge, London, 2009.

Önis, Ziya, "Organisation of export-oriented industrialisation: the Turkish foreign trade companies in a comparative perspective", in Nas, Tevfik F. and Odekon, Mehmet (eds), *Economics and Politics of Turkish Liberalisation*, Lehigh University Press and Associated University Press, London, 1992, pp. 73–100.

Oufriha, Fatima-Zohra, "Aspects of the brain drain in Algeria", in Zahlan, A.B. (ed.), *The Arab Brain Drain*, Ithaca Press, London, 1981, pp. 100–114.

Owen, Roger, *Cotton and the Egyptian Economy*, Oxford University Press, Oxford, 1969.

Owen, Roger, *The Middle East in the World Economy, 1800–1914*, Methuen, London, 1981.

Page, John with MacDonald, Lawrence, *The East Asian Miracle: Economic Growth and Public Policy*, Oxford University Press for the World Bank, Oxford, 1993.

Paine, Susan, *Exporting Workers: The Turkish Case*, Cambridge University Press, Cambridge, 1974.

Péridy, Nicolas, "Towards a new trade policy between the USA and the Middle Eastern Countries: eliminating trade resistance and export potential", *The World Economy*, Volume 28, Issue 4, 2005, pp. 491–518.

Pfeifer, Karen, "How Tunisia, Morocco, Jordan and even Egypt became IMF 'Success Stories' in the 1990s", in Middle East Research and Information Project (MERIP), *Reform or Reaction? Dilemmas of Economic Development in the Middle East*, Middle East Report, Number 210, Spring, 1999, pp. 23–27.

Platteau, Jean Philippe, "Behind the market stage where real societies exist: the role of public and private order institutions", *Journal of Development Studies*, Volume 30, Number 3, 1994, pp. 533–77.

Pomfret, Richard, *Diverse Paths of Economic Development*, Harvester Wheatsheaf, New York, 1992.

Poulson, Barry W., *Economic Development: Private and Public Choice*, West Publishing, Minneapolis, 1994.

Prebisch, Raul, "Commercial policy in the underdeveloped countries", *American Economic Review*, Volume 74, Number 2, 1964, pp. 305–26.

Presley, John R., *Directory of Islamic Financial Institutions*, Macmillan, London, 1988.

Rahman, Afzalur, *Economic Doctrines of Islam: Banking and Insurance*, Muslim Schools Trust, London, 1979.

Razin, Assaf and Sadka, Efraim, *The Economy of Modern Israel: Malaise and Promise*, University of Chicago Press, Chicago, 1993.

Richards, Alan and Waterbury, John, *A Political Economy of the Middle East: State, Class and Economic Development*, Westview Press, Boulder, 3rd edition, 2007.

Richards, Alan, Martin, Philip and Nagaar, Rifaat, "Labour shortages in Egyptian agriculture", in Richards, Alan and Martin, Philip (eds), *Migration, Mechanisation and Agricultural Labour Markets in Egypt*, Westview Press, Boulder, Col., 1983, pp. 21–44.

Rima, Ingrid Hahne, *Development of Economic Analysis*, 5th edition, Irwin, Homewood, Ill., 1991.

Rivlin, Paul, *Arab Economies in the Twenty-First Century*, Cambridge University Press, Cambridge, 2009, pp. 61–94.

Robbins, Philip J., "Politics and the 1986 electoral law in Jordan", in Wilson, Rodney (ed.), *Politics and the Economy in Jordan*, Routledge, London, 1991, pp. 184–207.

Rodinson, Maxime, *Islam and Capitalism*, Penguin Books, Harmondsworth, Middlesex, 1966.

Roncaglia, Alessandro, *The International Oil Market*, Macmillan, London, 1985.

Rosenstein-Rodan, Paul N., "Problems of industrialisation of Eastern and Southeastern Europe", *Economic Journal*, Volume 53, Number 210–11, June–September 1943, pp. 202–11.

Rostow, W.W., *The Stages of Economic Growth: A Non-Communist Manifesto*, Cambridge University Press, Cambridge, 1961.

Roy, Delwin, "The hidden economy of Egypt", *Middle Eastern Studies*, Volume 28, Number 4, 1992, pp. 689–711.

Sabagh, George (ed.), *The Modern Economic and Social History of the Middle East in its World Context*, Cambridge University Press, 1989.

Sabagh, Georges, "Migration and social mobility in Egypt", in Kerr, Malcolm and El Sayed, Yassin (eds), *Rich and Poor States in the Middle East: Egypt and the New Arab Order*, Westview Press, Boulder, Col., 1982, pp. 71–95.

Sacks, Wolfgang, "Progress and development", in Ekins, Paul and Max-Neef, Manfred, *Real Life Economics: Understanding Wealth Creation*, Routledge, London, 1992, pp. 156–61.

Saidi, Nasser, *Corporate Governance in MENA Countries: Improving Transparency and Disclosure*, Lebanese Transparency Association, Beirut, 2004.

Sardar, Ziauddin, *Islamic Futures: The Shape of Ideas to Come*, Mansell, London, 1985.

Sarno, Lucio, "Real exchange rate behavior in the Middle East: a re-examination", *Economic Letters*, Volume 66, Issue 2, 2000, pp. 127–36.

Schumpeter, Joseph, *The Theory of Economic Development*, Harvard University Press, Camrbidge, Mass., 1934.

Seccombe, Ian and Wilson, Rodney, *Trade and Finance in Jordan*, Durham University, Centre for Middle East and Islamic Studies, Occasional Paper No. 33, 1987.

Sen, Amartya, *Development as Freedom*, Anchor Books, New York, 1999.

Seymour, Ian, *OPEC: Instrument of Change*, Macmillan, London, 1980.

Share, Monther, "The use of Jordanian workers' remittances", in Khader, Bichara and Badran, Adnan (eds), *The Economic Development of Jordan*, Croom Helm, London, 1987, pp. 32–44.

Sherbiny, Naiem and Serageldin, Ishmail, "Expatriate labour and economic growth: Saudi demand for Egyptian labour", in Kerr, Malcolm and Yassin, El Sayed (eds), *Rich and Poor States in the Middle East*, Westview Press, Boulder, Col., 1982, pp. 225–57.

Shwadran, Benjamin, *Middle East Oil: Issues and Problems*, Schenkman, Cambridge, Mass., 1977.

Siddiqi, Muhammad Nejatullah, *Insurance in an Islamic Economy*, Islamic Foundation, Leicester, 1985.

Siddiqi, Muhammad Nejatullah, *Muslim Economic Thinking: A Survey of Contemporary Literature*, Islamic Foundation, Leicester, 1981.

Soderling, Ludvig, *Is the Middle East and North Africa Region Achieving its Trade Potential?*, IMF Working Paper, Number 05/90, Washington, May 2005.

Talha, Larbi, *Le Salariat immigré dans la crise*, Éditions du Centre National de la Recherche Scientifique, Paris, 1989.

Teitelbaum, Michael, "Relevance of demographic transition theory for developing countries", *Science*, Number 188, 1977, pp. 420–25.

Thirlwall, A.P., *Financing Economic Development*, Macmillan, London, 1976.

Tinbergen, Jan, *Central Planning*, Yale University Press, Cambridge, Mass., 1976.

Todaro, Michael P. and Smith, Stephen C., *Economic Development*, Pearson, Harlow, 2009.

Tosun, Cevat, Dallen, Timothy and Öztürk, Yüksel, "Tourism growth, national development and regional inequality in Turkey", *Journal of Sustainable Tourism*, Volume 11, Numbers 2–3, 2003, pp. 133–61.

Turner, Louis and Bedore, James, *Middle East Industrialisation: A Study of Saudi and Iranian Downstream Investments*, Royal Institute for International Affairs, Saxon House, London, 1979.

Turner, Louis, *Oil Companies in the International System*, George Allen & Unwin, London, 1983.

Viswanathan, Prema and Richardson, John, *Saudi Arabia's Petrochemical Industry Faces New Challenges*, International Chemical Information Services (ICIS), Singapore, 5 May 2010.

Walker, Tony, "Public sector liability for Egypt", *The Financial Times*, 18 March 1993, p. 6.

Watt, W. Montgomery, *Islamic Fundamentalism and Modernity*, Routledge, London, 1989.

Wei, Shang-Jin, *Corruption in Economic Development: Beneficial Grease, Minor Annoyance or Major Obstacle*, Staff Paper, Kennedy School of Government, Harvard University, 1999, pp. 1–28.

Weiss, Deiter, "Ibn Khaldun on economic transformation", *International Journal of Middle Eastern Studies*, Volume 27, Issue 1, 1995, pp. 29–37.

Wikan, Unni, *Life Among the Poor in Cairo*, Tavistock Publications, London, 1980.

Wilber, Charles K. and Jameson, Kenneth P., *The Political Economy of Development and Underdevelopment*, McGraw Hill, New York, 6th edition, 1995.

Wilson, Rodney, "Islam et capitalisme reconsidérés", *Maghreb-Machrek*, Number 187, 2006, pp. 29–44.

Wilson, Rodney with Al-Salamah, Abdullah, Malik, Monica and Al-Rajhi, Ahmed, *Economic Development in Saudi Arabia*, Routledge Curzon, London, 2004.

Wilson, Rodney, "Japan's exports to the Middle East: directional and commodity trends and price behaviour", *Middle East Journal*, Volume 38, Number 3, 1984, pp. 454–73.

Wilson, Rodney, "Development of transport infrastructure for inter-state trade throughout the eastern Arab world", in Nonneman, Gerd (ed.), *The Middle East and Europe: An Integrated Communities Approach*, Federal Trust for Education and Research, London, 1992, pp. 175–78.

Wilson, Rodney, "Economic democracy: state direction and popular participation", in *Proceedings of the British Society for Middle Eastern Studies Conference*, St Andrews University, St Andrews, 1992, pp. 521–31.

Wilson, Rodney, "The role of commercial banking in the Jordanian economy", in Khader, Bichara and Badran, Aidnan (eds), *The Economic Development of Jordan*, Croom Helm, London, 1987, pp. 45–61.

Wilson, Rodney, "Development of transport infrastructure for inter-state trade throughout the Eastern Arab world", in Nonneman, Gerd (ed.), *The Middle East and Europe: An Integrated Communities Approach*, Federal Trust, London, 1992.

Wilson, Rodney, "Education priorities for a service dominated economy: the case of Kuwait", *Teaching Public Administration*, Volume 9, Number 1, Spring 1989, pp. 52–59.

Wilson, Rodney, "Globalisation, governance and leadership development in the Middle East", in Metcalfe, Beverly Dawn and Mimouni, Fouad (eds), *Leadership Development in the Middle East*, Edward Elgar, Cheltenham, 2011, pp. 61–85.

Wilson, Rodney, "Islam and business", *Thunderbird International Business Review*, Volume 48, Number 1, 2006, pp. 109–23.

Wilson, Rodney, "The evolution of the Saudi banking system and its relationship with Bahrain", in Niblock, Tim (ed.), *State, Society and Economy in Saudi Arabia*, Croom Helm, London, 1982, pp. 278–300.

Wilson, Rodney, "Western, Soviet and Egyptian influences on Iraq's development planning", in Niblock, Tim (ed.), *Iraq: The Contemporary State*, Croom Helm, London, 1982, pp. 219–40.

Wilson, Rodney, *Banking and Finance in the Arab Middle East*, Macmillan, London, 1983.

Wilson, Rodney, *Cyprus and the International Economy*, Macmillan, London, 1992.

Wilson, Rodney, *Euro-Arab Trade: Prospects to the 1990s*, Economist Intelligence Unit Special Report, Number 1105, London, 1988.

Wilson, Rodney, *Islamic Business: Theory and Practice*, Economist Intelligence Unit Special Report, Number 221, London, 1985.

Wilson, Rodney, *The Economies of the Middle East*, Macmillan, London, 1979.

Young, Arthur, *Saudi Arabia: The Making of a Financial Giant*, Longmans for New York University Press, New York, 1983.

Yousef, Tarik, "Development, growth and policy reform in the Middle East and North Africa since 1950", *Journal of Economic Perspectives*, Volume 18, Number 3, Summer 2004, pp. 91–115.

Zarrouk, Jamal Eddine, "Intra-Arab trade: determinants and prospects for expansion", in El Naggar, Said (ed.), *Foreign and Intratrade Policies of the Arab Countries*, International Monetary Fund, Washington, D.C., 1992.

Zweimüller, Josef, "Schumpeterian entrepreneurs meet Engel's law: the impact of inequality on innovation driven growth", *Journal of Economic Growth*, Volume 5, Number 2, 2000, pp. 185–206.

# Index

# The Transformation of the Gulf

Politics, Economics and the Global Order

Edited By **David Held, Kristian Ulrichsen**

This book examines the political, economic and social transformation of the six member-states of the Gulf Cooperation Council (GCC) and the ways in which these states are both shaping, and being reshaped by, the processes of globalisation. Adopting a multidisciplinary approach, the volume combines thematic chapters focusing on issues such as globalisation, nationalism and identity, political thinking, and economic diversification and redistributive policymaking with empirical chapters studying specific aspects of reform and change.

Contributions from experts in the field provide cutting-edge snapshots of a region in flux and collectively offer a roadmap of its repositioning in the global order, examining the interaction between global processes and internal dynamics of change and resistance that inject new dimensions into debates over the loci of local and global transformations and the manner in which each plays off the other.

Situating the Gulf States firmly within their global twenty-first century context, this book will hold particular appeal to theorists of globalisation as well as to scholars of comparative politics, international political economy and area studies.

October 2011: 234x156: 376pp
Pb: 978-0-415-57452-5
Hb: 978-0-415-57451-8
Eb: 978-0-203-81321-8

For more information and to order a copy visit
www.routledge.com/9780415574525/

Available from all good bookshops

# State Reform and Development in the Middle East

Turkey and Egypt in the Post-Liberalization Era

By **Amr Adly**

**Series:** Routledge Studies in Middle Eastern Economies

The economies of Turkey and Egypt, remarkably similar until the early 1980s, have since taken divergent paths. Turkey has successfully implemented a policy of export-led industrialization whilst Egypt's manufacturing industry and exports have stagnated.

In this book, Amr Adly uses extensive primary research to present detailed comparisons of Turkey's and Egypt's state administrative and private sector capacities and links between the two. The conclusion the author draws is that the external contexts for both were so alike that this cannot account for their diverging paths. Instead, the author suggests a counterintuitive yet compelling explanation; that a democratic polity is far more likely than an authoritarian one to engender a successful developmental state.

Emerging in the wake of the January revolution in Egypt, when hopes for democratization were raised, this book provides a fresh perspective on the topical subject of state reform and development in the Middle East and will be of interest to students and scholars alike.

November 2012: 234x156: 272pp
Hb: 978-0-415-62419-0
Eb: 978-0-203-10017-2

For more information and to order a copy visit
www.routledge.com/9780415624190/

Available from all good bookshops

# Industrialization in the Gulf

A Socioeconomic Revolution

Edited By **Jean-François Seznec, Mimi Kirk**

**Series:** Routledge Studies in Middle Eastern Economies

In recent years, we have witnessed huge economic and socio-political change in the Gulf. This book examines the rapid industrial-ization of the region and how local economies are starting to diversify away from petroleum, exploring how this transformative process is starting to impact on the region's economy and social make-up.

With contributions from some of the top scholars and practitioners in the area, this book discusses crucial topics related to the region's transformation, from issues of economic development and relations with Iran to foreign labour and women's education and work outside the home. Chapters explore how in addition to the massive growth in investments and products such as oil, gas, chemicals, metals, and cement, this growth has triggered numerous societal changes, such as labour migration, educational reforms, declining natality, and shifting gender roles.

Covering in detail a broad range of issues, this book will appeal not only to Middle East experts, particularly those with an interest in the Persian Gulf, but also to development experts and political scientists.

August 2010: 234x156: 220pp
Hb: 978-0-415-78035-3
Eb: 978-0-203-84665-0

For more information and to order a copy visit
www.routledge.com/9780415780353/

Available from all good bookshops

# The Israeli Central Bank

Political Economy, Global Logics and Local Actors

By **Daniel Maman, Zeev Rosenhek**

**Series:** Routledge Studies in Middle Eastern Economies

This book examines the local and global political and institutional processes that have led to the strengthening of the Israeli central bank within the context of the now predominant neoliberal regime. Using Israel as a case study to identify broader patterns around the world, the authors examine the strengthening of central banks as a key dimension of the institutionalisation of the global regime.

Drawing on an in-depth analysis of the political economy of the Israeli central bank since the mid-1980s, the authors show how the Bank of Israel mobilized global logics in order to strengthen its position vis-à-vis competing actors, especially the Ministry of Finance, and to promote the institutionalisation of the neoliberal regime. Employing a conflict-centered theoretical perspective, the authors elucidate the character of this institutional transformation and the mechanisms that were involved. Chapters examine the different phases of the process of central bank strengthening, focusing on the actors involved, the interactions between them, and the political strategies they employed, and analyse the consequences of the process for the shift in macro-economic management and in the mode of state involvement in the economy.

Addressing the political and institutional processes that have led to the fundamental transformation of Israeli political economy, this book is a valuable addition to the existing literature on the Israeli banking system, political economy and globalisation.

February 2011: 234x156: 180pp
Hb: 978-0-415-57328-3
Eb: 978-0-203-83044-4

# Political Economy of the Gulf Sovereign Wealth Funds

A Case Study of Iran, Kuwait, Saudi Arabia and the UAE

By **Sara Bazoobandi**

**Series:** Routledge Studies in Middle Eastern Economies

Using four Gulf sovereign wealth funds as case studies – Iran, Kuwait, Saudi Arabia and the UAE – this book examines and analyses the history, governance and structure, and investment strategies of the above-mentioned funds, in the context of on-going debates about their transparency. The book discusses how most Gulf sovereign wealth funds were established under colonial rule, and have operated in the global financial system for many decades.

With the increase of oil revenues, it goes on to look at how the funds have broadened their asset classes and their institutional development. Debate over the transparency of sovereign wealth funds has highlighted various global practices. Recently, organisational measures have been introduced for calculating possible risks from non-commercial investment incentives of funds, whose politically-driven investment strategies are viewed as potentially a major threat to the national security of their host countries. Highlighting a number of incidents that triggered the transparency debate, the book scrutinises the reaction of some of the Gulf sovereign wealth funds to these recent regulatory codes and strategies. It is a useful contribution to Development, Political Economy and Middle East Studies.

November 2012: 234x156: 194pp
Hb: 978-0-415-52222-9
Eb: 978-0-203-08088-7